Spirituality in Social Work and Education

Spirituality in Social Work and Education
Theory, Practice, and Pedagogies

Janet Groen, Diana Coholic, and John R. Graham, editors

WILFRID LAURIER
UNIVERSITY PRESS

This book has been published with the help of a grant from the Canadian Federation for the Humanities and Social Sciences, through the Aid to Scholarly Publications Program, using funds provided by the Social Sciences and Humanities Research Council of Canada. Wilfrid Laurier University Press acknowledges the financial support of the Government of Canada through the Canada Book Fund for its publishing activities.

Library and Archives Canada Cataloguing in Publication

    Spirituality in social work and education : theory, practice, and pedagogies / Janet Groen, Diana Coholic, and John R. Graham, editors.

Includes bibliographical references and index.
Issued also in electronic formats.
ISBN 978-1-55458-626-4

    1. Social service—Religious aspects. 2. Social work education—Religious aspects. 3. Spirituality. I. Groen, Janet, 1959– II. Coholic, Diana, 1966– III. Graham, John R. (John Russell), 1964–

HV530.S65 2012   361.3'201   C2012-903296-4

Electronic monograph.
Issued also in print format.
ISBN 978-1-55458-642-4 (PDF).—ISBN 978-1-55458-849-7 (EPUB)

    1. Social service—Religious aspects. 2. Social work education—Religious aspects. 3. Spirituality. I. Groen, Janet, 1959– II. Coholic, Diana, 1966– III. Graham, John R. (John Russell), 1964–

HV530.S65 2012   361.3'201   C2012-903297-2

Cover design by Martyn Schmoll. Front-cover image by Daniel Airam, Artist Painter, www.danielairam.com. Text design by Angela Booth Malleau.

© 2012 Wilfrid Laurier University Press
Waterloo, Ontario, Canada
www.wlupress.wlu.ca

This book is printed on FSC recycled paper and is certified Ecologo. It is made from 100% post-consumer fibre, processed chlorine free, and manufactured using biogas energy.

Printed in Canada

Contents

Acknowledgements

John R. Graham, who is the Murray Fraser Professor in the Faculty of Social Work at the University of Calgary, would like to recognize the McConnell Foundation, which funds the Murray Fraser Professor.

Janet Groen, Diana Coholic, and John R. Graham would like to acknowledge the Laurentian University Research Fund for the book-completion grant they received.

Chapter 1
Introduction

Janet Groen, Diana Coholic, and John R. Graham

How is "spirituality" defined and conceptualized within the professions and disciplines of social work and education? Why have educators and social workers become increasingly interested in spirituality, and what are the rationales for its incorporation into professional practices? How do social work and education scholars currently teach professional students about spirituality? What are the challenges in doing so, and what are some of the rewards? What are researchers interested in studying within the field of spirituality, and what are the most useful future directions for this research? Where are we headed within social work and education regarding the incorporation of spirituality? These are some of the queries and issues that this book explores.

This book is the first of its kind in that it enabled an interdisciplinary interchange between education and social work, and presents ideas from each discipline. We believe that this type of collaboration is needed and timely. For instance, within social work there has been growing consolidation, particularly after 2001, of a group of scholars and practitioners committed to newer approaches of exploring spiritually sensitive social work, and to creating a learned society that meets yearly at a large national/international conference in order to mobilize the development and transfer of knowledge in this area (Graham, Coholic, & Coates, 2006). A smaller but parallel movement has also been occurring within education, with peer-reviewed publications and conference presentations focusing on the historical and theoretical understandings of spirituality within education (English, 2005; Fenwick, English, & Parsons, 2001; Miller, 2000; Van Brummelen, Koole, & Franklin, 2004), and its applications within various settings such as the workplace (English, Fenwick, & Parsons, 2003; Fenwick & Lange, 1998; Gockel, 2004; Groen, 2004b), community development (Bean, 2000; Gillen, 1998), and higher education (Chickering, Dalton, & Stamm, 2006). Across both the fields of social work and education, scholars have grappled with common issues, including how to define spirituality, integrate it into the classroom, and render it a meaningful concept for practitioners, students, and researchers (Coholic, 2006; English & Tisdell, 2010; Graham, Trew, Schmidt, & Kline, 2007; Groen, 2009; Groen & Jacob, 2006; Miller, 2000; Todd & Coholic, 2007; Vokey, 2000).

Spirituality includes one's search for meaning and life purpose, connection with self, others, the universe, and a higher power that is self-defined, either within or without a particular faith orientation. In Western education, an inclusive perspective of spirituality that moves beyond a solely religious orientation is developing to include "an awareness of something greater than ourselves, a sense that we are connected to all human beings and to all of creation" (English & Gillen, 2000, p. 1). Spirituality remains a growing and yet hitherto not fully developed area in all professional disciplines for a variety of reasons, including the fact that "some helping professionals are concerned with blurring professional and personal boundaries with clients. A lack of clarity surrounding definitions of spirituality and religion creates confusion and can lead to fears of proselytizing" (Metheaney & Coholic, 2009).

Accordingly, scholars in both social work and education argue that it is important to differentiate religion from spirituality. With regard to religion, religiosity, and faith traditions, Graham and Shier defined each, starting with

> Durkheim's definition of religion: "a unified set of beliefs and practices relative to sacred things, that is to say, things set apart and forbidden, beliefs and practices which unite into one single moral community … all those who adhere to them" (Durkheim, 1915, p. 62, as cited in Graham & Shier, 2009, p. 218), a concept that considers dimensions associated with both actions and beliefs but acknowledges the collective nature of religions. Religiosity has been defined by dimensions that assess the degree to which a person or group is religious (Cornwall, Albrecht, Cunningham, & Pitcher, 1986, as cited in Graham & Shier, 2009, p. 218). "Faith," "faith tradition" and "religious tradition" are used interchangeably, and each refers to specific religions that have emerged over time (Smith, 1998, as cited in Graham & Shier, 2009, p. 218).

Religion, in this sense, is based on both individual and collective relationships, belief systems, and practices. Spirituality, though, is typically defined in ways that help to explore individual experiences or cognition. For example, Canda and Furman (2010, p. 5) define spirituality as "a universal quality of human beings and their cultures related to the quest for meaning, purpose, morality, transcendence, well-being, and profound relationships with ourselves, others, and ultimate reality." Likewise, "spiritual relationships are defined as relationships to self, others, a higher power, or the environment that brings forth a sense of inner strength, peace, harmonious interconnectedness, and meaning in life" (Walton, 1996, as cited in Laurence, 2000, p. 233). Spirituality also "contributes to personal values and social action and relates to symbolic and unconscious knowledge construction processes" (English & Tisdell, 2010, p. 287).

While both concepts (i.e., religion and spirituality) are important for a profession that is concerned with individuals and communities, and the internal dynamics of the human psyche in relation to individual self-determination and collective socio-cultural interactions, this book's focus is mainly spirituality. A discussion of both religion and spirituality within social work and education is beyond its scope. Also, the interests and expertise of the authors reflect how spirituality (rather than religion) has been taken up by both professions. This has occurred in part because spirituality is more palatable for practitioners and teachers, more inclusive of diverse belief systems, and more consistent with professional values that honour people's interpretations of their experiences, strengths, and cultures.

This book is a collaborative project by a group of academics working within the fields of social work and education. The three editors came together because of their common backgrounds and mutual interest in studying spirituality within their respective professions. In 2009, Diana Coholic was visiting the University of Calgary as a researcher when she and John Graham met with Janet Groen, who they knew had a longstanding interest in spirituality in adult education. A year later, at the University of Calgary in June 2010, there were two major events: the tenth anniversary of the Canadian Society for Spirituality and Social Work's founding, which coincided with the Fifth North American Conference on Spirituality and Social Work. Coholic, Graham, and Groen (hereafter, "we") attended this conference, and that was where we finalized our ideas for the book, including the potential list of authors.

As the editors, we are uniquely placed to draw together an anthology on this topic. Graham has the most extensive background in the area and has written extensively about religion, spirituality, and social work since the early 1990s, publishing in four broad areas related to spirituality. The first is historical, including the religious origins of social work (Graham, 1992, 1994; Graham, Coholic, & Coates, 2007), as well as religion's relationship to certain professional practices within the discipline (Graham & Bradshaw, 2000). Second, as co-founder in 2001 of the Canadian Society for Spirituality and Social Work (CSSSW; www .spiritualityandsocialwork.ca), he has co-organized ten bi-annual conferences, and as a result has co-edited compilations that capture the discipline's promising scholarship (Coates, Graham, & Schwartzentruber, 2007; Coates & Graham, 2004, 2006; Graham & Coates, 2005). Third, Graham also has expertise in the area of international social work, based on nearly 20 years of work with Muslim communities in the Middle East (Al-Krenawi & Graham, 2009, 2011) and more recently in Canada (Graham, Bradshaw, & Trew, 2009a, 2009b, 2010). Much of that work focused on Islam itself as a means of expressing helping relationships (Al-Krenawi & Graham, 2000b), the roles of traditional healing (Al-Krenawi & Graham, 1996; Al-Krenawi, Graham, & Maoz, 1996; Al-Krenawi & Graham, 1997a, 1997b, 1999), and strategies to render social work culturally respectful (Al-Krenawi & Graham, 2000a). His international work has allowed him to reflect also on the role of spirituality in internationalizing the discipline (Graham, 2006) and the importance of spirituality as a tool for localizing (sometimes referred to as indigenizing) the discipline's knowledge base worldwide (Bradshaw & Graham, 2007). The fourth area is based on recent funded research on subjective well-being (SWB) in the human services, and SWB's relationship to both mindfulness (Graham & Graham, 2009; Shier & Graham, 2011) and spirituality (Graham & Shier, 2011).

Coholic has a background as a clinical social worker, and began her study in this field with doctoral research that explored how feminist social workers made sense of spirituality and incorporated it into their practices (Coholic, 2003). She met Graham in 2002 at the first Canadian Conference on Spirituality and Social Work, and from there became involved in the CSSSW, helping to organize several conferences and coediting the special issue of a journal based on conference paper presentations (Coholic, Cadell, & Nichols, 2008). Over the past ten years, her research interests have developed into investigating the effectiveness of arts-based and mindfulness-based group methods for improving resilience in at-risk young people (Coholic, 2011b; Coholic, Lougheed, & Cadell, 2009; Coholic, Lougheed, & LeBreton, 2009; Coholic & LeBreton, 2007). Her approach to mindfulness is holistic and the group methods that she is studying make space for children and youth to discuss spiritual and existential issues (Coholic, 2011a).

Groen also began her study in this area with doctoral research that explored how spirituality manifested in the workplace through the eyes of adult educators (Groen 2004a, 2004b). Over the ensuing years, Groen's research has focused on spirituality and adult learning, utilizing a transformative learning framework within higher education classrooms (Groen & Jacob, 2006; Groen, 2008; Groen, 2010a) and, more broadly, the emerging research and teaching focus on spirituality in the professional faculties of business, education, and social work (Groen, 2009). Returning to her roots in environmental studies, Groen (2010b) is currently engaged in research that explores the significance of links between environmental adult education and spirituality, "to generate a heightened awareness and sensibility, a sense of global responsibility, a new kind of spiritual literacy" (King, 2010, p. 245).

Likewise, we recruited contributing authors based on established expertise in their respective areas as evidenced by their scholarship, including solid publication records and active research programs. Regarding the education scholars, Leona English is a pioneer of research in the area of adult education and spirituality, and has published prolifically on spiritual, international, and feminist issues in adult education (English, 2004, 2005). Daniel Vokey's research interests include integrating Eastern and Western perspectives on the development of practical wisdom, drawing on his background in moral philosophy, his expertise in adventure-based education, and his study and practice of Shambhala Buddhism (Vokey, 2001, 2005). Veronika Bohac Clarke has taught a graduate course titled Spirituality in a Postmodern Age at the University of Calgary for the past several years, and has researched and published in the areas of values, character education, and spirituality (2002). John Miller has been working in area of holistic education for over thirty years, and has published extensively in the areas of holistic learning and contemplative practices in education (Miller, 1994, 2006). Finally, Ian Winchester has a special interest in the mind and spirituality from a philosophical vantage point and is currently engaged in a multidisciplinary study of spiritual healers.

With regards to the social work scholars, John Coates was a founding member of the CSSSW and has published widely in the area of spirituality and social work, focusing much of his attention on the area of environmentalism and its connection with spirituality (Coates 2003, 2005). Susan Cadell has also been involved with the CSSSW for many years, and her expertise lies in the areas of post-traumatic growth and palliative care. She has studied these phenomena in people caring for loved ones with HIV/AIDS, and in parents with seriously ill children (Cadell, 2007; Cadell, Janzen, & Fletcher, 2004). Richard Csiernik's research has explored workplace wellness and its connections with spirituality, and students' spiritual growth (Csiernik, 2005; Csiernik & Adams, 2003). Sarah Todd has explored the intersections between social justice work and spirituality, and has also written about the challenges related to teaching spirituality to social work students (Todd, 2007; Todd & Coholic, 2007).

Given the expertise of all of the authors, we encouraged them to write in a more personal style than that used for most academic papers, asking them to draw on their practices and scholarship. We were interested in hearing about people's experiences teaching and researching in spirituality and education/social work, and based on their experiences, what ideas they had for future directions for this area of study and practice. We believe that these narratives are more interesting and informative for the reader, and will hopefully encourage new scholars to take up work in the identified areas based on what has been done to date, which constitutes a substantial foundation of knowledge.

Importantly, from the outset, we had in mind a book that would enable dialogue and knowledge translation among the authors and between their two disciplines. We hoped this process would enrich and help to further develop each author's own work in this area. In line with the current emphasis on interdisciplinary collaboration, we also hoped that this collaborative process could, in some small way, further the discourse within each profession regarding spirituality. Certainly, part of the rationale for bringing together scholars in education and social work stemmed from the many overlapping commonalities in histories, values, and areas of engagement with children, families, and communities in these two professions. Also, based on our initial conversations, we knew that these disciplines are grappling with similar issues in their respective fields concerning the conceptualization and incorporation of spirituality, the rationales for this incorporation, and the complexities inherent in a spiritually sensitive pedagogy. Again, we hoped that insights could be gleaned from beyond our respective disciplines. And so we worked carefully with each author to align him or her with a counterpart in the other academic discipline. The authors wrote over the course of the 2010–2011 academic year, and very often there was dialogue among them. In the end, we grouped the authors into three convergent theme areas and facilitated a discussion among them using conference calls. This process allowed for further adjustments to the chapters, and fostered considerable interdisciplinary learning.

The book is divided into three sections according to broad topics that helped to facilitate the dialogue between the authors, and organize the book's material. The first section explores the historical and theoretical underpinnings of spirituality in education and social work. Examination of our respective heritages uncovers the religious roots within our professions and reveals a present understanding of spirituality that calls for active engagement in challenging oppression and working toward social justice. "History both within and beyond our field has shown that the justice work of many well-known social activists has been fueled by their spiritual commitments … it is through spirituality that many of us engage that sense of hope" (English & Tisdell, 2010, p. 285). English launches this section, critically reflecting on the spirituality agenda in adult education, and makes the argument that a spiritual heritage is evident across human service work, since religious groups have been actively engaged in education, health, and social work throughout the world. She challenges us to engage in uncomfortable conversations that probe deeper issues such as the oppressive and social control dimensions of some religious and spiritual traditions.

Graham and Shier echo English, arguing that spirituality has always been an undercurrent in social work theory. However, its early origins reflected a religious rather than spiritual understanding. They trace the place of religion and spirituality in the historical arc of the profession in Canada, the current status of "spirituality" and "religion" terms within English language social work scholarship, and conclude by looking at the future role of religion and spirituality in the education and training of social workers. Coates, reflecting on the role of spirituality by addressing environmental challenges in an effective and substantial way, reinforces the notion that spirituality pushes us to ask difficult questions and consider how our existing world view of modern society, despite increasing harbingers of environmental destruction, continues to wreck havoc on the natural world. He demonstrates that an infusion of spirituality within our respective professions can play a significant role in fostering active and engaged scholarship and practices that are environmentally and socially just.

Groen, in the concluding chapter of the first section, explores how historical and theoretical underpinnings of spirituality in the fields of social work and education translate into the daily teaching and research practice of current academics in these respective fields. Specifically, she reports on the cross-faculty dialogue that occurred among six of the authors in this book, equally representing education and social work, exploring how their interest in integrating spirituality into teaching practices emerged; how they understood spirituality, and how this translated into course content; and finally, how spirituality was interpreted and valued by their respective students, faculties, universities, and disciplines.

The second section shifts the focus to the pedagogical implications of incorporating spirituality in our practice as instructors in the higher education environment. The varied level of acceptance and ensuing tensions that come from including spirituality, implicitly or explicitly, within the programs and coursework of our respective faculties are illuminated by these three authors. "The language of spirit is considered anti-thetical to normalized institutional paradigms in pedagogical practices" (Shahjahan, 2009, p. 121). In his chapter, Vokey argues that devoting time to understanding and promoting spirituality in our programs and coursework is critical if we seek to support faculty and students in becoming more just, caring, and effective helping professionals. However, he cautions that the inclusion of spirituality in the classroom must be intentional about reaching a shared understanding across and within traditions, and that there are a variety of legitimate ways spirituality can be expressed and supported in the academy. In response to this warning, Vokey presents a curriculum framework for professional faculties (e.g., education, nursing, business, and social work) addressing the challenges and opportunities that pluralism presents to the goal of promoting spirituality in a secular age, and includes recommended strategies and processes for implementing it.

The next two authors explore the pedagogy of spirituality through their own experiences as instructors in a university setting. Todd grapples with the challenge of creating a liminal space in her social work courses between some students' antipathy toward spirituality and/or religion and others' deep attachment to the very same set of practices and beliefs. After exploring its historical roots in higher education and the field of social work, she focuses on how to integrate spirituality implicitly into the core courses of the social work curriculum using post-structural and critical pedagogical approaches. In contrast, Bohac Clarke reflects on her experiences teaching one of several graduate courses in the Faculty of Education at the University of Calgary, where the content is explicitly focused on spirituality. After Bohac Clarke presents a compelling case for "teaching spirituality" within professional faculties, she outlines the central components of her course, Spirituality in a Postmodern Age, utilizing Wilber's (2006) integral theory as her theoretical framework.

The third section of the book explores issues related to practising and teaching from a spiritually sensitive perspective. Within the social work profession, "knowledge regarding spiritually sensitive social work practice continues to develop and demonstrates the usefulness of holistic practice methods," and many have reported on the benefits of spirituality in both practice and theory (Metheaney & Coholic, 2009). Among educators and education scholars, interest in the role and impact of spirituality has grown in recent years, in part due to reaction against a curriculum that has focused largely on instrumental knowledge, or instruction on what it takes to be successful and "get ahead" (Austin, 2004). Coholic provides an overview of current and emerging spiritually sensitive social work practices including a focus on group work, culturally competent practices, and mindfulness-based practices. She explains that there is enough of a foundation for researchers to further explore the effectiveness of holistic practices, continuing to develop our knowledge in this area and answering current calls for evidence-based practices.

Miller takes up the specific thread of mindfulness, which is a rapidly growing area of research across helping and health professions. His chapter focuses specifically on how practising mindfulness can lead to improved "teacher presence," similar to the concept of "therapeutic presence" in helping professions. Mindful teachers can better connect with their students and build effective relationships for learning. Winchester then reports on research that explores how traditional healers practice. Alternative health practices, many of which are based on spiritual beliefs and viewpoints, are increasingly being utilized by the general population, and research that explores these practices is needed. Cadell and Csiernik both explore the matter of trauma but with different foci. Cadell discusses the emerging area known as post-traumatic growth, arguing that researchers have not paid enough attention to spiritual growth and change as a result of trauma. Csiernik examines social work students who suffer traumatic and stressful experiences during their field placements, and how spirituality can aid them in processing these events.

Within Western social work and education, we have experienced incredible growth over the past ten years in research and literature that has explored and discussed spiritually sensitive issues. It is very difficult (if not impossible) to keep abreast of all of these developments occurring across a wide variety of professions and disciplines. At the same time, spiritually sensitive social work and education is not yet "mainstream." In fact, some would argue that it is still fairly marginalized. However, those of us already working in this area should mentor newer and emerging practitioners, teachers, students, and scholars who will further advance this scholarship and practice. We strongly encourage students and practitioners to remember that there are now many of us who can assume these roles. We also need to continue interdisciplinary collaborations, as many of us are struggling with similar challenges, questions, and dilemmas, and these types of collaborations can foster rich, interesting, and valuable discourse. This anthology is a small step in that direction. We have all been enriched by the experience and hope that the reader also finds the material that follows to be useful and thought-provoking.

References

Al-Krenawi, A., & Graham, J. R. (1996). Social work and traditional healing rituals among the Bedouin of the Negev, Israel. *International Social Work, 39*, 177–188.

Al-Krenawi, A., & Graham, J. R. (1997a). Nebi-Musa: A therapeutic community for drug addiction in a Muslim context. *Transcultural Psychiatry, 34*, 377–398.

Al-Krenawi, A., & Graham, J. R. (1997b). Spirit possession and exorcism: The integration of modern and traditional mental health care systems in the treatment of a Bedouin patient. *Clinical Social Work Journal, 25*, 211–222.

Al-Krenawi, A., & Graham, J. R. (1999). Gender and biomedical/traditional mental health utilization among the Bedouin-Arabs of the Negev. *Culture, Medicine, and Psychiatry, 23*, 219–243.

Al-Krenawi, A., & Graham, J. R. (2000a). Culturally sensitive social work practice with Arab clients in mental health settings. *Health and Social Work, 25*, 9–22.

Al-Krenawi, A., & Graham, J. R. (2000b). Islamic theology and prayer: Relevance for social work practice. *International Social Work, 43*, 289–304.

Al-Krenawi, A., & Graham, J. R. (2009). *Helping professional practice with indigenous peoples: The Bedouin-Arab case.* New York, NY: University Press of America.

Al-Krenawi, A., & Graham, J. R. (2011). Mental health help seeking among Arab university students in Israel, differentiated by religion. *Mental Health: Religion and Culture, 14*, 157–167.

Al-Krenawi, A., Graham, J. R., & Maoz, B. (1996). The healing significance of the Negev's Bedouin Dervish. *Social Science and Medicine, 43*, 13–21.

Austin, W. A. (2004). Why spirituality deserves a central place in higher education. *Spirituality in Higher Education Newsletter, 1*(1), 1–12.

Bean, W. (2000). Community development and adult education: Locating practice in its roots. *New Directions for Adult and Continuing Education, 85*, 67–76.

Bohac Clarke, V. (2002). In search of school spirit: The cloud of unknowing in public education. *International Electronic Journal for Leadership in Learning, 6*(10). Retrieved from www.ucalgary.ca/iejll/bohac_clarke

Bradshaw, C., & Graham, J. R. (2007). Localization of social work practice, education and research: A content analysis. *Social Development Issues, 29*, 92–111.

Cadell, S. (2007). The sun always comes out after it rains: Understanding posttraumatic growth in HIV carers. *Health & Social Work*, *32*(3), 169–176.

Cadell, S., Janzen, L., & Fletcher, M. (2004). *Parents finding meaning: Examining the post traumatic growth and the role of support with two bereavement programs.* Research presentation at the National Hospice Palliative Care Organization's First Pediatric Palliative Care Conference, Dearborn, MI.

Canda, E. R., & Furman, L. D. (2010). *Spiritual diversity in social work practice: The heart of helping* (2nd ed.). New York: Oxford University Press.

Chickering, D., Dalton, J., & Stamm, L. (2006). *Encouraging authenticity and spirituality in higher education.* San Francisco, CA: Jossey-Bass.

Coates, J. (2003). *Ecology and social work: Toward a new paradigm.* Halifax, NS: Fernwood Press.

Coates, J. (2005). Environmental crisis: Implications for social work. *Journal of Progressive Human Services*, *16*(1), 25–49.

Coates, J., & Graham, J. R. (Eds.). (2004). Spiritual diversity and social work. *Currents: New Scholarship in the Human Services*, *3*(2).

Coates, J., & Graham, J. R. (Eds.). (2006). Spirituality and social work. *Critical Social Work*, *7*(1).

Coates, J., Graham, J. R., & Schwartzentruber, B. (Eds.). (2007). *Canadian social work and spirituality: Current readings and approaches.* Toronto, ON: Canadian Scholars' Press.

Coholic, D. (2003). Incorporating spirituality in feminist social work perspectives. *Affilia: Journal of Women and Social Work, 18*, 49–67.

Coholic, D. (2006). Mindfulness meditation practice in spiritually influenced group work. *Arete, 30*, 90–100.

Coholic, D. (2011a). Exploring how young people living in foster care discuss spiritually sensitive themes in a holistic arts-based group program. *Journal of Religion, Spirituality and Social Work—Social Thought, 30*(3), 193–211.

Coholic, D. (2011b). Exploring the feasibility and benefits of arts-based, mindfulness-based practices with young people in need: Aiming to improve aspects of self-awareness and resilience. *Child and Youth Care Forum, 40*(4), 303–317.

Coholic, D., Cadell, S., & Nichols, A. W. (Eds.). (2008). Social Thought [Special Issue]. *Journal of Religion, Spirituality and Social Work, 27*(1–2).

Coholic, D., & LeBreton, J. (2007). Working with dreams in a holistic arts-based group: Connections between dream interpretation and spirituality. *Social Work with Groups, 30*(3), 47–64.

Coholic, D., Lougheed, S., & Cadell, S. (2009). Exploring the helpfulness of arts-based methods with children living in foster care. *Traumatology, 15*, 64–71.

Coholic, D., Lougheed, S., & LeBreton, J. (2009). The helpfulness of holistic arts-based group work with children living in foster care. *Social Work with Groups, 32*, 29–46.

Csiernik, R. (2005). Wellness and the workplace. In R. Csiernik (Ed.), *Wellness and work: Employee assistance programming in Canada.* Toronto, ON: Canadian Scholars' Press.

Csiernik, R., & Adams, D. (2003). Social work students and spirituality: An initial exploration. *Canadian Social Work, 5*(1), 65–79.

English, L. (2004). Feminist identities: Negotiations in the third space. *Feminist Theology*, *3*(1), 97–125.

English, L. (2005). Historical and contemporary explorations of the social changes and spiritual directions of adult education. *Teachers College Record 107*(6), 1169–1192.

English, L., Fenwick, T., & Parsons, J. (2003). *Spirituality of adult education and training*. Malabar, FL: Krieger.

English, L., & Gillen, M. (2000). Editors' notes. *New Directions for Adult and Continuing Education, 8*, 1–5.

English, L., & Tisdell, E. J. (2010). Spirituality and adult education. In C. Kasworm, A. Rose, & J. Ross-Gordon (Eds.), *Handbook of adult and continuing education* (pp. 285–293). Thousand Oaks, CA: Sage.

Fenwick, T., English, L., & Parson, J. (2001). Dimensions of spirituality: A framework for adult educators. *Proceedings of the 20th National Conference of the Canadian Association for the Study of Adult Education, Laval University, Quebec*.

Fenwick, T., & Lange, E. (1998). Spirituality in the workplace: The new frontier of HRD. *Canadian Journal for the Study of Adult Education, 12*(1), 63–87.

Gillen, M. (1998). Spiritual lessons from the Antigonish Movement. In S. Scott, B. Spencer, & A. Thomas (Eds.), *Learnings for life: Canadian readings in adult education* (pp. 273–282). Toronto, ON: Thompson Education.

Gockel, A. (2004). The trend toward spirituality in the workplace: Overview and implications for career counseling. *Journal of Employment Counseling, 41*(4), 156–167.

Graham, J. R. (1992). The Haven, 1878–1930. A Toronto charity's transition from a religious to a professional ethos. *Histoire Sociale/Social History, 25*, 283–306.

Graham, J. R. (1994). Charles Eric Hendry (1903–1979): The pre-war formational origins of leader of post-World War II Canadian social work education. *Canadian Social Work Review, 11*, 150–167.

Graham, J. R. (2006). Spirituality and social work: A call for an international focus of research. *Arete, 30*, 63–77.

Graham, J. R., Bradshaw, C., & Trew, J. (2009a). Adapting social work in working with Muslim clients: Insights for education. *Social Work Education: The International Journal, 28*, 544–561.

Graham, J. R., Bradshaw, C., & Trew, J. (2009b). Addressing cultural barriers with Muslim clients: An agency perspective. *Administration in Social Work, 33*, 387–406.

Graham, J. R., Bradshaw, C., & Trew, J. (2010). Cultural considerations for social service agencies working with Muslim clients. *Social Work, 55*, 337–346.

Graham, J. R., & Coates, J. (Eds.). (2005). Spirituality and social work. *Critical Social Work, 6*.

Graham, J. R., Coholic, D., & Coates, J. (2006). Spirituality as a guiding construct in the development of Canadian social work: Past and present considerations. *Critical Social Work, 7*(1). Retrieved from http://www.criticalsocialwork.com/

Graham, J. R., Coholic, D., & Coates, J. (2007). Spirituality as a guiding construct in the development of Canadian social work: Past and present considerations. In J. Coates, J. R. Graham, & B. Schwartzentruber (with B. Ouellette) (Eds.), *Spirituality and Social Work: Select Canadian Readings* (pp.111–134). Toronto, ON: Canadian Scholars' Press.

Graham, S. M., & Graham, J. R. (2009). Subjective well-being, mindfulness, and the social work workplace: Insight into reciprocal relationships. In S. Hick (Ed.), *Mindfulness and social work* (pp. 103–120). Chicago, IL: Lyceum.

Graham, J. R., & Shier, M. (2009). Religion and social work: An analysis of faith traditions, themes, and Global North/South authorship. *Journal of Religion, Spirituality, and Social Work, 28,* 215–233.

Graham, J. R., & Shier, M. (2011). Making sense of their world: Aspects of spirituality and subjective well-being of practicing social workers. *Journal of Religion, Spirituality, and Social Work, 21*(5), 1–19.

Graham, J. R., Trew, J., Schmidt, J., & Kline, T. (2007). Influences on the subjective well-being of practising social workers. *Canadian Social Work, 9*(1), 92–105.

Groen, J. (2004a). The creation of soulful spaces: An exploration of the processes and the organizational context. *Organization Development Journal, 22*(3), 8–19.

Groen, J. (2004b). The experience and practice of adult educators in addressing the spiritual dimensions of the workplace. *Canadian Journal for the Study of Adult Education, 18*(1), 72–92.

Groen, J. (2008). Paradoxical tensions in creating a teaching and learning space within a graduate education course on spirituality. *Teaching in Higher Education, 13*(2), 193–204.

Groen, J. (2009). Moving in from the fringes of the academy: Spirituality as an emerging focus in the Canadian professional faculties of business, education and social work. *Journal of Educational Thought, 43*(3), 223–244.

Groen, J. (2010a). An insider's view: Reflections on teaching a graduate education course on spirituality in the workplace. *Journal of Management, Religion and Spirituality, 7*(4), 335–349.

Groen, J. (2010b). The spiritual retreat centre as a place of re-enchantment. *Proceedings of the 29th National Conference of the Canadian Association for the Study of Adult Education, Montreal, QC.*

Groen, J., & Jacob, J. (2006). Spiritual transformation in a secular context: A qualitative research study. *International Journal of Teaching and Learning in Higher Education, 18*(2), 75–88.

King, U. (2010). Earthing spiritual literacy: How to link spiritual development and education to a new earth consciousness. *Journal of Beliefs and Values, 31*(3), 245–260.

Laurence, P. (2000). Exploring spirituality. In J. Beversluis (Ed.), *Sourcebook of the world's religions: An interfaith guide to religion and spirituality* (pp. 232–235). Novata, CA: New World Library.

Metheaney, J., & Coholic, D. (2009). Exploring spirituality in mental health: Psychiatrist and social worker viewpoints. *Critical Social Work, 10.* Retrieved from http://www.uwindsor.ca/criticalsocialwork/exploring-spirituality-in-mental-health-social-worker-and-psychiatrist-viewpoints.

Miller, J. (1994). *The contemplative practitioner.* Westport, CT: Bergin and Garvey.

Miller, J. (2000). *Education for the soul: Toward a spiritual curriculum.* Toronto, ON: OISE Press.

Miller, J. (2006). *Educating for wisdom and compassion: Creating conditions for timeless learning.* Thousand Oaks, CA: Corwin.

Shahjahan, R. (2009). The role of spirituality in the anti-oppressive higher-education classroom. *Teaching in Higher Education, 14*(2), 121–131.

Shier, M., & Graham, J. R. (2011). Mindfulness, subjective well-being, and social work: Insight into their interconnection from social work practitioners. *Social Work Education, 30,* 29–44.

Todd, S. (2007). Feminist community organizing: The spectre of the sacred and the secular. In J. Coates, J. R. Graham, & B. Swartzentruber (with B. Ouellette) (Eds.), *Spirituality and social work: Selected Canadian readings.* Toronto, ON: Canadian Scholars' Press.

Todd, S., & Coholic, D. (2007). Christian fundamentalism and anti-oppressive social work pedagogy. *Journal of Teaching in Social Work, 27*(3–4), 5–25.

Van Brummelen, H., Koole, R., & Franklin, K. (2004). Transcending the commonplace: Spirituality in the curriculum. *Journal of Educational Thought, 38*(3), 237–253.

Vokey, D. (2000). Longing to connect: Spirituality in public schools. *Paideusis,13*(2), 23–41.

Vokey, D. (2001). *Moral discourse in a pluralistic world.* Notre Dame, IN: University of Notre Dame Press.

Vokey, D. (2005). Spirituality and educational leadership: A Shambhala Buddhist view. In C. Shields, M. Edwards, & A. Sayani (Eds.), *Inspiring practice: Spirituality and educational leadership* (pp. 87–99). Philadelphia, PA: Pro-Active Press.

Wilber, K. (2006). *Integral spirituality.* Boston, MA: Integral Books.

Section One

Historical and Theoretical Underpinnings

"Spirituality" as a focus for research and practice in the professions of education and social work has experienced rapid development and burgeoning interest in the past decade. However, assuming that this is a "new" area of exploration for us negates compelling evidence that spiritualty has been an underlying value and force over the past century in both social work and education. The first four chapters of this book explore the historical and theoretical underpinnings of spirituality within our respective professions, revealing that while we both share a common religious orientation, we have moved beyond it to an understanding of spirituality that values diverse belief systems, and works to uncover and address oppressive beliefs and practices.

English in adult education, and Graham and Shier in social work, demonstrate that there is evidence of spiritual heritage across human service work, since early religious groups actively participated in health, education, and social work. In turn, this heritage has informed our current interpretation: although spirituality is moving beyond a religious orientation, it must be tightly interwoven with a social justice agenda.

Coates and Groen both demonstrate how our understanding of spirituality is foundational to how we engage in the world. Coates explores our relationship to the natural environment and argues that a deeper, more inclusive view of spirituality compels us to question our mechanistic world view and destructive practices, especially when it comes to the environment. Groen, also arguing for a more holistic understanding of spirituality, considers how six academic colleagues (contributors in this book) sought to incorporate spirituality in their practice within a higher education culture that reinforces a cognitive and rational orientation to teaching and research. The future for a teaching and research agenda that seeks to incorporate spirituality is unclear. While the authors note the diminishing number of courses that focus specifically on the topic of spirituality in either social work or education, there is an expanding research agenda in the area of spiritualty in both the faculties.

Chapter 2

For Whose Purposes? Examining the Spirituality Agenda in Adult Education

Leona English

The more sand in the oyster, the more chemical the oyster produces until finally, after layer upon layer of gel, the sand turns into a pearl. And the oyster itself becomes more valuable in the process.... [In thinking of this] I discovered the ministry of irritation. (Chittister, 2008, pp. 15–16)

Adult education has its roots in religious impulses and directions, from the early days of the Presbyterian Minister Alfred Fitzpatrick (1920/1999) setting up the literacy initiative Frontier College in the railway camps, to Mary Arnold and Moses Coady working with the Antigonish Movement in the 1920s and 1930s in northeastern Nova Scotia (Neal, 1998), to abstinence crusaders such as Letitia Youmans speaking at the Chautauqua Institute, a major social gospel arena in upstate New York during the late 1800s (English, 2005a). In general, human service work can be said to have spiritual connections, since religious groups have always been at the forefront of education, health, and social work the world over. In adult education, the connections have been especially strong since my field is so close to the community and has grappled, often while lacking the necessary funds, with fundamental human needs: adult literacy, ESL and settlement services, and the right to a sustainable livelihood.

Like the many streams of transformative learning embedded in my field (Taylor, 2008), there have been a number of versions of spirituality and education. The oldest texts concerning these come from the pen of Basil Yeaxlee, who published his dissertation entitled *Spiritual Values in Adult Education* in the United Kingdom in 1925. His book heralded a very humanistic and religious type of spirituality that assumed it was largely church-going people who would see spirituality as part of their religious and daily practice. The fact that Yeaxlee was employed by the YMCA at that time indicated his own religious connections.

In my field, spirituality in the sense of creating and doing good work has always been important, and it appears that both faith-based organizations (FBOs) and secular non-profits continue to support good work in the community today (Botchwey, 2007). While motivations and spiritual impulses may differ, at heart the focus is similar. As noted in Graham and Shier's chapter, we share a similar history with social work.

This chapter explores the tension between spirituality as a sacred and secular phenomenon. I begin with a brief overview of the roots of spirituality in the field of adult education, and then move on to identify critical social science issues affecting spirituality, such as emotion, race, geography, gender, and social class. Building on these insights, I examine spirituality at three sites of adult education: workplace training, higher education, and community development. Finally, I propose a number of critical points to consider when integrating spirituality into adult education. I have two guiding questions: For what purpose is spirituality being promoted in these settings? And whose interests does it serve?

Situating Spirituality in Our Field

Nothing could be harder to dismiss than the role of religion and spirituality in the histories and life stories of adult education's scholars and practitioners. The number of ministers and people who have religious training in adult education is quite high. Peter Willis, Peter Jarvis, Carolyn Clark, and Michael Newman are just a few of those who have acknowledged their work in and affiliation with organized religion, and they are all very much imbued with the spirituality of social change (English, 2005a; Jarvis & Walters, 1993). This interlocking of purpose between justice and spirituality has stood the test of time. Most adult education initiatives in Canada and the US, including the Antigonish Movement, Highlander, and Chautauqua, were rooted in and influenced by various religious movements, and many of them appear to have had tensions with organized religious leaders. Admittedly, their definition of spirituality is far more sacred than our secular version today. Yet I do not take the position that spirituality and religion are totally separate; rather, some people express their spirituality through religious practice (i.e., in more formalized and institutional ways) and others through alternate means. Acknowledging the contributions of religious groups and their continued support of spiritual practices and beliefs, I value the wisdom of O'Sullivan (1999), who reminds me that "it must also be acknowledged that religious movements have also been the focal point of social transformation and revolutionary vision" (p. 267).

Historically, spirituality and adult education were entwined, with many of the early figures in the field coming of age through religious groups and impulses. One only has to think of those famous initiatives like Mondragon, Chautauqua, Highlander, Frontier College, and the Antigonish Movement to see evidence of religious impulses and supports. I look at several of these to illustrate this point.

Frontier College

From a Canadian perspective, Frontier College is one of the most innovative programs in adult education history; indeed, it is the oldest adult education institution in Canada. Begun in 1899 by Alfred Fitzpatrick, Frontier College was a grassroots movement of hired educators working alongside railway workers during the day and teaching them to read and write at night (Cook, 1987). A Presbyterian minister, Fitzpatrick had grown up in Nova Scotia in a religious family, and took that experience with him throughout his life, promoting literacy and the social gospel simultaneously. His own book, *University in Overalls* (1920/1999), chronicles his dreams about education and his plans for Frontier College's expansion to grant post-secondary degrees, eventually becoming an alternative university. Though some of his dreams did not materialize, including this one, Frontier College is a milestone in our history. It continues today at the new frontier: on city streets and in shelters, among Native communities and disabled persons. It embodies Fitzpatrick's vision of adult education, which he described in his oratorical and faintly preachy style as "[t]his office is the college, and the vast domain of Canada is your campus" (p. 7). Significantly, he presaged Freire and Illich's resistance to institutional education in his 1936 unpublished manuscript "Schools and other Penitentiaries" (Fitzpatrick, 1920/1999, p. 24). However, his main contribution was bringing literacy to the men working in the railway and lumber camps.

Chautauqua

Another example of the connections between adult education, spirituality, and social justice is Chautauqua, a village of learning begun by John Heyl Vincent, a Methodist minister, and Lewis Miller, an industrialist, in Western New York State. It began in 1874 as a two-week retreat and summer school for Sunday school teachers in the Methodist church (Kilde, 1999; Scott, 1999). This summer school was intended to parallel the normal school experience for teachers. Jane Addams (Founder of Hull House, a settlement house for the poor in Chicago) and noted suffragettes Susan B. Anthony and Julia Ward Howe were attendees. Influenced by social gospel, Chautauqua became a supportive environment for those with religious and social justice leanings, and even for those with Marxist ideas, since faith and Marxism are not necessarily contradictory (Reiser, 2003). Chautauqua hosted a temperance meeting which sparked the creation of the Woman's Christian Temperance Union (WCTU), one of the most successful women's activism movements of the late nineteenth and early twentieth centuries. American and international temperance leader Frances

Willard was also an attendee of this summer retreat. Unlike society as a whole, Chautauqua welcomed activist women and gave them a place to speak and be heard. It was a site of religious learning and political action that supported suffrage and women's organizing, including the formation of associations that were forerunners of the Parent Teacher Association (PTA) and Mothers Against Drunk Driving (MADD) (Kilde, 1999; Scott, 1999). It became a critical venue for women, though some authors such as Kilde have challenged the community's elitism and lack of diversity.

The Antigonish Movement

The Antigonish Movement is an often-cited example of the intersection between spirituality and adult education. A social justice and economic cooperation movement that started in the first half of the twentieth century, it had strong ties with the Roman Catholic Church and St. Francis Xavier University, its operational base (Welton, 2001). The movement involved not only Father Moses Coady and his cousin Father Jimmy Tompkins (giants of Catholic social justice) but also a cadre of strong women who worked alongside them. They organized study clubs, established libraries (Sister Dolores Donnelly), edited the cooperative newspaper (Zita O'Hearn Cameron), hosted a radio show (Sister Marie Michael MacKinnon), organized a handicraft program (Sister Irene Doyle), established cooperative housing (Mary Arnold), and in general supported the activities of the movement (Neal, 1998). The spiritual dimensions of this movement were rooted in Catholic teachings about social justice, and it involved a massive collective effort to work with the economically disenfranchised, educating and mobilizing them to build farming, fishing, and mining cooperatives. This movement was not an effort to proselytize, rather it worked for justice, to create the conditions that encourage human potential to flourish. In many ways, it actually worked counter to the agenda of officials in the church, resulting in Father Jimmy being forced out of the university and his official role in the movement, and banished to a remote, rural parish. One suspects he knew the movement was effective when he was ousted. A tenacious man, he truly believed in human potential and using every teachable moment. A quote about his dedication (and some would say stubbornness) illustrates this point: "he wouldn't even let the cat out for you. But he'd stay up half the night nagging *you* to do it" (Lotz & Welton, 1997, p. 7).

Frontier College, Chautauqua, and the Antigonish Movement are but three examples of justice and spirituality's historical position in adult education. They show how the times served as incubators for important ideas and supported vigorous actions. Yet they also show that adult education has engaged in its own share of colonizing. Early leaders, such as Yeaxlee (1925), clearly saw themselves as part of a religious endeavour to bring others into their faith community. Their vision was often based in a liberal, white, Western and Christian stance. Given their social location, it was likely difficult for them to envisage a broad-based and inclusive effort to educate. They were rooted in their time and privilege.

Dimensions of Spirituality

Yet my field's discourse and preoccupations have shifted with the times. Its signature publication, the *Handbook of Adult and Continuing Education*, tells the tale of change and development in how the field has interpreted spirituality. Since its first publication in 1934, each decennial edition of the handbook has included chapters on religious education, which usually was understood as being synonymous with spirituality. The 2010 handbook shifted the language from religion to spirituality for the first time in its history (English & Tisdell, 2010). This change likely came about because the increasing paternalism and neo-colonialism of some religious institutions is increasingly off-putting to educators who have a social change agenda and who see their own spiritual practices as justice-oriented. Indeed, it hard to argue with the change, given the overall status of many religious groups at this time in history. It is this critical eye and discerning spirit that guides this chapter's exploration of the "spirituality of irritation" (Chittister, 2008).

Although it can be a contested area, spirituality has the potential to enable adult educators to grapple with many critical issues in civil society. For many (and this area has been delved into numerous times), spirituality is about a connection to meaning and to a divine being, and requires the individual to reach out to the world in search of justice and right living (English & Tisdell, 2010). These understandings of spirituality have become embedded in adult education's literature and working definitions. In the following sections, I look at factors that affect and are affected by spirituality.

Negativity and the Spectrum of Emotions

Popular culture to the contrary, spirituality is about more than achieving bliss. Indeed, like its religious antecedents in adult education history, spirituality includes approaches to both good and bad times: the negotiation of health and illness, poverty and wealth, justice and injustice (Whitehead & Whitehead, 1994). The potential for spirituality to help negotiate the wide range of life experiences is shown in the Ignatian exercises, a prayer form in which participants experience the full spectrum of human emotion over an extended period of time. Groen also references the Ignatian exercises in her chapter for this book. E. and J. Whitehead (1994), writing from the Christian tradition, note that negative ideas and emotions are part of the human condition; in their words, "to be human is to be aroused" (p. 3). They speak about the power of anger to address corruption and wrongdoing, and call our communities to right action. They remind us that the judicious expression of emotion is part of our sense of integrity and righteous living, not something to fear or avoid. Rather, emotions are a deep and integral part of our spirituality, and enable us to be fully human. In adult education circles, teachers often relate stories about labour and economic justice leader Moses Coady, who did not mind speaking truth to problems and did not gloss them over. At a meeting of the Canadian Association for Adult Education, then-president Moses Coady was overheard responding to a critic, "I'm not a leftist, I'm where the righteous ought to be" (Kidd, 1975, p. 242). The many stories about Coady, his cousin Father Jimmy Tompkins and others in the adult education toolbox are rife with the full spectrum of human emotion and all are imbued with a rich spirituality of justice that never soft-peddled or resorted to paternalism or complacency. One exemplar of spirituality in adult education is Freire (1970), who refuted the possibility of neutrality in educating, preferring instead to recognize that education is always political. Freire, steeped as he was in liberation theology from his home in Brazil, exile in Chile, and many years at World Council of Churches in Geneva, knew well the need to link justice and spirituality. In his literary work, he was fond of saying that we need to read the world before we read the word (Freire & Macedo, 1987).

Race and Ethnicity

Spirituality is connected to and influenced by our race and ethnicity. I am reminded daily that my own definition of spirituality is affected by my white background, and that my family has a strong attachment to working-class, Irish Roman Catholicism. I have prayed the stations of the cross, eaten fish on Friday, and known an intimate relationship with the Irish saints Brigid and Patrick. This ethnic identity helps me to understand why people return to rituals from their youth—they can provide comfort and support, and help them understand their vocation in adult education. Chittister reminds me that these rituals have carried my religious tradition—graces, masses, benedictions, rosaries, candles, and sick kits. The benefit of examining our own ethnic, racial, and spiritual biography is that it helps us understand how we relate to others as spiritual beings with different experiences.

The Africadian community, which is well represented in Nova Scotia, has a strong tradition of group singing, charismatic services, and vibrant preaching. Their spirituality has long been influenced by their location, culture, and traditions. I was reminded of how different this spirituality was from mine when I went to a wake for an Africadian co-worker who was Baptist. A sixty-year-old single mom, Susie had raised three children about thirty kilometres from our Scottish-Canadian town, though it is likely that she and her family rarely went there, except for work. At the visitation there was singing and rejoicing, with none of the usual Scottish traditions, such as lining up to shake hands with the family of the deceased that are so common in Nova Scotia. Spirituality here clearly has a religious and outward expression, as well as a strong cultural one. At that wake, I was reminded of how race and ethnicity affect our experience of, and affiliation to, a variety of spiritual traditions and our adult education practices. Black and local First Nations stories are not told in adult education history courses, and they are noticeably absent from the Antigonish Movement histories and texts, though these peoples have been here all along.

Culture and Geography

Overlapping with race are the factors of culture and geography that affect how adult educators' spirituality is lived out. While interviewing adult educators from Africa and India, I found that my Muslim and Hindu participants spoke freely of how they brought their religious traditions to bear on their work and how they acted as motivators, yet sometimes could cause local conflicts. One Ghanaian educator named Selma told me that she struggled with the conflicting expectations from her own class and religious group. Her move away from Ghana to study in the five-month Canadian certificate program was regarded as a crisis by her in-laws, who saw this act of independence as a violation of Islam. When I asked if she had conflicts with Islam, Selma responded that "religion is a big conflict ... more with the way we have taken Islam than with the way it actually is. They [some religious leaders] say that if a woman is being educated at some standard, I will not have time for religion. But that is not true, as I am practising it here" (English, 2005b, p. 95). What comes through this interview transcript is that religion is part of her life, though she must negotiate the various conflicts (which from my standpoint appear to be about power and control, not spirituality, although they are entangled with it) around its intersection with culture. Spirituality rarely comes easily and is the site of much learning in her life and adult education practice.

Gender

Gender, too, is a major aspect of spirituality. In the quote at the beginning of this chapter, Benedictine nun Joan Chittister (2008) speaks to her conflict with patriarchal religion because of her gender, which has developed into "a ministry of irritation" (p. 16). Even when dealing with social justice groups outside the church, gender (and often feminism) plays a role. A Canadian woman whom I interviewed about her national adult education work for justice pointed to how a local women's group regarded her suspiciously for her religious affiliation, and religious groups regarded her suspiciously because of her association with women's organizations. This study participant noted that "when you go off ...

for funding, you never mention [religion]. You have another language you would use. Going overseas opened up my eyes a lot to Roman Catholicism. I became much more critical of the church, as I think I have become much more critical of everything" (English, 2004, p. 107). As a committed feminist, she incorporates a strong justice element into her spirituality, and couples this with a clear and critical perspective that she applies to all life experiences.

Social Class

Intermingled with gender is social class. A steady script of religion *versus* spirituality has been promoted in the middle-class bastion of higher education, and some educators have made a concerted effort to emphasize a generic and all-inclusive spirituality. One wonders if these nuances and distinctions are not in some way connected to the attempt to shun religious institutions, part of the backlash against belief that has been fuelled by writers such as Hitchens (2007) and Dawkins (2008), along with others supporting atheism. Clearly, how we live our spirituality is influenced by our social class and position. I am abundantly aware of class when I listen to popular radio host Mary Hynes interview spiritual writers on the CBC radio show *Tapestry* every Sunday. There is a great deal of chuckling and chortling (no laughing), talk of "daring irreverence," and a version of spirituality that often seems fairly ethereal and removed from the everyday world of literacy, community development, and health education activities. In adult education's past, the emphasis of spirituality was more likely to be on community activism and social improvement. I am reminded of a story I read about Father Jimmy Tompkins, who was attending an adult education conference in the United States. When a fellow delegate approached him and said, "I understand you are making good Catholics of all those Nova Scotia fishermen," Father Tompkins retorted, "God help us, can you tell me any Catholic way of canning lobsters?" (Kidd, 1975, p. 244). Clearly, he was more interested in the roll-up-your-sleeves type of spirituality, given the great social and economic needs present in his day and region.

All of these elements—emotion, race, culture, gender, and class—factor into how one develops a spirituality and enacts it in the adult education community. For some of the people mentioned above, spirituality has strong overtones of religion; it is influenced by religion and affects it in turn. For others, spirituality knows no such religious or institutional bounds, and is lived out in a public or secular way (Berry, 1988). I see spirituality as having a broad reach, connected to a strong sense of self and the divine, and expressed in outreach, action, and relationships to others. It often involves challenges, and its practitioners must be critically self-reflexive, always asking: Who does this serve? Who is disenfranchised by it? Adult educators have the task of examining their own spirituality as well as cultivating it in others.

Spirituality in Adult Education Contexts

It is true that spirituality has infiltrated all arenas. What was once taboo has entered the mainstream. Writers like Norris (2008) and Dillard (1984) have become popular among the religious and non-religious alike. Within the field of adult education, spirituality has been lived out in many different venues, all of them educational yet influenced by different actors and socio-cultural factors. And a fair share of spiritual writers have contributed to adult education literature (e.g., English, 2005a; Groen, 2004a, 2004b). Interest in spirituality has spread to business, industry, nursing, and social work, among other fields, all of which are asking how spirituality can be integrated into teaching, work practices, and leisure activities. Yet it seems that most writers in the social sciences and nursing are only playing with making spiritual concepts palatable to their hearers. Nurses have worked with expanding the term "caring" (Dean, 2005); social workers have mixed spirituality with therapy and healing (Bullis, 1996); business has used spirituality in combination with human resources and professional development (Driscoll & Wiebe, 2007), and oriented it to the bottom line. And for all of these professions, it was a struggle to define spirituality, legitimate it, and encourage it. It got to the point where there were more books on spirituality in the business and workplace section of the bookstore than there were in religion. This conversation has not taken place without both costs and benefits. In the following sections, I examine some of the adult education communities of practice in which spirituality has been explored.

Workplace Education

There is a burgeoning literature on spirituality in workplace education and organizational literature (Driscoll & Wiebe, 2007; Groen, 2004a, 2004b; Weick & Putnam, 2006), some of it sympathetic to the need to bring in spirituality, but a great deal more cautioning the worker to beware of the employer's motives. Significantly, there is more theorizing on this topic than actual research of those who are actively promoting spirituality in the workplace. Yet the relationship between spirituality and workplace education has blossomed, as evidenced by multiple publications in this area, the section produced by the Academy of Management dedicated to spirituality, and special issues of journals such as *Advances in Developing Human Resources* (McLean & Johansen, 2006) devoted to the topic. In the same way employers assume that happier people work better and produce more, they also assume that spiritually rich people make more money or somehow improve the bottom line (Bell & Taylor, 2004).

An example of a university faculty concerned about workplace spirituality is Sobey's Business School at St. Mary's University in Halifax, Nova Scotia. Its Centre for Spirituality and the Workplace hosts speakers and seminars on the topic. This is intended to be a place where people can gather to study and learn about how spirituality might be incorporated into the workplace in an authentic way. In a 2007 article, Driscoll and co-writer Wiebe addressed the increasing technical approach to spirituality, and the need that many have to mechanize and control spiritual matters. They pointed out that spiritual matters have been taken over (or colonized) by corporate interests, and these left little to chance or revision. Driscoll and Wiebe critiqued the broadening of spirituality's definition to the point where it is difficult to find any frame of reference. Is everything spiritual? They made a compelling argument for the careful use of spirituality. As they pointed out, the link between "happiness and productivity is not a new idea" (2007, p. 340) and words such as empowerment, creativity, and values are all old ways of saying spiritual. Though one can argue that these words may or may not be used in a spiritual sense, they do give us something to think about. In sum, Driscoll and Wiebe, like many writers in this area, struggled with finding a workable solution to the issues they identified. What we, and they, are left with is the caution to be vigilant, authentic, and careful.

Sometimes this integration of spirituality in the workplace is intended to be part of a cultural sensitivity project. Papuni and Bartlett (2006) studied the integration of Maori and Pakeha perspectives into adult learning in Aotearoa/New Zealand workplaces. They were troubled by the fact that there was a colonial bias against incorporating Maori spirituality. Similarly, Beck (2006) looked at the integration of Jewish adult learning in the workplace. Clearly, the use of a culture or its spirituality needs to be undertaken with great care, and must have the full support and involvement of the culture concerned. Otherwise, charges of colonialism may be well founded.

Religiously oriented contexts such as parish offices, seminaries, schools of theology, church-based school boards, and even Jewish charities have a stated mandate to cultivate and nurture spirituality. This can indeed be challenging, as spirituality may become routinized and scheduled, or as religious educator Joan Marie Smith (1985) said, conditions can be created for the "dailyness of the sacred" (p. 102). Like her, I have experienced these taken-for-granted religious practices that are basically uncritically accepted and rarely examined. Some have stated that seminaries, for instance, can be quite lacking in spirituality. To the surprise of some readers (not to those who have spent time teaching and studying in such environments), Philip Sheldrake, a theologian and noted writer on spirituality made this observation in his work. Alternately, spirituality may be imposed, as when leaders mandate prayer and religious compliance, or support indoctrination without discussion or the opportunity for exemption. In all cases, it is necessary to be respectful of variances in commitment. Only an examined and continuously critiqued environment can be an exemplar for others.

All of this discussion on workplace spirituality raises the fear that employers will move into workers' personal space and invade their lifeworld. The threat of over-spiritualizing the work world is a real one, since it has the potential to erode personal boundaries and spaces. I believe that as a society, we need to be careful well-intentioned employers do not infringe on the authentic practices of employees, and that they do not trivialize spirituality to the degree that all aspects of life are seen as spiritual. We need to question our own practices: What is the purpose, and whose values are being furthered? My opinion of this literature and experience in the workplace is that the only defensible purpose for acknowledging or cultivating the spirituality of workers ought to be for providing assistance for human flourishing, not the bottom line. Workplace educators need to be wary about adopting specific spiritual and religious practice without paying attention to context, purpose, and authenticity.

Higher Education

Another place where spirituality has become firmly ensconced is in the academy, to the point that there is now major research going on examining how spirituality has been incorporated into higher education over the past few decades. For instance, Duerr, Zajonc, and Dana (2003) were asked to study 100 colleges that the Fetzer Institute had funded in order to integrate transformative and spiritual learning into their classes, a signal of the scope and importance attached to spiritualizing higher education. What was significant about this study is that spirituality was only integrated into the traditional subjects of the arts and humanities, raising the question of why the researchers thought scientists would self-select out of an opportunity to engage spirituality in their teaching.

A number of institutions have deliberately cultivated courses on spirituality. For instance, professors at the University of Calgary "collectively instruct seven graduate courses that focus on some aspect of spirituality and education" (Groen, 2008, p. 193). This is a very high number, and may constitute the most offered by an education faculty (outside of a school of theology) anywhere in the West. Faculty member Groen's influence, which she describes in her own chapter in this book, has directly affected this change and growth. She is not alone, since similar courses are being offered by many institutions, suggesting that we are now beyond the mistrust of spirituality in adult education and it is considered mainstream. For instance, in his chapter in the *Handbook of Adult Development and Learning*, Irwin (2006) simply stated that he was interested in Buddhist meditation as a spiritual act. Rather than addressing whether spirituality is acceptable, he showed interest in ways to encourage it to support adult development. The same can be said of Palmer (1998), who has written extensively about teaching and spirituality. In *The Courage to Teach*, Palmer focused on the importance of cultivating the "inner landscape of the educator's life" in order to focus on the starting place for effective teaching: one's spiritual life, quality of thought, and moral fibre.

Clearly, higher education has accepted spirituality to some degree. This is certainly true of religiously affiliated schools and colleges, but we must ask: is spirituality the purpose of higher education in general? How can we guard against our classes becoming meditation centres? Is spirituality seen only as introspection? What is the content—history, culture, and religion—of spirituality, and can we develop this in our teaching? As I noted in the section on spirituality and emotion, spirituality is not all about feathers, candles, and soft music. In other words, educators must take care not to use spirituality as an escape to a spiritual place in our classrooms; life is spiritual in all its messiness. So, while I support the recognition and cultivation of spirituality, I also support boundaries for it, and I refuse to limit spirituality to prayer practices. As the Benedictines make clear in their motto, *ora et labora*, work is also prayer. And so is reading, relating, imagining, and studying.

Community Development

Spirituality has recently achieved great recognition in both domestic and international community development (e.g., Chile & Simpson, 2004; Walters & Manicom, 1996), after centuries of dealing with the colonization efforts of churches and governments in many developing nations (VerBeek, 2000). This recent interest is seen most clearly in the emphasis on appreciative inquiry in development discourse and practice, an educative process that stresses the positive aspects of the community situation and values the hopes and dreams of participants (Cooperrider, Whitney, & Stavros, 2008; Hammond, 1998). It is also seen in the dedication of special issues for journals such as *Gender and Development* to the topic of religion and development (Sweetman, 1999) and in journal articles that focus on faith-based organizations (a term increasingly used instead of religious institutions) in local development (Botchwey, 2007). Botchwey makes the point that faith-based organizations are "silent partners in a web of institutional capital" (p. 37). She correctly asserts their integral role in offering a number of services in the community.

Of course, the concerted effort of the liberation theologians who work in South America to bridge the divide between development and religion is the oft-cited example of the link between spirituality and development (e.g., Gutierrez, 1988). As I noted already, this liberation theology movement had a significant effect on Freire (1970), and indirectly on many working in adult education influenced by his work. More recently, adult educator Parrish (Parrish & Taylor, 2007) looked at spirituality in community-based religious organizations such as the Catholic Worker Movement, which is clearly religious yet not traditionally so. And Pyrch (2007) examined the spiritual notions of hope in the practice of participatory action research, a vital and radical form of community development. He saw the practice as restorative for him and other participants.

What becomes clear in all these community development scenarios is the degree to which spirituality has entered relatively seamlessly into the everyday lexicon of community development. That it is present and talked about speaks to the hunger that many have for a deeper sense of life and meaning in their work, and the need to be part of a collective enterprise. Yet I do want to ask critical questions about how we engage spirituality and religion in development contexts. Have we seriously thought about the possibility that we might re-victimize our participants, especially those who have suffered at the hands of religious colonizers, such as Canada's First Nations? Are we working *with* participants, or have we come carrying our own spirituality agenda? Care needs to be taken to learn from past mistakes and experiences with cultures that are economically, culturally, and socially vulnerable.

Implications for Teaching and Learning

Adult education is a field that purports to be imbued with a critically reflective practice orientation that allows us to dig in deep to inform our thinking and future directions in the area of spirituality. As critically reflective practitioners, we realize that education is rife with contradictions and consequences of which we are, at best, only dimly aware (Brookfield, 2000). Consequently, through critical reflective practice we need to continuously assess the power relations in our spiritually informed work. Power is always already there, but we need to keep looking for it and tracing it in our relationships with learners. The challenge is not to rid the education context of power dynamics, according to Mary Parker Follett, but rather to see how power over learners can become power with learners (Brookfield). A critical question is how and why we are so interested in having spirituality involved in adult education, what our assumptions are, and what the expected outcomes are. Critically reflective practice is one route to constantly examining and re-examining our activity and our motivations. In terms of spirituality and adult education, there are numerous questions, and many will remain unresolved but often contemplated. The true bottom line for many of us is quite benign: We want to increase awareness, discussion, enactment, and cultivation of spirituality in our students' sphere, in their work, and in them as individuals. Here I propose some directions for educational practice.

The first direction is to disentangle spirituality from exclusive ties to "being nice." We need to remember that like justice, spirituality can be both fair and kind. Spirituality that is only oriented to increasing our personal bliss is problematic. From studying our history we can become more convinced that spirituality is about hard work, social justice, and sometimes entanglements with the deeper side of life. In adult education settings, whether they are workplaces, community projects, or classrooms, this may mean taking part in uncomfortable conversations and being willing to probe deeper issues such as the oppressive and social control dimensions of some religious and spiritual traditions and practices.

The second direction relates to the first. That is, we may need to engage in the "ministry of irritation" as Chittister (2008) called it when she described herself as the one who is charged to stir things up. To work for spirituality is to do more than pray and meditate—it is to work for justice, or to link our discussions to justice issues and support economic, social, and cultural development. Promoters of workplace education need to be aware of the changes that might result as a consequence of an emphasis on spirituality. A spirituality that works only to promote our own good is vacuous.

A third direction relates to the imagination (Chile & Simpson, 2004). Spirituality in our past has been related to vision and forward-looking thinking. In the words of bell hooks (1999), "One of the things that we must do as teachers is twirl around and around, and find out what works with the situation that we're in. Our models might not work. And that twirling, changing, is part of the empowerment" (p. 128). She empowers with love and heart. Using one's imagination does not mean flights of fancy, but it does mean creative engagement with the world and its needs. To be spiritually alive in community development is to think of possibilities, "to pursue a reasoned, compassionate, committed and democratic knowledge base" (Pyrch, 2007, p. 199). We need to ask if we are willing to let participants dream and imagine, and if we will create "a sanctuary in times of alienation and fear" (p. 199) as part of the imaginative process.

Another direction is for us, as adult educators, to tone down our expectations. We need to realize the spirit cannot be controlled and not think that spirituality will bring us instant peace, justice, and happiness. Vanier (1979), who founded the L'Arche Community for people with intellectual disabilities, observed that "it is difficult to make people understand that the ideal doesn't exist, that personal equilibrium and the harmony they dream of come only after years and years of struggle, and that even then they come only as flashes of grace and peace" (p. 17). We need to practise patience with the questions, the process, and ourselves.

Finally, as adult educators we need to think about future directions for our work. Do we have colleagues in cognate areas such as nursing and global studies who can work with us? How can we bring our research skills to bear in a systematic way on the experience of spirituality in adult education? Is it possible to bring our strengths in critically reflective dialogue to bear on conversations about spirituality in higher education? These are some of the threads that we might weave into our ongoing investigations.

Acknowledgements

This chapter grew out of a lecture I gave at St. Andrew's Hall, the Vancouver School of Theology, in December, 2007. I would like to thank my colleague, the Reverend Dr. Roberta Clare, for inviting me to give that address.

References

Beck, J. (2006). Jewish adult learning in the workplace. *Advances in Developing Human Resources, 8*(3), 364–372.

Bell, E., & Taylor, S. (2004). "From outward bound to inward bound": The prophetic voices and discursive practise of spiritual management development. *Human Relations, 57*(4), 439–466.

Berry, T. (1988). *The dream of the earth.* San Francisco, CA: Sierra Club.

Botchwey, N. D. (2007).The religious sector's presence in local community development. *Journal of Planning Education and Research, 27*, 36–48.

Brookfield, S. D. (2000). The concept of critically reflective practice. In A. L. Wilson & E. R. Hayes (Eds.), *Handbook of adult and continuing education* (New ed., pp. 33–50). San Francisco, CA: Jossey-Bass.

Bullis, R. K. (1996). *Spirituality in social work practice.* London, UK: Taylor & Francis.

Chickering, A. W., Dalton, J. C., & Stamm, L. (2006). *Encouraging authenticity and spirituality in higher education.* San Francisco, CA: Jossey-Bass.

Chile, L., & Simpson, G. (2004). Spirituality and community development: Exploring the link between the individual and the collective. *Community Development, 39*(4), 318–331.

Chittister, J. (2008). *Joan Chittister: In my own words* (Comp., ed., and intro. Mary Lou Kownacki). Ligouri, MI: Ligouri.

Cook, G. L. (1987). Educational justice for the campmen: Alfred Fitzpatrick and the foundation of Frontier College, 1899–1922. In M. R. Welton (Ed.), *Knowledge for the people: The struggle for adult learning in English-speaking Canada* (pp. 35–51). Toronto, ON: OISE Press.

Cooperrider, D., Whitney, D., & Stavros, J. M. (2008). *The appreciative inquiry handbook for leaders of change* (2nd ed.). San Francisco, CA: Crown, Custom & Berrett-Koehler.

Dawkins, R. (2008). *The God delusion.* Boston, MA: Houghton Mifflin.

Dean, A. (2005). Spirituality as a component in nursing care. *Kentucky Nurse, 53*(1), 12.

Dillard, A. (1984). *Holy the firm.* New York, NY: Harper & Row.

Driscoll, C., & Wiebe, E. (2007). Technical spirituality at work: Jacques Ellul on workplace spirituality. *Journal of Management Inquiry, 16*(4), 333–348.

Duerr, M., Zajonc, A., & Dana, D. (2003). Survey of transformative and spiritual dimensions of higher education. *Journal of Transformative Education, 1*(3), 177–211.

English, L. M. (2004). Feminist identities: Negotiations in the third space. *Feminist Theology, 3*(1), 97–125.

English, L. M. (2005a). Historical and contemporary explorations of the social change and spiritual directions of adult education. *Teachers College Record, 107*(6), 1169–1192.

English, L. M. (2005b). Third-space practitioners: Women educating for civil society. *Adult Education Quarterly, 55*(2), 85–100.

English, L. M., & Tisdell, E. J. (2010). Spirituality and adult education. In C. Kasworm, A. Rose, & J. Ross-Gordon (Eds.), *Handbook of adult and continuing education* (pp. 285–293). San Francisco, CA: Jossey-Bass.

Fitzpatrick A. (1999). *The university in overalls: A plea for part-time study.* Toronto, ON: Thompson Education. (Original work published 1920).

Freire, P. (1970). *Pedagogy of the oppressed.* New York, NY: Continuum.

Freire, P., & Macedo, D. P. (1987). *Literacy: Reading the word & the world.* South Hadley, MA: Bergin & Garvey.

Groen, (2004a). The creation of soulful spaces: An exploration of the processes and the organizational context. *Organization Development Journal, 22*(3), 8–19.

Groen, J. (2004b). The experience and practice of adult educators in addressing the spiritual dimensions of the workplace. *Canadian Journal for the Study of Adult Education, 18*(1), 72–92.

Groen, J. (2008). Paradoxical tensions in creating a teaching and learning space within a graduate education course on spirituality. *Teaching in Higher Education, 13*(2), 193–204.

Gutiérrez, G. (1988). *A theology of liberation: History, politics and salvation.* Maryknoll, NY: Orbis Books.

Hammond, S. A. (1998). *The thin book of appreciative inquiry* (2nd ed.). Plano, TX: Thin Books.

Hitchens, C. (2007). *The portable atheist: Essential readings for the nonbeliever.* Philadelphia, PA: Da Capo.

hooks, b. (1999). Embracing freedom: Spirituality and liberation. In S. Glazer (Ed.), *The heart of learning: Spirituality in education* (pp. 113–129). New York, NY: Jeremy Tarcher.

Irwin, R. R. (2006). Spiritual development in adulthood: Key concepts and models. In C. Hoare (Ed.), *Handbook of adult learning and development* (pp. 307–325). Oxford University Press.

Jarvis, P., & Walters, N. (Eds.). (1993). *Adult education and theological interpretations.* Malabar, FL: Krieger.

Kidd, R. (March 1975). The social gospel and adult education in Canada. In R. Allen (Ed.), *The social gospel in Canada: Papers of the interdisciplinary conference on the social gospel in Canada, University of Regina.* Ottawa, ON: National Museums of Canada.

Kilde, J. H. (1999). The "predominance of the feminine" at Chautauqua: Rethinking the gender–space relationship in Victorian America. *Signs, 24*(2), 449–486.

Lotz, J., & Welton, M. R. (1997). *The life and times of Father Jimmy.* Wreck Cove, NS: Breton Books.

McLean, G. N., & Johansen, B.-C. (2006). World views of adult learning in the workplace [Special issue]. *Advances in Developing Human Resources, 8*(3).

Neal, R. (1998). *Brotherhood economics: Women and cooperatives in Nova Scotia.* Sydney, NS: UCCB Press, Cape Breton Books.

Norris, K. (2008). *Acedia and me: A marriage, monks and a writer's life.* Penguin.

O'Sullivan, E. (1999). *Transformative learning: Educational vision for the 21st century.* New York, NY: Zed Books, in association with University of Toronto Press.

Palmer, P. (1998). *The courage to teach: Exploring the inner landscape of a teacher's life.* San Francisco, CA: Jossey-Bass.

Papuni, H. T., & Bartlett, K. R. (2006). Maori and Pakeha perspectives of adult learning in *Aotearoa*/New Zealand workplaces. *Advances in Developing Human Resources, 8*(3), 400–407.

Parrish, M. M., & Taylor, E. W. (2007). Seeking authenticity: Women and learning in the Catholic Worker Movement. *Adult Education Quarterly, 57*(3), 221–247.

Pyrch, T. (2007). Participatory action research and the culture of fear: Resistance, community, hope and courage. *Action Research, 5*(2), 199–216.

Reiser, A. C. (2003). *The Chautauqua movement: Protestants, progressives and the culture of modern liberalism, 1874–1920.* New York, NY: Columbia University Press.

Scott, J. C. (1999). The Chautauqua movement: Revolution in popular higher education. *Journal of Higher Education, 70*(4), 389–412.

Sheldrake, P. (1998). The role of spiritual direction in the context of theological education. *Anglican Theological Review, 80*(3), 366–381.

Smith, J. (1985). Ecumenical spirituality and the religious educator. In James Michael Lee (Ed.), *The spirituality of the religious educator* (pp. 88–105). Birmingham, AL: Religious Education Press.

Sweetman, C. (1999). Gender and Development [Special Issue]. *Gender, Religion, and Spirituality, 7*(1).

Taylor, E. W. (2008). Transformative learning theory. *New Directions for Adult and Continuing Education, 119,* 5–15.

Vanier, J. (1979). *Community and growth: Our pilgrimage together.* Toronto, ON: Griffin House.

Ver Beek, K. A. (2000). Spirituality: A development taboo. *Development in Practice, 10*(1), 31–43.

Walters, S., & Manicom, L. (Eds.). (1996). Introduction. In *Gender in popular education: Methods for empowerment* (pp. 1–22). London, UK: Zed books.

Weick, K. E., & Putnam, T. (2006). Organizing for mindfulness: Eastern wisdom and Western knowledge. *Journal of Management Inquiry, 15,* 275–287.

Welton, M. R. (2001). *Little Mosie from the Margaree: A biography of Moses Michael Coady.* Toronto, ON: Thompson Education.

Whitehead, J. D., & Whitehead, E. E. (1994). *Shadows of the heart: A spirituality of the negative emotions.* New York, NY: Crossroad.

Yeaxlee, B. (1925). *Spiritual values in adult education* (2 vols.). Oxford University Press.

Chapter 3

Religion and Spirituality in Social Work Academic Settings

John R. Graham and Micheal L. Shier

This chapter is a collaboration between a professor (Graham) who has been writing on the topic of spirituality in social work since the early 1990s, and a very impressive graduate student (Shier) completing a Ph.D. at the University of Pennsylvania (the words here are Graham's). They have published together on the topic before (Graham & Shier, 2009, 2011; Shier & Graham, 2012), and some of that work made its way into the present chapter. Graham previously conveyed many of his experiences in writing about spirituality (Graham, 2006, 2008; see also Al-Krenawi & Graham 2009). Much of his early research was based on the religious origins of the profession (Graham, 1991, 1992, 1994). He later became involved in international social work, and a good portion of that, like the previous scholarship he published, was oriented toward spirituality. But back then, it was not an easy topic to write about. As he commented a few years ago,

> A lot of [that] early scholarship with long-standing collaborator and friend
> Professor Alean Al-Krenawi looked at various ways of understanding traditional
> healing in the Middle East (among Dervish, Koranic healers, and others) in
> relation to professional disciplines such as social work (Al-Krenawi & Graham,
> 1996a, b, 1997a, b, 1999b, c; Graham & Al-Krenawi, 1996). This research was
> strongly indebted to epistemologies other than our own, and indeed it appeared
> not only in social work journals but also in such disciplinary venues as anthropol-
> ogy, area studies, bereavement studies, family therapy, health sciences, psychol-
> ogy, psychiatry, sociology, and women's studies (Al-Krenawi & Graham, 1996b,
> 1997a, 1999a, b, d, 2003a, 2004, 2005; Al-Krenawi, Graham, & Sehwail, 2002;
> Al-Krenawi, Graham, & Slonim-Nevo, 2002). Later we moved into understand-
> ing Islam as a force in social work writ large (Al-Krenawi & Graham, 2000,
> 2003a). Our research was wonderfully collaborative with Muslim commun-
> ities in the Arab Middle East: the Bedouin-Arab of the Negev, communities

in Palestine, Jordan, Egypt, the United Arab Emirates, and other parts of the Muslim world (Al-Krenawi & Graham, 2004, 2005, 2006; Al-Krenawi, Graham, Dean, & El-Thabet, 2004; Al-Krenawi, Graham, & Sehwail, 2002, 2004).

However, disseminating this scholarship within social work, particularly in the early 1990s, was a hard slog. I recall 15 years ago receiving letters from editors of American journals that I would not expect to receive today. Most could be paraphrased as follows: "thank you for your submission; it is analytically and methodologically sound and makes a contribution to the literature; but it is of insufficient interest to our readership, and so we regretfully decline the submission." How strange, it seemed to me then (as now), that professional journals—the ones in which we wanted to publish—appeared so fundamentally resistant to research on spirituality. Or was it resistant to spirituality as a topic outside of America? (Graham, 2006, p. 65)

How different it is today. The 2001 creation of the Canadian Association for Spirituality and Social Work (now known as the Canadian Society for Spirituality and Social Work: CSSSW) changed things in our country. Co-founded by Barbara Swartzentruber, John Graham, John Coates, and Brian Ouellette, the CSSSW has organized eight conferences, each with its own special edition journal arising out of that work. Through the frankly yeoman work of CSSSW founders and subsequent people involved with the organization and the leadership of John Coates in many areas, including CSSSW's website, there is a strong national organization, and a growing constituency within and outside the academy fully willing to legitimate spirituality as a topic of genuine professional concern.

But working with the spiritual traditions of social work has had further complexities beyond this. To begin with, social work has an ambivalent relationship with the academy, having emerged as an academic discipline only after previously established practices were well under way in voluntary charitable communities, working houses, and poor law offices (Graham & Al-Krenawi, 2000). Graham shall always regard social work as a discipline that is constantly striving to catch up to a theoretical tradition; the practices usually occur first, and how we make sense of these things—how we conceive them as scholars—come next. Rarely is it the other way around. When it has been—for instance, as when psychodynamic theories emerged in casework from the late 1920s to mid-1960s—there was always a very practical approach taken that emphasized the hands-on aspects of getting the job done: creating and sustaining rapport, facilitating communication, and understanding professional roles in the context of agency functions (Dore, 1990). To some extent, spirituality has always been an undercurrent to social work theory, something implicitly understood as important—perhaps so much so that it was taken for granted, assumed not to be important, or even believed to be non-existent. In Canada, it leapt out of the closet shortly after the CSSSW was established. The last great taboo of the profession exposed itself to a surprisingly receptive (at least to me) social work community.

Social work originated as an academic discipline in the 1890s in the United Kingdom, and the first decade of the twentieth century in the United States. A traditional narrative many have repeated claims that those in the profession sought to dispense with its religious roots once it became part of an academic setting and positioned social work to be a discipline that was both professional and scientific (as the term was understood at the start of the twentieth century) (Lubove, 1965; Woodroffe, 1962). More recent scholarship, however, insists on the persistence of religious norms as part of the profession's modus vivendi (Graham, 1992; Leiby, 1985); and even the Canadian welfare state itself is properly understood to have a very strong basis in religious thinking and principles (Gauvreau & Christie, 1996).

The discipline's origins therefore extend to the earliest notions of human caring, and can be rightly seen as an outcome of institutional arrangements that gradually developed from the Middle Ages onward. Those people responsible for paving the way for the historic emergence of social work therefore would not have understood the term "spirituality" the way that we read it in the early twenty-first century. Indeed, religious rather than spiritual nomenclature and concepts frequently conveyed the rationale, processes, and intended outcomes for coming to the assistance of other people. But as Graham and Shier outline in this chapter, "spirituality" is nonetheless a useful concept for tracing the emergence of social work as an academic and applied professional discipline, particularly over the *longue durée* leading to our present time.

In this chapter, Graham and Shier do three things. First, they outline the history of the profession, emphasizing the place of religion and spirituality within that trajectory. Limited space requires much of that analysis to concentrate on Canada, but part of the narrative is anchored to the European colonial heritage from which social work and its allied institutional structures emerged. Next, they consider the current status of "spirituality" and "religion" as terms within English language social work scholarship, and equally important, as applied concepts in the field. In a final section, they reflect on social work's encounter with religion and spirituality in their own training and education of future social workers.

History of Social Work

Despite its modest roots which began growing a little over 100 years ago, social work today is practised in much of the world. The International Federation of Social Workers (IFSW, established 1956) succeeded the International Permanent Secretariat of Social Workers (1928), and grew from a small organizational framework in seven nations to include countries in Africa, Asia/Pacific, Europe, Latin America and the Caribbean, and North American regions as members (www.ifsw.org). The International Association of Schools of Social Work (established 1928) initially comprised 51 schools mostly from Europe, but today has membership worldwide. The 2006 Canadian Census claimed that there are almost 49,000 social workers in Canada, nearly 80% of whom are women.

A previous generation of historians tended to look at social work as a product of industrialization, urbanization, and transition from religiously inspired helping to secular, professional practice. The history of social work therefore emphasizes a teleology of progress—religious sentiment replaced with emergent social science theory; faith-based practices supplanted with professional and deliberate skills from the emerging fields of social casework, community development, and policy practice—and after the Second World War, empirically based practice dominated all (Graham, Coholic, & Coates, 2007; Graham, Al-Krenawi, & Bradshaw, 2000).

Canada's first school of social work opened in 1914 at the University of Toronto, following the late-nineteenth-century establishment of a formal training program at a settlement house in east London, later affiliated with the University of London. The school's establishment in the first decade of the twentieth century was concurrent with that of social work schools at Columbia University and the University of Chicago (Graham & Al-Krenawi, 2000). Over the course of the interwar period, Freudian and later Rankian theories held sway in the emerging field of social casework, and a variety of community development and group work theories paralleled (and were often influenced by) a growing corpus of social scientific thought.

The religious roots of social work in Canada precede European settlement to the extent that Aboriginal peoples cared for one another and expressed in those actions some reference to spirituality. Starting in the sixteenth century, the French and later the English brought with them European approaches to eleemosynary activities that included Roman Catholic and Protestant institutions, respectively. By the mid-nineteenth century, there was an elaborate system of social care in Canada that was frequently anchored to these traditions. But these would change over the course of the next 100 years.

A Toronto charity for women established in 1878 called the Haven is a perfect example for understanding this Canadian transition. By the 1890s, the organization had started to display more secular, professional tenets in service delivery, and by 1930 a secular, professional social work ethos had replaced the organization's religious foundations. By examining one such case study in detail, it is possible to provide insight into the Canadian profession's spiritual and religious origins (Graham, 2007).

One of the religiously inspired volunteers associated with the Haven was William Lyon Mackenzie King, the future prime minister of Canada, then merely an undergraduate student at the University of Toronto. As he wrote in his diary,

> I am going to seek to know more of Christ and to live a better life....I want to give my whole life to Him.... I am learning more of our Saviour every day.... I must become more earnest in my work for the Master, it will not do to be half-hearted. I hope I can do more and more every day to lift up the fallen, I hope that my life may be a pure and holy one devoted to Christ alone. (Graham, 2007, p. 51)

Religious sentiments were everywhere in the Haven's annual reports. As its 1879 report asserted, an "undercurrent of vice" rushed "madly through every large centre of population." "Never in the world's history," the report continued, "was such a glamour thrown around sin; never was vice presented in such a multitudinous of forms" (Toronto Women's Christian Association, 1879, as cited in Graham, 2007, p. 57). Religious terminology was often used to describe a resident's plight. In 1878, for example, the Haven volunteer Harriet Gamble urged young women to "avoid evil," lest they "be swallowed up in the vortex of sin." The organization's services were also conceptualized in religious terms. As the 1879 Toronto Women's Christian Association (WCA) Annual Report noted, all work undertaken by its volunteers was meant to glorify God, as well as to save sinners:

> The Divine Master has taught us that one soul exceeds in the value [of] the whole world, and we know that within the casket of these sin-stained, sin-marred bodies, there lives, dwarfed and depraved though it may be, an immortal and redeemed spirit, and we are willing to labour a lifetime that, even one of these priceless gems may be laid at the feet of Jesus. (Graham, 2007, pp. 52–53)

Gradual changes, though, started to occur in the mid-1880s. Residential inmates, as they were then called, started to be classified according to terms such as "older" and "younger," more or less "depraved" and "shameless," those with young children and those without (Graham, 2007, p. 56). The first reference to a Nursery Matron was made in 1898, and by 1907 the organization appointed a superintendent who had written on the growing presence of the "white slave trade" (the perceived rise in numbers of young women who earned money selling sex); the person who held that 1907 appointment later became a part-time lecturer in the University of Toronto's newly formed Department of Social Science, which ultimately became a School and later Faculty of Social Work (Graham, 2007, p. 57). In the post–First World War period, social casework ascended fairly rapidly, to a large extent because of the pressures placed upon it by an emerging Federation for Community Service (FCS), the precursor to the United Way that was a formal associative arrangement of Toronto charities to which the Haven belonged after 1918. Federation dollars spoke loudly, and by 1930 nearly half of the Haven's budget came from the FCS. A 1924 federation report strongly urged the organization to hire trained social service workers and to keep systematic records of intervention. The following year, the organization hired its first graduate of a social work program, and with this came formal social investigations, the classification of residents according to psychiatric terminologies, and formal staff training at various national conferences on practice-related issues. In 1926, social work became one of three distinct divisions within the organization, and ten years later the organization assumed a mandate for working with one resident population, the "mentally retarded" (Graham, 2007, pp. 59–61).

As the Haven changed over this fifty-year period, so did social work in Canada. Both reflected and were increasingly influenced by the broad changes in religious and social life in the nation. As Graham, Coholic, and Coates (2007) argued, the Social Services Council of Canada (established 1907) was the creation of a number of diverse representatives from the trade union movement, Anglican, Methodist, Presbyterian, and Baptist churches, and others. Historians Gauvreau and Christie see the rise of the twentieth-century welfare state as the ultimate ascendance of United Church theology (1996). The welfare state itself was highly indebted to a Canadian social democratic tradition, and here again several Protestant clergy were important in the establishment and leadership of the Cooperative Commonwealth Federation (renamed the New Democratic Party in 1961), a social democratic political party elected to national and provincial legislatures: Methodist cleric and party founder J. S. Woodsworth (1874–1942) and Baptist Minister Tommy Douglas (1904–1986). Woodsworth's famous 1911 *My neighbor: A study of city conditions, a plea for social service*, captures the social gospel tradition perhaps as well as any other Canadian source. It is possible to argue that "the welfare state owes much to faith traditions and that many of the country's oldest social service institutions have roots that are in some way associated with religious institutions or with personnel who were motivated by faith" (Graham, Coholic, & Coates, 2007, pp. 26–27).

Religion and Spirituality in Social Work Scholarship

Previous research has assessed the focus of scholarship on religion and spirituality in social work (Canda, Nakashima, Burgess, & Russel, 1999; Graham, 2006, 2008; Graham & Shier, 2009). This section is intended to provide a general overview of this scholarship. While the terms religion and spirituality are sometimes used interchangeably, research conducted on each is distinct—focusing on, for example, the spirituality of a person or cultural aspects of a specific religious faith tradition. Social work researchers somewhat agree with current discussions on the interrelationship between the two concepts (Canda & Furman, 2010), but the development of empirical and conceptual scholarship on each is still divided. Because of the socio-cultural aspects of major faith traditions for individuals, families, and communities, it is necessary to understand the differences and similarities between religiously sensitive social work practice and spiritually sensitive social work practice (Graham & Shier, 2009). Definitions for the two terms provide some insight into the difference between these two approaches in social work practice.

With regard to religion, religiosity, and faith traditions, Graham and Shier (2009) define each using

> Durkheim's definition, [with] religion: "a unified set of beliefs and practices relative to sacred things, that is to say, things set apart and forbidden, beliefs and practices which unite into one single moral community ... all those who adhere to them" (Durkheim, 1915, p. 62), a concept that considers dimensions associated with both actions and beliefs but acknowledges the collective nature of religions. Religiosity has been defined by dimensions that assess the degree to which a person or group are religious (Cornwall, Albrecht, Cunningham, & Pitcher, 1986). "Faith," "faith tradition," and "religious tradition" are used interchangeably, and each refers to specific religions that have emerged over time (Smith, 1998, p. 218)

Within this definition, religion is based upon both individual and collective relationships, belief systems, and practices. Spirituality, though, is typically defined in ways that help to describe individual experiences or cognition. For example, Canda and Furman (2010) define spirituality as "a universal quality of human beings and their cultures related to the quest for meaning, purpose, morality, transcendence, well-being, and profound relationships with ourselves, others, and ultimate reality" (p. 5). Likewise, "spiritual relationships are defined as relationships to self, others, a higher power, or the environment that brings forth a sense of inner strength, peace, harmonious interconnectedness, and meaning in life (Walton as cited in Laurence, 2000, p. 233). Both concepts (religion and spirituality) are important for a profession concerned with individuals and communities and the internal dynamics of the human psyche in relation to individual self-determination and collective, socio-cultural interactions.

Scholarship of Religion and Social Work

Graham and Shier (2009) did a literature review and analysis of scholarship on 15 different faith traditions and social work for the period 1970 to 2007: the faith traditions included Bahá'í, Buddhism, Confucianism, Christianity, Druze, Hinduism, Islam, Judaism, Sikhism, Taoism, Traditional or Aboriginal Spirituality, Wicca, and Zoroastrianism. In summary, they found that there have been an increasing number of publications over the last four decades about religious faith traditions in social work scholarship (Graham & Shier, 2009). Furthermore, within the last two decades specifically, there has been growing interest in multiple faith traditions. This scholarship is appearing, not surprisingly, in publications such as *Social Work and Christianity, Jewish Social Work Forum, Journal of Jewish Communal Service, Journal of Religion and Spirituality in Social Work: Social Thought*, and in *Families in Society, International Social Work, Social Science and Medicine*, and *Social Work*, among many others. The lead author's country of affiliation for the majority of this scholarship was the United States, and approximately 75% of all lead authors of the 1,205 abstracts reviewed were affiliated with United States, Israel, England, or Canada. Graham and Shier (2009) only reviewed English language scholarship, and utilized databases that provide access to primarily North American and European journals. While this was a limitation of their literature review study, the findings were similar to other studies done on spirituality in social work (Graham, 2006) and topics related to social work theory and practice (Al-Krenawi & Graham, 2003a; Bradshaw & Graham, 2007; Healy, 1999, 2001; Midgely, 1981). As Graham puts it,

> Much of social work's written, English-language knowledge base continues to be produced in the Global North, particularly its English language countries, but is consumed in the Global North and South (Al-Krenawi & Graham, 2003a; Lyons, 1999). Social work, after all, emerged in the Global North, and was transplanted to the Global South during the interwar period as a product of what has been described (accurately, in my view) as "academic colonialization" (Atal, 1981). After World War II, schools of social work in the Global South proliferated, with cultural assumptions, and with the predominance of professional writing, originating in the North, profoundly influencing teaching, research, and practice in the Global South. (2006, p. 68)

Graham and Shier (2009) also identified four primary themes in this scholarship. Through a process of inductive analysis, they found that the publications discussed (1) how religion impacts social work, (2) how religion and social work are interrelated, (3) how religion impacts social processes and issues, and (4) how considering religion can improve religious/cultural sensitivity and/or competency. Each theme is discussed in more detail in their article. Table 3.1 provides a general overview of the subthemes for each category.

Literature related to the theme in the first column of Table 3.1 was most prevalent over the four-decade study period. A decreasing amount of scholarship is associated with each column following this category. Within this scholarship, more emphasis has been placed over the last two decades on specific faith traditions. The result is a growing body of literature in two of the primary themes: scholarship focusing on religious and cultural sensitivity in social work practice, and scholarship describing the impact of religion on social work practice and education (column 1 and column 4, Table 3.1).

While Graham and Shier (2009) pointed out that there is an overlap between all four primary thematic categories, they did not identify how the categories

Table 3.1* Thematic Breakdown of Content Analysis on Journal Articles about Religion and Social Work

Religious/cultural sensitivity in practice	Impact of religion on social environment, processes, and issues	Interrelationship between religion and social work	Impact of religion on social work practice and education
1. Factors from specific faith traditions to consider in practices 2. Religion and ethno-cultural identity of client groups 3. Incorporating religion in social work scholarship – Best practices – Interventions	1. Impact of religion on social interaction(e.g., within families, in communities) 2. Impact of religion on individual and public perceptions of social issues 3. Impact of religion on socio-cultural, economic, and political context of the social environment (e.g., gender constructs, resource distribution, modernization, development)	1. Historical context of religion and social work. – Christianity as the foundation of the profession – Link between religious values and beliefs and social work principles of practice and ethical guidelines 2. Role of religious organizations and practice comparable to non-sectarian social welfare organizations – Mutually reinforcing practices and roles (e.g., practices in the Eastern faith traditions of Confucianism and Buddhism)	1. Impact of religion on social work practice – Religion contributes to the reasons people access or seek services (i.e., the help-seeking process) – Religion contributes to the process of relationship development between client and worker 2. Impact of religion on social work education – Religion is a construct to consider in social work theory (i.e., religion or spirituality is another construct to consider when assessing the person in the environment) – Religion impacts students of social work (i.e., it impacts how they perceive and experience social work education).

*Table adapted from the thematic description provided in Graham and Shier (2009).

were interrelated. Further analysis of these thematic categories, extending that earlier analysis, finds a distinctive pattern between the categories (see Figure 3.1). The two categories of "Impact of religion on the social environment, processes, and issues" and "Interrelationship between religion and social work" act as rationales for the remaining two categories. The categories of "Impact of religion on social work practice and education" and "Religious/cultural sensitivity in practice," are mutually reinforcing. Future research should explore the relationship between categories that are not mutually reinforcing and/or informing.

In Canada specifically, research has also investigated the impact of specific faith traditions within our multicultural context. Graham, Bradshaw, and Trew (2008, 2009a, 2009b, 2010) have investigated the unique needs of some Muslim clients accessing social services. Their study provided an overview of cultural and religiously sensitive social work practice with Muslim service users in four Canadian cities. A number of other studies are presented in a recent edited collection by Coates, Graham, and Swartzentruber with Ouellette (2007). In that book, Snyder and Bowman (2007) identified considerations that should be taken when working in a social work capacity with Old Order Mennonites. Este (2007) found evidence of the significance of black churches for African-Canadians. Zapf (2007) highlights the relationship between Aboriginal spiritual practices and the environment. He argues that in some traditional knowledge systems, the environment is considered a person's "partner," essentially challenging the perspective that religion is just an aspect of the person's environment to consider. These discussions challenge the way social workers view clients and their surrounding social and physical environments, and question many of the

Figure 3.1. Interrelationship between Major Themes

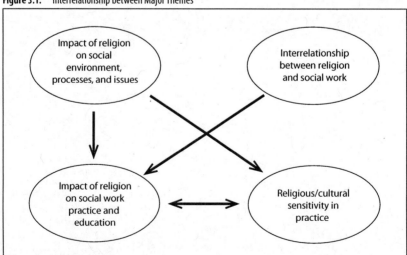

essentialist qualities of social work theory and practice. As a collective, these studies suggest that practice needs to be adapted to meet the religious cultural aspects of these diverse individuals, groups, and communities.

Scholarship of Spirituality and Social Work

In comparison to religion, research on spirituality in social work has received less attention. Researchers have been challenged on how to adequately measure the influences of spirituality for individuals, families, communities, and societies. Canda and Furman (2010) highlight several aspects of spirituality to consider in their "operational model of spirituality" (p. 82). They focus on spirituality as a holistic concept of the person and identify spiritual drives, experiences, functions of spirituality, development processes related to spirituality, aspects of a person's spiritual perspectives (i.e., beliefs or values, and so on), and expressions of religiosity. Each of these aspects of spirituality for a person is measurable— whether that means gathering empirical data through interviewing, or developing instruments that measure religiosity or how people respond to adverse life situations.

Some of this research has been completed. For instance, Shier and Graham (2011) found that social workers engage in mindfulness practices around several themes related to life experiences and thought processes. These social workers were engaging in a spiritual process. Would it be fair to assume that their clients do not do the same? Of course, this question is somewhat facetious. People seeking help from social workers likely engage in similar processes, which could contribute to their overall well-being; and this in turn contributes to the overall subjective well-being of the social workers participating in that study. Cadell, Janzen, and Haubrich (2007) also investigated aspects of spirituality involved in caring for someone who has HIV/AIDS, and the grief following that person's death. They found that people with these experiences contemplated aspects of their own existence and longevity, and reconstructed meaning after the loss of the individual. Todd (2007) found similar connections in her research with feminist community organizers. She identified how these women made sense of their experiences based on personal religious and spiritual stories.

More recently, researchers have conducted several studies with social work practitioners who have identified aspects of spirituality being incorporated into their own practice (Gilligan & Furness, 2006) and with distinct population groups. For example, Kvarfordt and Sheridan (2007) found that social workers working with children and adolescents utilized spiritually based interventions with that demographic group. A similar finding was uncovered among social workers practising with the elderly (Murdock, 2005). Other research has found the need to consider the topic of spirituality and religion when working with clients experiencing terminal illness, bereavement, adoption, and foster care

(Furman, Benson, Grimwood, & Canda, 2004; Zahl, 2006), or when working with specific immigrant populations (Lee & Chan, 2009). The social needs of specific client groups differ, as do their spiritual needs. This is an important consideration for social work education and any attempt to create a single model of spiritually focused social work intervention.

Likewise, location is a necessary consideration. The role of spirituality in social work practice is different from one international context to the next (Stirling, Furman, Benson, Canda, & Grimwood, 2010; Zahl, 2003). For instance, social workers practising in the United Kingdom and the United States were more accepting of religion and spirituality in their direct practice than their Norwegian counterparts, and United States social workers were more accepting than those in the United Kingdom (Furman, Zahl, Benson, & Canda, 2007; Furman, Zahl, Benson, Canda, & Grimwood, 2005; Zahl, 2003; Zahl, Furman, Benson, & Canda, 2007).

Why social workers follow a spiritually sensitive practice approach is also an important question. For example, Stewart and Koeske (2006) found that the religious and spiritual beliefs of social work students along with the local culture helped to predict attitudes toward the use of spiritually based interventions (Mattison, Jayaratne, & Croxton also had a similar finding in 2000). This is important because it suggests that social workers may not include the spirituality based needs of their clients given their own personal beliefs or local environment and culture. If the inclusion of spirituality within the social work curriculum is necessary in more mainstream ways—as most of the research on the subject suggests—understanding student, practitioner, and professor perceptions of spirituality and religion in social work practice becomes even more important. In Canada, there is an omission in scholarship investigating the general attitudes of social workers and students about spirituality and religion in practice. Attitudes vary by country; therefore it would be useful to assess the general perceptions of practitioners in Canada, a unique example because of the colonial history and multicultural context (including social work practice experience with a diversity of Aboriginal populations) and diverse geography.

Religion and Spirituality in Social Work Education

Some schools of social work within North America have a long-standing association with formal religious denominations. These include a Roman Catholic tradition at Fordham University in New York City and at Catholic University of America in Washington, DC, a Protestant tradition at Calvin College in Grand Rapids, Michigan, and Judaism at Yeshiva University in New York City.

Formal associations of spirituality or religion and social work have also developed in recent years, linking social work practitioners, academics, and all other interested members throughout the world. Examples include the Canadian

Society for Spirituality and Social Work (CSSSW), the Society for Spirituality and Social Work in the United States of America (SSSW), the North American Association of Christians in Social Work (NACSW), and the Center for Spirituality and Social Work (CSSW).

Along with these, religion has been considered in accreditation and professional regulatory associations in North America. For instance, the Canadian Association of Social Workers (CASW) Code of Ethics makes reference to discrimination based on religion. More generally, under direct guidelines of practice, reference is also made to social workers' religious beliefs and articulates the need to recognize conflict between personal and professional values. Where in social work education, though, are these religious beliefs held by the practitioner discussed?

While scholarship and research on spirituality and religion has developed separately—primarily because of spirituality's measurability issues and the link between religion, religiosity, and culture—the terms religion and spirituality in relation to social work education have developed more connectively, with the latter an extension of the former. As a result, this following section is not broken into two separate parts like the previous section was.

Religion, Spirituality, and Social Work Education

Earlier writings about religion in social work education discussed its impact specifically on social work practice (Loewenberg, 1988). Religion and faith can act as guides for people as they make sense of themselves and the contexts in which they live (Beattie, 2007; Beyer, 2000; Cnaan, Wineburg, & Boddie, 1999; Taylor, 2007). Furthermore, religion has become an aspect of diversity to consider in models of anti-oppressive and culturally respectful social work practice (Al-Krenawi & Graham, 2003b).

As an extension of the earlier literature on religion in social work, an alternative approach to the field has focused instead on spirituality (Graham, 2006). A spirituality focus has gained some favour because it offers a framework to understand multiple religions and those spiritually based thoughts, processes, and actions that have no formal connection to a specific faith tradition (Canda & Furman, 1999). In the second edition of Canda and Furman's book (2010), the overlap between social worker, client, and spirituality is made conceptually clearer, since academics and practitioners have been thinking more about the intersection between spirituality and social work practice in recent years (Barker, 2007). What this growing body of literature has argued is that spirituality in social work education is more than just teaching students how to respect diversity or understand how their clients see the world. Spirituality is just as much a part of them (Collins, 2005; Lee & Barrett, 2007) as social workers and people, and the way they engage with their clients, as it is about their clients' specific spiritual needs. Spirituality in social work practice can also be about identifying how practitioners make sense of their own identities and relationships with clients. This second point has long been considered in reflective social work practice, and in multiple models of social work practice used with individuals and communities (Graham & Shier, 2011; Shier & Graham, 2011).

Making the link between aspects of religiosity and spirituality, Carroll (1998) identified two dimensions of spirituality that are important for social workers to consider in practice. The first dimension refers to the essence of individual existence and the underlying motivation for personal development and fulfillment. In many ways, this can be considered spirituality. The other dimension, related to religiosity in some ways, consists of those behaviours and actions that contribute to how people develop meaning in life and their relationship to some higher being. Examples of the latter are a mindfulness exercise, the actual psychological process of self-reflection, or the physical acts of prayer and meditation.

Within social work education, these contexts of spirituality have been less understood. Curriculum content about spirituality and religious traditions is sparse in social work (Canda & Furman, 2010; Sheridan, 2009; Whiting, 2008). Likewise, Canadian curriculum has minimal content related specifically to spirituality and religion (Coholic, 2003; Morgan, Berwick, & Walsh, 2008). If they are available, these topics are presented generally in courses on diversity, or offered as a special elective course (Rothman, 2009). Some have made attempts to rectify this. Carroll (1998), for example, relates her two-dimensional model to social work practice, emphasizing the use of particular tools to help people connect to their essence. The main focus of most pedagogical material though has been on the social worker–client relationship and methods of intervention to assist in the spiritual functioning of the client (Bullis, 1996; Canda & Furman, 1999; Van Hook, Hugen, & Aguilar, 2001; Hodge, 2002). Derezotes (2006) offers a comprehensive application of conceptual literature and empirical research on the subject of spirituality and social work to practice with specific groups or in particular domains. Likewise, spirituality is a component of a client's self-determination to consider when engaging in helping processes and relationships (Crisp, 2010). This body of literature helps teach social workers how to think about the client's religiosity and other spiritual aspects. A limitation, though, is that most of this literature is not empirically based. Instead, it is focused primarily on guidelines of how to incorporate spiritual dimensions in direct practice (Baskin, 2002; Ouellette, 2007). Specifically, the literature predominantly discusses certain areas of practice like assessment (Hodge, 2001, 2003) and intervention (Abels, 2000; Canda & Smith, 2001) in a spiritually sensitive way (see also Sheridan & Amato-von Hemert, 1999; Stewart, Koekse, & Koeske, 2006; Tan, Bowie, & Orpilla, 2004, among others). Some recent literature has begun to explore the role of field education in bringing about discussions of spirituality in educational settings (Galloway, Wilkinson, & Bissell, 2008; Moss, 2008). Further research is required within social work education to assess the utility of these approaches to spiritually sensitive social work practice.

Canda and Furman (2010) provide a useful approach for thinking of issues of spirituality in social work practice. They developed an alternative to wholly mainstream emic and etic perspectives, arguing that it is more about the openness and relationship capacity between client and worker, and less about positioning oneself as either an insider or outsider. Canda and Furman's (2010) approach seeks to implement practices defined by universal truths of human behaviour and interaction. While this is a useful framework for thinking about spirituality and explaining the way clients define meaning while engaged in a helping relationship, what about religion? Social workers practising in multicultural contexts or homogenous cultural environments will always find themselves in either an emic or etic position in relation to religion and the religiosity of a person they are working with. Social workers need spiritual and religious sensitivity in their practice. Two figures and the discussion of each in Canda and Furman (2010) demonstrate this point—there are several different ways that people might experience or perceive the intersection between religion and spirituality (see Figures 3.1 and 3.2, pp. 77–78). Social work practice, education, and training should be conducive to all interpretations.

Conclusion

This chapter provided a brief overview of the concepts of religion and spirituality in social work research, practice, and education, with an emphasis on the Canadian context. Religion and spirituality have been entrenched in the development of practices and theory for the profession, but much work needs to be done in the classroom to open up further discussion of how religion and spirituality are manifested in contemporary social work. A useful place to begin is in those classrooms where professors have already incorporated religion and spirituality into their teaching. While curriculum content in the area of spirituality and religion is sparse within social work educational settings, some instructors and professors have been incorporating these ideas. How has that affected students in those classes? Do they perceive or rationalize client experiences when they enter the field to work the same way or differently than students not exposed to this teaching? What is the impact of spirituality and religion taught in the social work classroom? The omission of these questions in the literature significantly constrains spiritually minded instructors of social work from being able to demonstrate the impact spiritual teaching has on social worker development in a number of areas, such as multicultural practice or relationship development with clients.

Also, instructors must give further consideration to the intended goals of incorporating spirituality and religion in more mainstream social work settings. Other researchers have suggested areas for improvement or focus within the social work curriculum. Lodge, Baughman, and Cummings (2006) suggest devoting more material within the social work curriculum to help students better understand specific faith groups. Likewise, Chung and Singh (1991) stated there was a need to integrate information about different religious values, as well as social and interpersonal understanding. Also, educators must provide more content on how to effectively respond to religious and spiritual issues in practice (Graff, 2007; Northcut, 2004). Hodge (2005) suggested that educators should address issues of religious discrimination and become attuned to the spiritual diversity that social workers might encounter in practice settings. While these goals might be useful, are there others to consider? And with what aspects of general social work practice, beyond assessment and intervention, should professionals be considering the religious and spiritual needs of clients? These and other questions will require further empirical investigation if discussions of spirituality are to be fully incorporated into core social work coursework and field placement settings.

One final point that requires consideration and possible investigation is the link between social work curricula and that of other disciplines. The literature presented in this chapter was primarily concerned with religion and spirituality in social work educational settings, but students of social work engage in a broader range of disciplines while at university. Are some students taking religious studies or anthropology and sociology courses where they might learn some of these ideas? While social work should be striving to meet the immediate training needs of professional social workers as they transition from academic to workplace settings, it might be useful to engage with other disciplines in the university to help meet these educational needs.

References

Abels, S. (Ed.). (2000). *Spirituality in social work practice: Narratives for professional helping*. Denver, CO: Love Publishing.

Al-Krenawi, A., & Graham, J. R. (2003a). Principles of social work practice in the Muslim Arab world. *Arab Studies Quarterly, 25*(4), 75–91.

Al-Krenawi, A., & Graham, J. R. (2003b). *Multicultural social work with diverse ethno-racial communities in Canada*. Toronto, ON: Oxford University Press.

Al-Krenawi, A., & Graham, J. R. (2009). Localizing social work: Bedouin-Arab of the Negev. In G. G. James, R. Ramsay, & G. Drover (Eds.), *International social work: Canadian perspectives* (pp. 224–240). Toronto, ON: Thompson Education.

Atal, Y. (1981). *Building a nation: Essays on India*. Delhi, India: Abhinav.

Barker, S. L. (2007). The integration of spirituality and religion content in social work education: Where we've been, where we're going. *Social Work and Christianity, 34*(2), 146–166.

Baskin, C. (2002). Circles of resistance: Spirituality in social work practice, education, and transformative change. *Currents: New Scholarship in the Human Services, 1*(1). Retrieved from http://www.ucalgary.ca/SW/currents/articles/documents/Currents_baskin_v1_n1.pdf

Beattie, T. (2007). *The new atheists: The twilight of reason and the war on religion.* London, UK: Darton, Longman, & Todd.

Beyer, P. (2000). Secularization for the perspective of globalization. In W. H. Swatos & D. V. A. Olson (Eds.), *The secularization debate* (pp. 81–94). Lanham, MD: Rowman and Littlefield.

Bradshaw, C. M., & Graham, J. R. (2007). Localization of social work practice, education, and research: A content analysis. *Social Development Issues, 29*(2), 92–111.

Bullis, R. K. (1996). *Spirituality in social work practice.* Washington, DC: Taylor & Francis.

Cadell, S., Janzen, L., & Haubrich, D. J. (2007). Engaging with spirituality: A qualitative study of grief and HIV/AIDS. In J. Coates, J. R. Graham, & B. Swartzentruber (with B. Ouellette) (Eds.), *Spirituality and social work: Selected Canadian readings* (pp. 175–190). Toronto, ON: Canadian Scholars' Press.

Canda, E. R., & Furman, L. D. (1999). *Spiritual diversity in social work practice: The heart of helping.* New York, NY: The Free Press.

Canda E. R., & Furman, L. D. (2010). *Spiritual diversity in social work practice: The heart of helping* (2nd ed.). New York, NY: Oxford University Press.

Canda, E. R., Nakashima, M., Burgess, V., & Russel, R. (1999). *Spiritual diversity and social work: A comprehensive bibliography with annotations.* Alexandria, VA: Council on Social Work Education.

Canda, E. R., & Smith, E. (2001). *Transpersonal perspectives on spirituality in social work.* Binghamton, NY: Haworth Press.

Carroll, M. M. (1998). Social work's conceptualization of spirituality. *Journal of Religion and Spiritualty in Social Work, 18*(2), 1–13.

Census of Canada. (2006). *Major Field of Study* – Classification of Instructional Programs, 2000 (423), Age Groups (10A) and Sex (3) for the Population 15 Years and Over With Trades or College Certificates or Diplomas of Canada, Provinces, Territories, Census Metropolitan Areas and Census Agglomerations, 2006 Census – 20% Sample Data. Ottawa, Canada: Queen's Printer. Retrieved from http://www12.statcan.gc.ca/census-recensement/2006/dp-pd/tbt/Rp-eng.cfm?LANG=E&APATH=3&DETAIL=0&DIM=0&FL=A&FREE=0&GC=0&GID=0&GK=0&GRP=1&PID=93613&PRID=0&PTYPE=88971,97154&S=0&SHOWALL=0&SUB=0&Temporal=2006&THEME=75&VID=0&VNAMEE=&VNAMEF, and http://www12.statcan.gc.ca/census-recensement/2006/dp-pd/tbt/Rp-eng.cfm?LANG=E&APATH=3&DETAIL=0&DIM=0&FL=A&FREE=0&GC=0&GID=837928&GK=0&GRP=1&PID=92104&PRID=0&PTYPE=88971,97154&S=0&SHOWALL=0&SUB=0&Temporal=2006&THEME=74&VID=0&VNAMEE=&VNAMEF

Chung, D. K., & Singh, R. N. (1991). Advocacy and cultural competent social work practice: An integrated approach. *Information and Referral, 13*(1–2), 45–64.

Cnaan, R. A., Winehurg, R. J., & Boddie, S. C. (1999). *The newer deal: Social work and religion in partnership.* New York, NY: Columbia University Press.

Coates, J., Graham, J. R., and Swartzentruber, B. (with Ouellette, B.) (Eds.) (2007). *Spirituality and social work: Selected Canadian readings.* Toronto, ON: Canadian Scholars' Press.

Coholic, D. (2003). Student and educator viewpoints on incorporating spirituality in social work pedagogy: An overview and discussion of research findings. *Currents: New Scholarship in the Human Services, 2*(2). Retrieved from http://www.ucalgary .ca/files/currents/v2n2_coholic.pdf

Collins, W. L. (2005). Embracing spirituality as an element of professional self-care. *Social Work and Christianity, 32*(3), 263–274.

Cornwall, M., Albrecht, S. L., Cunningham, P. H., & Pitcher, B. L. (1986). The dimensions of religiosity: A conceptual model with an empirical test. *Review of Religious Research, 28*(3), 226–244.

Crisp, B. R. (2010). *Spirituality and social work.* Surrey, UK: Ashgate.

Derezotes, D. S. (2006). *Spiritually oriented social work practice.* Boston, MA: Pearson.

Dore, M. M. (1990). Functional theory: Its history and influence on contemporary social work practice. *Social Service Review, 64*(3), 358–374.

Durkheim, E. (1915). *The elementary forms of the religious life: A study in religious sociology* (J. W. Swain, Trans.). New York, NY: Macmillan.

Este, D. (2007). Black churches in Canada: Vehicles for fostering community development in African-Canadian communities: A historical analysis. In J. Coates, J. R. Graham, and B. Swartzentruber (with B. Ouellette) (Eds.), *Spirituality and social work: Selected Canadian readings* (pp. 299–322). Toronto, ON: Canadian Scholars' Press.

Furman, L. D., Benson, P. W., Grimwood, C., & Canda, E. R. (2004). Religion and spirituality in social work education and direct practice at the millennium: A survey of UK social workers. *British Journal of Social Work, 34*(6), 767–792.

Furman, L. D., Zahl, M. A., Benson, P. W., & Canda, E. R. (2007). An international analysis of the role of religion and spirituality in social work practice. *Families in Society, 88*(2), 241–254.

Furman, L. D., Zahl, M. A., Benson, P. W., Canda, E. R., & Grimwood, C. (2005). A comparative international analysis of religion and spirituality in social work: A survey of UK and US social workers. *Social Work Education, 24*(8), 813–839.

Galloway, G., Wilkinson, P., & Bissell, G. (2008). Empty space or sacred place? Place and belief in social work training. *The Journal of Practice Teaching & Learning, 8*(3), 28–47.

Gauvreau, M., & Christie, N. (1996). *A full-orbed Christianity: The Protestant churches and social welfare in Canada, 1900–1940.* Kingston, ON: McGill-Queen's University Press.

Gilligan, P., & Furness, S. (2006). The role of religion and spirituality in social work practice: Views and experiences of social workers and students. *British Journal of Social Work, 36*(4), 617–637.

Graff, D. L. (2007). A study of baccalaureate social work students' beliefs about the inclusion of religious and spiritual content in social work. *Journal of Social Work Education, 43*(2), 243–256.

Graham, J. R. (1991). The Downtown Churchworkers' Association: The emergence of a social welfare ethos in the Anglican Diocese of Toronto, 1912–1988. In A. Irving, (Ed.), *Social welfare in Toronto: Two historical papers* (pp. 1–65). Toronto, ON: Faculty of Social Work, University of Toronto.

Graham, J. R. (1992). The Haven, 1878–1930. A Toronto charity's transition from a religious to a professional ethos. *Histoire Sociale/Social History, 25*(50), 283–306.

Graham, J. R. (1994). Charles Eric Hendry (1903–1979): The pre-war formational origins of leader of post-World War II Canadian social work education. *Canadian Social Work Review, 11*(2), 150–167.

Graham, J. R. (2006). Spirituality and social work: A call for an international focus of research. *Arete, 30*(1), 63–77.

Graham, J. R. (2007). The Haven, 1878–1930: A Toronto charity's transition from a religious to a professional ethos. In J. Coates, J. R. Graham, & B. Schwartzentruber (with B. Ouellette) (Eds.), *Canadian social work and spirituality: Current readings and approaches* (pp. 47–64). Toronto, ON: Canadian Scholars' Press.

Graham, J. R. (2008). Who am I? An essay on inclusion and spiritual growth through community and mutual appreciation. *Journal of Religion & Spirituality in Social Work, 27*(1/2), 5–24.

Graham, J. R., & Al-Krenawi, A. (2000). Contested terrain: Two competing views of social work at the University of Toronto, 1914–1945. *Canadian Social Work Review, 17*(2), 245–262.

Graham, J. R., Al-Krenawi, A., & Bradshaw, C. (2000). The Social Work Research Group/NASW Research Section/Council on Social Work Research: 1949–1965, an emerging research identity in the American profession. *Research on Social Work Practice, 10*(5), 622–643.

Graham, J. R., Bradshaw, C., & Trew, J. (2008). Social workers' understanding of the Muslim client's perspective. *Journal of Muslim Mental Health, 3*, 125–144.

Graham, J. R., Bradshaw, C., & Trew, J. (2009a). Adapting social work in working with Muslim clients: Insights for education. *Social Work Education: The International Journal, 28*(5), 544–561.

Graham, J. R., Bradshaw, C., & Trew, J. (2009b). Addressing cultural barriers with Muslim clients: An agency perspective. *Administration in Social Work, 33*(4), 387–406.

Graham, J. R., Bradshaw, C., & Trew, J. (2010). Cultural considerations for social service agencies working with Muslim clients. *Social Work 55*(4), 337–346.

Graham, J. R., Coholic, D., & Coates, J. (2007). Spirituality as a guiding construct in the development of Canadian social work: Past and present considerations. In J. Coates, J. R. Graham, & B. Schwartzentruber (with B. Ouellette) (Eds.), *Canadian social work and spirituality: Current readings and approaches* (pp. 23–46). Toronto: Canadian Scholars' Press.

Graham, J. R., & Shier, M. L. (2009). Religion and social work: An analysis of faith traditions, themes, and global north/south authorship. *Journal of Religion & Spirituality in Social Work, 28*(1/2), 215–233.

Graham, J.R., & Shier, M. L. (2011). Making sense of their world: Aspects of spirituality and subjective well-being of practicing social workers. *Journal of Religion and Spirituality in Social Work: Social Thought, 30*(3), 253–271.

Healy, L. (1999). International social work curriculum in historical perspective. In R. J. Link & C. S. Ramanathan (Eds.), *All our futures: Principles and resources for social work practice in a global era* (pp. 14–29). New York, NY: Brooks/Cole.

Healy, L. (2001). *International social work: Professional action in an interdependent world.* New York, NY: Oxford University Press.

Hodge, D. R. (2001). Spiritual genograms: A generational approach to assessing spirituality. *Families in Society: The Journal of Contemporary Human Service, 82*(1), 35–48.

Hodge, D. R. (2002). Does social work oppress Evangelical Christians? A new "class" analysis of society and social work. *Social Work, 47*(4), 401–414.

Hodge, D. R. (2003). *Spiritual assessment: Handbook for helping professionals.* Botsford, CT: North American Association of Christians in Social Work.

Hodge, D. R. (2005). Spirituality in social work education: A development and discussion of goals that flow from the profession's ethical mandates. *Social Work Education, 24*(1), 37–55.

Laurence, P. (2000). Exploring spirituality. In J. Beversluis (Ed.), *Sourcebook of the world's religions: An interfaith guide to religion and spirituality* (pp. 232–235). Novata, CA: New World Library.

Lee, E. O., & Barrett, C. (2007). Integrating spirituality, faith, and social justice in social work practice and education: A pilot study. *Journal of Religion and Spirituality in Social Work, 26*(2), 1–12.

Leiby, J. (1985). Moral foundations of social welfare and social work: A historical view. *Social Work, 30*(4), 323–330.

Lee, E. O., & Chan, K. (2009). Religious/spiritual and other adaptive coping strategies among Chinese American older immigrants. *Journal of Gerontological Social Work, 37*(4), 517–533.

Lodge, D. R., Baughman, L. M., & Cummings, J. A. (2006). Moving toward spiritual competency: Deconstructing religious stereotypes and spiritual prejudices in social work literature. *Journal of Social Service Research, 32*(4), 211–231.

Loewenberg, F. M. (1988). *Religion and social work practice in contemporary American society.* New York, NY: Columbia University Press.

Lubove, R. (1965). *The professional altruist: The emergence of social work as a career, 1880–1930.* Cambridge, MA: Harvard University Press.

Lyons, K. (1999). *International social work: Themes and perspectives.* Aldershot, UK: Ashgate Arena.

Kvarfordt, C. L., & Sheridan, M. J. (2007). The role of religion and spirituality with children and adolescents: Results of a national survey. *Journal of Religion and Spirituality in Social Work, 26*(3), 1–23.

Mattison, D., Jayaratne, S., & Croxton, T. (2000). Social workers' religiosity and its impact on religious practice behaviours. *Advances in Social Work, 1*(1), 43–59.

Midgely, J. (1981). *Professional imperialism: Social work in the third world.* London, UK: Heinemann.

Morgan, V. J., Berwick, H. E., & Walsh, C. A. (2008). Social work education and spirituality: An undergraduate perspective. *Transformative Dialogues: Teaching and Learning Journal, 2*(2), 1–15.

Moss, B. (2008). Pushing back the boundaries: The challenge of spirituality for practice teaching. *The Journal of Practice Teaching & Learning, 8*(3), 48–64.

Murdock, V. (2005). Guided by ethics: Religion and spirituality in gerontological social work practice. *Journal of Gerontological Social Work, 45*(1/2), 131–154.

Northcut, T. B. (2004). Pedagogy in diversity: Teaching religion and spirituality in the clinical social work classroom. *Smith College Studies in Social Work, 74*(1), 349–358.

Ouellette, B. (2007). Introduction. In J. Coates, J. R. Graham, & B. Swartzentruber (with B. Ouellette) (Eds.), *Spirituality and social work: Selected Canadian readings* (pp. 89–92). Toronto, ON: Canadian Scholars' Press.

Rothman, J. (2009). Spirituality: What we can teach and how we can teach it. *Journal of Religion & Spirituality in Social Work, 28*(1), 161–184.

Sheridan, M. (2009). Ethical issues in the use of spiritually based interventions in social work practice: What are we doing and why? *Journal of Religion and Spirituality in Social Work, 28*(1), 99–126.

Sheridan, M. J., & Amato-Von Hermert, K. (1999). The role of religion and spirituality in social work practice: A survey of practitioners. *Journal of Social Work Education, 35*(1), 125–141.

Shier, M. L., & Graham, J. R. (2011). Mindfulness, subjective well-being, and social work: Insight into their interconnection from social work practitioners. *Social Work Education, 30*(1), 29–44.

Shier, M. L., & Graham, J. R. (2012). Social work, religion, culture and spirituality. In K. Lyons, T. Hokenstad, M. Pawar, and N. Huegler (Eds.), *The Sage handbook of international social work.* London, UK: Sage.

Smith, J. Z. (1998). Religion, religions, religious. In M. C. Taylor (Ed.), *Critical terms for religious studies* (pp. 269–84). University of Chicago Press.

Snyder, L., & Bowman, S. (2007). Communities of cooperation: Human services work with Old Order Mennonites. In J. Coates, J. R. Graham, & B. Swartzentruber (with B. Ouellette) (Eds.), *Spirituality and social work: Selected Canadian readings* (pp. 273–298). Toronto, ON: Canadian Scholars' Press.

Stewart, C., & Koeske, G. F. (2006). Social work students' attitudes concerning the use of religion and spiritual interventions in social work practice. *Journal of Teaching in Social Work, 26*(1–2), 31–49.

Stewart, C., Koeske, G. F., & Koeske, R. D. (2006). Personal religiosity and spirituality associated with social work practitioners' use of religious-based intervention practices. *Journal of Religion and Spirituality in Social Work, 25*(1), 69–85.

Stirling, B., Furman, L. D., Benson, P. W., Canda, E. R., & Grimwood, C. (2010). A comparative survey of Aotearoa New Zealand and UK social workers on the role of religion and spirituality in practice. *British Journal of Social Work, 40*(2), 602–621.

Tan, P. P., Bowie, S., & Orpilla, G. (2004). A Caribbean perspective on spirituality in social work practice. *Caribbean Journal of Social Work, 3*(1), 74–88.

Taylor, C. (2007). *A secular age.* Cambridge, MA: Harvard University Press.

Todd, S. (2007). Feminist community organizing: The spectre of the sacred and the secular. In J. Coates, J. R. Graham, & B. Swartzentruber (with B. Ouellette) (Eds.), *Spirituality and social work: Selected Canadian readings* (pp. 161–174). Toronto, ON: Canadian Scholars' Press.

Van Hook, M., Hugen, B., & Aguilar, M. (Eds.) (2001). *Spirituality within religious traditions in social work practice.* Pacific Grove, CA: Brooks/Cole.

Whiting, R. (2008). For and against: The use of a debate to address the topic of religion and spirituality in social work education. *Journal of Practice Teaching & Learning,* *8*(3), 79–96.

Woodroffe, K. (1962). *From charity to social work.* London, UK: Routledge.

Zahl, M. A. (2003). Spirituality and social work: A Norwegian reflection. *Social Thought: Journal of Religion in the Social Services, 22*(1), 77–90.

Zahl, M. A. (2006). Incorporating a spiritual dimension in social work practice. *Socialno Delo, 45*(3–5), 127–133.

Zahl, M. A., Furman, L. D., Benson, P. W., & Canda, E. R. (2007). Religion and spirituality in social work practice and education in a cross-cultural context: Findings from a Norwegian and UK study. *European Journal of Social Work, 10*(3), 295–317.

Zapf, M. K. (2007). Profound connections between person and place: Exploring locations, spirituality, and social work. In J. Coates, J. R. Graham, & B. Swartzentruber (with B. Ouellette) (Eds.), *Spirituality and social work: Selected Canadian readings* (pp. 229–242). Toronto, ON: Canadian Scholars' Press.

Chapter 4

Prisoners of the Story: A Role for Spirituality in Thinking and Living Our Way to Sustainability

John Coates

> *Many of the deepest thinkers and many of those most familiar with the scale of the challenges we face have concluded that the transitions required can be achieved only in the context of ... the rise of a new consciousness. For some, it is a spiritual awakening—a transformation of the human heart. For others it is a more intellectual process of coming to see the world anew and deeply embracing the emerging ethic of the environment and the old ethic of what it means to love thy neighbor as thyself.* (Speth, 2008, pp. 199–200)

Up to now, social work (as with most other professions and society in general) has failed to engage in and effectively respond to environmental challenges in a substantial way. For example, social workers have not significantly altered their practices in response to the flood of research and media attention over the past two decades concerning environmental destruction, and in particular, global warming. While some have critiqued religion and spirituality for supporting industrial enterprise and for getting in the way of effective ecological policy and action (such as Besthorn 2002; White, 1967), in this chapter I argue that spirituality can play a significant role in the development of effective professional responses to environmental and social justice issues, and can help us make the transition to a society that proactively engages in the struggle for a better world.

I begin with an overview of the current environmental predicament and ask why the scientific knowledge and media attention has not led to substantial change. Second, I point out that Western society, and the professions that emerged to serve its citizens, are prisoners of a story—the story or world view of modernity. This story enabled progress, medical cures, and work-saving technologies, but it also limited our thinking to symptoms rather than root causes. Third, I present an alternative narrative—one reflecting a spiritually grounded holistic consciousness that restores the universal human need for meaning to a central place in our lives. Fourth, I outline some practical steps that show how spiritually aligned professional action can be a guide for moving us closer to a profession and society in which environmental and social justice prevail.

As an academic with a deep concern about the scope, severity, and long-term effects of environmental degradation (see also Orr, 2009), I have been deeply discouraged by my profession and society's refusal to take this predicament seriously. As I investigated this reluctance, it became clear that the root is embedded in the foundational values and assumptions of industrial society and the professions that support it. The environmental crisis reveals the paradox of modernity—despite its many benefits, it is founded on exploitation. It is imperative that we review our current way of being and thinking in order to look critically at the paradigm of modernity, and explore alternatives. The famous quote attributed to Einstein applies here: "We can't solve problems by using the same kind of thinking we used when we created them" (n.d.). Yet paradigm-shifting innovations and thinking (Barker, 1990) are difficult to grasp because we see what we believe (what Barker called "the paradigm effect"). Spirituality is an essential aspect of a holistic consciousness, an alternative to modernity and a foundation for professional practice and societal policy that provides hope for a sustainable future for our children.

The Current Predicament

Environmental issues such as climate change, habitat destruction, pollution, and species extinctions have increasingly taken up the front pages of newspapers and magazines and served as the subject of documentaries. Authors of recent books and journal articles have discussed more specific outcomes, such as the loss of migratory birds (Stutchbury, 2007) and the decline of wild fisheries (Greenberg, 2010); this decimation is so widespread and so exceptional that it has been labelled the *Sixth Extinction* (Glavin, 2006). The Earth is losing "an entire human language every two weeks ... a domesticated food-crop variety every six hours, and ... an entire species every few minutes" (Glavin, 2006, p. 2). In fact, the Zoological Society of London reported that since 1970, when Earth Day originated, over 25% of the wild species on Earth have disappeared. The society also estimated that 50% of the world's languages will disappear this century (as cited in Montenegro and Glavin, 2010).

The reality of global warming and habitat destruction is no longer arguable. While cycles of climate change and species loss have occurred over millennia, the speed and severity of the current ecological destruction points clearly to the role of human activity in this devastation. The primacy of economic growth and gross domestic product (GDP) in the mind of politicians, corporations, and economists, along with the corresponding overharvesting, industrial pollution, and habitat destruction, colludes with consumption, efficiency and convenience to hasten the decline of biocultural diversity. As a result, the world loses species, genetic diversity, and local knowledge, all events that impact quality of life for humans. Detailed reviews of these processes include Clark (1989), Godrej (2001), Hamilton (2003), and Jarman (2007). If one looks through the haze of economic rhetoric, it is not difficult to foresee the collapse of our current socio-economic system, as this "extractive economy" (Berry, 1988) is exhausting the renewable and non-renewable capacities of the Earth (see also Diamond, 2005; Korten, 2009). Goldsmith regards this system as "totally aberrant and destructive" (1998, p. xv).

However, despite the plethora of evidence and calls for change (Berry, 1999; Coates, 2003; IPCC, 2011; Korten, 2009), humanity has so far been unable to develop an effective or coordinated collective response. While there is substantial consensus on how we understand sustainability (Gladwin, Newbury, & Reiskin, 1997)—"meeting the needs of the present without compromising the ability of future generations to meet their own needs" (WCED, 1987, p. 8)—commitments to reaching this goal remain elusive. In fact, some notable political leaders, such as Stephen Harper and George W. Bush, have actively blocked more effective action. The vast majority of governments are not taking the personal and public actions called for by the scientific community (IPCC, 2007). In politics, illusion and ideology take precedence over the strong weight of scientific knowledge; for example, the Harper government in Canada has garnered international attention for its refusal to adhere to the Kyoto Protocol, its intransigence at the 2009 IPCC meetings (CANC, 2009), and its cancellation of the mandatory long-form Census despite a groundswell of academic and scientific opposition. For his part, George Bush was accused of committing "crimes against nature" when he rolled back environmental protection laws and weakened protections for air, water, and wildlife in the US (Kennedy, 2003).

The attention the media gives to the issue indicates that, overall, awareness about environmental problems is increasing (Norgaard, 2006), and bookstores and the Internet have many sources for people who wish to learn more about "going green" (such as May, 2006; Suzuki, 2010). This public discourse has resulted in many individuals changing their behaviours in modest ways, by doing such things as composting, using energy efficient light bulbs, and recycling; some are buying hybrid cars or making their homes more energy efficient. Such efforts are laudable, and to some extent helpful, but they are not happening on the scale necessary to seriously impact climate change. Despite some researchers referring to the environmental movement as the "largest, most densely organized political cause in human history" (Brown, 1995, p. xiv), political will has not mobilized. Explanations for the lack of political engagement are often ascribed to a denial of the risks involved (Norgaard, 2006); apathy, as if paralyzed or emotionally numbed by the scope of the problems (see Lifton 1981; Lertzman, 2008); a desire to hide in the midst of reality TV and other distractions (Hedges, 2009);

or a retreat into fundamentalism and nationalism (Lerner, 2003). In the absence of significant and widespread public and individual action, climate change will not be abated.

Many of the efforts made by people and organizations who are active regarding environmental concerns are consistent with a "conventional environmental consciousness" (Christopher, 1999) where a rationalist method and mechanistic view results in a technical approach to our relationship with the Earth, and results in reliance on a technological fix to solve the problems of waste and over-harvesting. This reflects a conventional environmentalist (Wapner, 2003), resourcist (Howard, 2008), or human welfare ecology (Eckersley, 1992) understanding of nature. The focus of conventional environmentalism is limited to reducing the effects of climate change through a more efficient use of resources, waste reduction, technological innovation, and resource conservation. Such actions are undertaken primarily to retain human access to resources and wilderness for recreation and enjoyment. What results, at best, is symptom reduction, since the core principle is to conserve nature *for* humans. The exploitive, extractive, and anthropocentric attitudes and actions are not challenged. Conventional efforts at symptom reduction will not bring about the needed transformation.

How do we understand the lack of action regarding, and even acknowledgement of this multidimensional systemic breakdown? How do we move people toward more effective engagement with environmental issues?

The Paradox of Modernity

The language and actions of conventional environmental activism are informed by the stories or narratives that form our core beliefs and values—our world view. The dominant world view today is modernity, the world view that celebrates rationality, science, self-interest, anthropocentrism, competition, and market economics. Modernity restricts our ability to target the root causes of environmental destruction, and limits the focus of concern and action to isolated technical solutions that, for many people, seem better left to scientists and experts. The emphasis on efficiency and reduction of waste, while important to environmental well-being, will never lead to sustainability because the core narrative results from dualistic thinking about domination and positivism: the Earth remains a resource for humans to use, and a place to absorb our waste (Coates, 2003, 2005).

The stories that humans fashion in an effort to explain to ourselves how nature works and what our role is in it "have profound implications for the kind of world we create" (Nordhaus & Shellenberger, 2007, p. 220) and the kind of personal actions and political directions that people and societies take. The technical rationality and anthropocentrism of modernity form a prison of the mind with impenetrable core assumptions that dictate certain approaches as worthwhile and others as unrealistic, impractical, or unthinkable (outside of our awareness). They reinforce "existing power structures and ideologies by suggesting that environmental protection is only a matter of technical reform, not holistic transformation" (Wapner, 2003, p. 3).

Modernism surfaced as a reaction to the rigid absolutism of religious authority and converged with the social relations of capitalism (Howe, 1994; Irving 1994). A major breakthrough in the advancement of civilization, modernism gave rise to science and the many recent improvements in wealthy people's lives: medical breakthroughs, car and air travel, electrical appliances (and the nuclear and coal-fired generating stations that make them work), air-conditioned transport that provides "fresh" fruits and vegetables to rich countries 12 months of the year, and factory farms and fishing armadas that fill grocery stores with a range of meat and fish. However, while the Renaissance and Enlightenment movements (each significant to the development of modernity) shifted the dominant narrative to the primacy of science and commerce, in both thought and behaviour the core narrative of modernity expanded to include progress, individualism, consumerism, and materialism. This system of thought not only "produces an intrinsically destructive relationship to nature" (Christopher. 1999, p. 361) but also has many structured inequalities that include patriarchy, economism, speciesism, and anthropocentrism (Spretnak, 1997).

Over the past century, what Capra (1982) termed the "dark side of growth" has increased in proportion to the advance and spread of technological innovation, and includes air and water pollution, soil erosion, habitat loss, overharvesting of forests and oceans, extinctions, global warming, desertification, and social maladies including poverty, war, and forced migration. This belief system that places the human as separate from and superior to the rest of nature also supports wealth accumulation, unrestrained economic growth, the removal of trade barriers, and the monoculture of capitalist democracy (Gladwin et al., 1997; Korten 1995, 2009). We are beginning to realize that systemic flaws exist, and as Montenegro and Glavin (2010) point out, biological and cultural extinctions "are different facets of the same phenomenon" (p. 2). The ceaseless consumption of the planet's limited supply of natural resources has been called a "Ponzi scheme" (Fein, 2010) where the rich and Western nations of the twentieth century have lived comfortably at the expense of the world's poor and future generations.

The paradox of modernity is that science and reason have enabled humanity to uncover the dynamics of nature, to deeply understand the interdependence of all things, to see Gaia in action through the self-organizing and self-healing capacities of Earth (Lovelock, 1979), to see the evolutionary process as one of increasing complexity and differentiation within an ever-expanding whole (Sahtouris, 1998; Swimme & Berry, 1992). It is modernity that has prepared us to recognize its flaws and the necessity of moving forward to a higher level of consciousness and action. The shift to a holistic consciousness must move beyond the dualism and determinism of modernity and be seen as an evolutionary process, a shift that embraces but transcends earlier stages (Wilber, 2007).

Environmental problems, when looked at in this way, can be understood best as resulting from our understanding of reality and human relationships with the Earth; they are social problems in their origins and effects. Like Lerner (2003), Coates (2003), and Gladwin et al. (1997), Scharmer (2003) sees that modernity's shackles extend deep into the public and private understanding of, and response to, crises such that the "root issue of the current crisis is in our thinking," or rather, "how we don't" (p. 4).

Modernity also acts in other ways to confound effective action. It not only separates humans from nature, it informs the bureaucratic style of organizations and professions such that work is divided into distinct silos with little connection or interdisciplinary collaboration. This approach is so entrenched that, despite the numerous crises that confront human society (economic, climate, energy, water, food, security, health care) each problem and every profession has their own discourses, journals, organizations, conferences and websites (Scharmer, 2009). While these efforts are well intentioned and address important issues, Scharmer argues that two pieces are missing: one, "a discourse across all these silos about how these issues are interconnected, and two, a discourse about the systemic root causes that continuously reproduce the whole cluster of crises" (p. 4).

We are prisoners of a story—prisoners of modernity. While there are notable exceptions, humanity at large has not yet developed the reflective consciousness that enables us to explore deeply and question our core values and beliefs. Environmental and social problems are not the result of a miscalculation that can be resolved by technological adjustment. They are the "logical and unavoidable consequences of modern (i.e., instrumental) rationality as expressed in the current structure of the most basic social and cultural institutions of modernity (i.e., modern capitalism, industrial technology, individualistic morality, and mechanistic science)" (Christopher 1999, p. 361). Coates reached a similar conclusion: "(t)he environmental crisis is not just having an impact on our lives. It is our way of life. It is the advancement of the industrial enterprise through the consumption of nature and the exploitation of people" (2005, p. 31). The world view of modernity is unable to meet the expectations of sustainability—inclusiveness, connectivity, equity, prudence, and security (Gladwin et al., 1997).

A New World View

An in-depth critique of modernity is required, as it is antithetical to informed and effective movement toward sustainability. Such a critique brings to our attention the need to develop a new response to essential existential questions: Why are we here? What does it mean to be human? And what is a proper relationship for humans to the rest of nature?

These fundamental questions need to be addressed, since what needs to be done can be determined only in light of the narrative that informs how we understand the human–Earth relationship. An effective human response to the significant, dramatic, and rapid changes that are anticipated globally over this century will depend upon a new sense of human identity and purpose. Scholars from many fields have called for new ways of thinking, a different set of foundational beliefs and assumptions, and a new world view (see Benyus, 1997; Berry, 1999; Coates, 2003; O'Murchu, 1997). We do not need to retreat back to nature nor abandon technology; we do, however, need to live by a new narrative or story, a new set of beliefs and values through which we, as Elshof (2010) writes, "free ourselves from the straitjacket of modernity and markets" (p. 75). Berry (1999) referred to this effort as the Great Work of our time.

Why are we here? What is the proper human–Earth relationship? These are questions concerning our ultimate meaning and purpose that, in light of environmental destruction and social injustice, call for a new consciousness and, as such, can be seen as essentially spiritual questions (see Canda & Furman, 2010; Faver 2009). This spiritual awareness is both cognitive and heartfelt, engaging our whole being and seeing the human as intimately connected to the web of all life. It has been called for under various names, including global consciousness (Earley, 1997), cultural and spiritual consciousness (Korten, 2006), ecological consciousness (Chefurka, 2011), conscious evolution (Sahtouris, 1998), and empathic consciousness (Rifkin, 2009). This holistic world view has a profound awareness of interdependence and the capacity of every living thing to contribute to the well-being of the whole. Within this whole-system consciousness, an individual's well-being and fulfillment are possible only to the extent that the well-being and fulfillment of the Other (including all living things) can be achieved: my well-being depends on that of my neighbours and a thriving Earth. The whole is inclusive and embraces diversity.

"As people realize that their well-being depends on the well-being of others and the Earth, we can begin to develop patterns of mutual support and behaviour which contribute to the common good" (Coates 2005, p. 33). When the common good is understood to include the entire community of Earth, we can establish and sustain a "mutually enhancing, human–Earth relationship" (Coates, 2005, p. 33). While it is possible to come to this realization from a philosophical analysis (see Elshof, 2010; Naess, 1989; Speth, 2008) this world view is essentially spiritual. Faver (2009) defines spirituality as "the process of taking our rightful place in the web of life" (p. 364); she sees spirituality incorporating interdependence (the web of life) and harmony with everything in nature (rightful place). For Canda and Furman (2010), spirituality is the "universal quality of human beings and their cultures related to the quest for meaning, purpose, morality, transcendence, well-being, and profound relationships with ourselves, others and ultimate reality" (p. 5). Striving to live a life of personal integrity and wholeness in the context of relationships between oneself and nature, society, and ultimate reality is a spiritual path. Humans can seek personal meaning and fulfillment not only through personal behaviour but also through the policies and practices of public institutions that are consistent with these sustainable values.

Social Work

A number of articles over several years have appeared in social work literature that speaks to the importance of the profession being engaged in environmental issues (Berger & Kelly, 1993; Besthorn 1997, 2003; Besthorn & Canda, 2002; Coates, 2003, 2005; Mary, 2008). However, there has not been a substantial shift in social work practice, which remains reactionary and primarily therapeutic (Besthorn, 1997; Coates, 2003; Zapf, 2009). Further, efforts at cross-cultural practice have largely been ineffective for similar reasons (see Gray, Coates, & Yellow Bird, 2008). The social work profession, like Western society, is domesticated and so strictly confined within the constraints of modernity that it is unable to resolve the problems that are embedded in and created by the dominant collective belief system. For example, the persistence of poverty both at home and abroad, along with the steady increase in the income gap between the rich and the poor despite a generation of efforts to ameliorate poverty, are reflective of a system of beliefs that is unable to overcome marginalization. Unmitigated environmental destruction, social injustice, and poverty are societal problems that are linked directly to the values and beliefs inherent in the structure of modern society.

A holistic and inclusive framework could enable the social work profession to see that the root of exploitation is unrestrained modernity and the industrial processes that adhere to it. The myth that material progress and abundance will solve the problems of marginalization, exploitation, and destitution can be transformed into whole-system consciousness, an identity where interdependence and inclusivity prevail.

The challenge remains in how to shift our thinking away from the domination of self-interest and individualism, and away from being "realistic" about, and subservient to, the power of market forces. Replacing this is a world view that celebrates and acts on the interdependence of all life and our co-creative capacity. For example, within modernity, nature and markets are separate and distinct, and serve substantially opposing values. It is important to realize that it is our thinking that creates and separates markets and nature, and it is our thinking that can help to create the "natures and markets (that) serve the kind of world we want and the kind of species we want to become" (Nordhaus & Shellenberger, 2007, p. 235).

However, the transition to a new world view is most often a struggle, with some writers arguing that it is important for people to feel threatened by social or natural problems that their existing way of understanding the world cannot resolve (Beck, 1995; Christopher, 1999). The dissonance may be essential to push one toward an alternative perspective, as modernity's emphasis on rationalism, individualism, and economism is so strong that it provides a "cultural condition-ing" (Korten, 1995) or "mythological insulation" (Livingston, 1994) where an appreciation of human–nature interdependence is "lost to conceptualization" (Rogers, 1994). This conditioning is so powerful that many people are unaware of the assumptions embedded in this world view, and so are not able to question, examine, or critique them.

Another restraint that has made inclusiveness elusive has been the tendency of the environmental movement, up to this time, to frame the struggle as dualis-tic: a win–lose scenario where markets, growth, and profit are opposed to fulfill-ment, well-being, and a vibrant, fecund nature. This polarization reflects how many in the sustainability movement have not been able to escape the dualism of modernity and grow to see environmental solutions from a whole-system perspective. A holistic world view and global consciousness are not in opposi-tion to modernity, for they build upon earlier knowledge and advancements, but they are transformational.

The interdependence and connectedness of all life enables an acceptance of the power and potential of human creativity for the benefit of all. It recognizes that all humans share similar aspirations for a life of meaning and fulfillment and that, in a broader and more advanced level of human existence, cooperation and community can be central to individual and social identity. The next step is both integrative and developmental—to act from a higher level of human evolution, where people are able to think and feel in more empathic ways and be open to new solutions and levels of creativity (see Korten, 2009; Scharmer, 2009). In order to more effectively address the challenges of sustainability, the new world view must be framed by "collective leadership, ecosystem awareness, and collective action that arises from common attention and will" (Scharmer, 2009, p. 11). The self-interest of each person expands to include the well-being and mutual benefit of everyone and all things. This reflects a shift in awareness that "extends the natural self-interest of the players to the entire eco-system" (Scharmer, 2009, p. 7).

Restor(y)ing Meaning in Our Lives

The long-term challenges faced by conventional environmentalists, social workers, and other professionals, include the reliance on scientific thinking, linear notions of progress, and the reluctance to bring spiritual and holistic consciousness into their arguments and politics. Having worked so hard for many years to separate church and state, and to keep the negative and exclusionary elements of religion out of professional practice and politics, many progressive activists and thinkers have limited spirituality to the personal level, and thereby confined the search for meaning to personal and individualistic realms. The focus of personal meaning at the individual level has restricted (unfortunately, in my opinion) environmental actions to personal choice (see for example, Gore, 2006) and resulted in progressive environmental change being kept on the sidelines of public and political action.

While knowledge about climate change informs people of its existence and consequences, knowledge itself is not a predictor of the intention to behave or act differently (Heath & Gifford, 2006). To bring about effective action on environmental and social issues, we need a different set of core beliefs and values—a new consciousness—within which to argue for new social and environmental policies and public practices. This consciousness can provide an avenue to express and live by a deeper meaning and commitment. In this world view, the Earth moves from the background of our lives to the forefront, as "something we share our lives with—something we nurture, have fun with, are stunned by, respond to, empathize with, find nourishment from, and, in turn, nourish" (Wapner, 2003, p. 4). While not necessarily a religious view, it is certainly a spiritual one, as it alters meaning-making and central values. It can be viewed as an expansion of the Golden Rule to all life. The great spiritual-religious traditions of the world have all taught that "(t)he deepest human pleasures come from living in a world based on justice, peace, love, generosity, kindness, and celebration of the universe" (Lerner, 2003, p. 10). Korten (2009), reflecting on his experience at the 1992 Earth Summit, noted that despite so many differences among people and cultures, "we all wanted the same thing: healthy, happy children, families and communities, living in peace and cooperation in healthy, natural environments" (p. 95). This is easy for almost everyone to appreciate, yet in industrially advanced countries and all others as well, access to clean water, nutritious food free of toxins, work that offers a livelihood, healthy uncontaminated environments for all creatures, peace, and hope for the future, are neither actual nor imaginable realities for their children (see also Lerner, 2003; Wapner, 2003).

The shift that merges the interests of self and other requires deep reflection and personal development, as it celebrates with awe and appreciation the robust fecundity of the Universe, the sacredness and interconnectedness of all things, and the revelatory power that resides in nature unfolding around us. To be fully effective, such a shift must also include empathy for the social problems that always accompany ecological degradation. The focus of life and politics shift to recreating communities that nourish wholeness.

Steps toward Holistic Consciousness

The emergence of a holistic consciousness is a significant shift in world view and is similar to what Mezirow (1978, 1990) referred to as "perspective transformation," a process that usually takes place over time, is experienced deeply, and involves (in addition to a critique of dominant values and beliefs), exposure to an alternative world view and the opportunity to discuss reactions. The self-awareness that develops and accompanies the transformation may involve the need to mourn what has been given up; dreams of success within the old paradigm often meant material possessions, privilege, and economic status (see Coates, 2003). An important aspect of this process, especially for students, is the realization that each person has a world view, even though he or she may not be aware of it. By virtue of socialization, most of us learn the world view of our culture.

Coates (2003), building on the work of Macy (1989), Elgin (2000), and Hubbard (1998), outlines several steps that facilitate the emergence of a holistic consciousness. One of the first steps is shaking off what Macy (1989) refers to as our "mistaken identity" (p. 201) of being separate and superior in favour of our profound interconnection to one another, to the rest of nature, and to the creative spirit that is present in all life. The realization of interdependence leads to transcendence from isolated, personal self-interest as we move toward an identity with all of humanity as a member of Earth's community. This "common connection to the community of life" (Elgin, 2000, p. 14) opens us to compassion (what Rifkin, 2009, calls empathy) for the needs of all on Earth. Many scholars, including Clark (1989), Earley (1997), O'Murchu (1997), Spretnak (1997), and Korten (2009) state that self-reflection, compassion, and planetary empathy

Table 4.1 Evolving World views

Modernity	Whole-system Consciousness
Dualism	Wholeness
Determinism	Emergence
Domination	Interdependence
Globalization	Local Well-being
Technological Dominance	Community
Communications	Engagement

are associated with spiritual development. This sense of interdependence and compassionate awareness is the first step toward a global consciousness, and shows itself primarily through ethics—behaviour and actions that reflect a sense of responsibility for the Other. Russell (1998) and Hubbard (1998) argue that as holistic consciousness develops among many individuals, they contribute to the development of the critical mass of consciousness that collectively can influence public action. Mullaly (1997) sees the development of critical mass as a prerequisite for social transformation.

The second step in the emergence of a holistic consciousness is developing awareness about the full scope and impact of the planetary crisis and the consequences of environmental destruction and social injustice (similar to feeling threatened, according to Beck, 1995; Christopher, 1999). Thinking critically regarding the systemic persistence of exploitation and injustice is challenging for most people raised in a culture that venerates modernity. The realization of systemic inequality, oppression, privilege, and exploitation can challenge one's values, identity, and sense of purpose. In line with this, English (in Chapter 2) discusses the importance of "disentangl[ing] spirituality from exclusive ties to being nice." This is why Hubbard (1998) argues that the second step involves opportunities for increased interaction with progressive others. This interaction provides the opportunity to share, support, challenge, and confirm, and also leads people to make decisions on collective acts that strengthen social and political awareness, resulting from a shift in personal beliefs and values. Graham and Shier (Chapter 3) discuss the important role that social work education can play in linking personal spiritual paths to social work practice.

Social workers can nurture the development of personal and collective global consciousness by supporting people in their transformation and providing opportunities for them to self-reflect, critique, and act on their new understanding. This can be an empowering process, as individuals act on their new sense of identity and capacity and begin to see the connection between their own fulfillment and the well-being of All. When it is evident that personal fulfillment can be achieved through acts that contribute to a well-functioning society, personal action advances society (Coates, 2003).

Further, social workers can play a significant role in this transformative and empowering process by helping people to accept and recognize their own unique value, talents, and potential. As people share experiences and learn how to give and receive support, they feel stronger and are free from any internalized self-blame for the severity of the crisis. The third step involves people discovering how their talents can be put to use for the benefit of the community. The creativity that emerges when people are freed from the constraints of modernity and encouraged to solve problems and act on concerns is considerable. Social workers can support individual actions and the development of teams whose members will support one another in their respective actions.

Informed by the spiritual essence of a global or holistic consciousness, an individual can undertake personal and social acts that reflect interdependence and the fulfillment of all. Spirituality enables and elicits personal lifestyle change and participation in social/political action to bring about ecological and social justice. It is a whole-system consciousness which we can use to break free of the constraints of modernity. By doing so, we are free to act from an understanding of human–Earth relationships that is communal and self-serving, and this perspective leads to actions that are both enriching and sustainable. Examples of this thinking and action include

1 Reframing the environmental challenge as a journey toward liberation rather than as one of loss and sacrifice.

The expectation that living sustainably requires a shorter work week and living with less has been interpreted by many to mean a lower income and diminished ability to provide for our families. Instead, it could be emphasized that sustainable living provides opportunities for release from the constraints of consumerism and the pressure of incessant competition that perpetuates social injustices and pits one person against another as opponents in the battle of self-interest. Sustainable actions and lifestyles can lead us to feel that we are doing our part by contributing to the ongoing evolutionary processes of the Earth, and participating in what Thomas Berry referred to as *The Great Work* (1999). Rather we can see our lifestyle as an opportunity for liberation from modernity, as we transition from participation in a culture of individualism, competition, and superiority, to one of mutual growth, equality, and interdependence, from being an exploiter of Earth's resources to participating in the ongoing evolution of the Earth (Coates 2003).

2 Acting from our essential connection to all humans and the Earth in its wholeness.

If we accept that all life is sacred, and that the divine is present in all things, then it is imperative for us break through the walls of dualism to place regard for all of nature (including humanity) at the forefront of our thinking and action. By recognizing our essential connection to all of life, we can more easily understand that how we treat one another effects everyone, and how we treat the environment impacts all of nature and has repercussions for humanity. Ecological destruction is social injustice. Once we understand the systemic nature of life on Earth, it is easier to see how, for example, the BP oil spill in the Gulf of Mexico not only killed many marine species and damaged oceans and shorelines, but impacted many thousands of people directly and the livelihoods of nearby fishers and packers. Industrial waste, such as byproducts of oil extraction from the tar ponds of Alberta are contaminating river systems and have become more toxic than the regenerative powers of the Earth can handle (Kelly et al., 2009). Science and spirituality can merge as we are called to play our part to ensure that the creativity and evolution of the Earth continues. Progressive, collective action can help the Earth heal. In such a story, we are called to engage both our hearts and minds to appreciate all things for what they really are, and what they can be (Green, 2010).

This awareness allows social work to pay more attention to the positive effect of our relationship with the rest of nature, such as with animals and other life forms (Green, 2010; Faver, 2009) and the use of outdoor activity and therapies (Clinebell, 1996).

3 Engaging in spiritual practices that enable personal transcendence and strengthen our sense of personal and social interdependence.

One of the great challenges of the modern day is to overcome the psychic barriers of modernity so that we are able to "see things as they are" (Gladwin et al., 1997, p. 260). Modernity has impacted our capacity for critical thinking and supported the use of psychological defence mechanisms to provide a false sense of security, limits to our personal growth, and constraints on our willingness to act (Gladwin et al., 1997). Spiritual and contemplative practices can assist us to see through self-deceptions, to connect thinking and feeling, and to expand our ego beyond self-interest. As we become free of distorted thinking and emotions, we are better able to overcome old habits of the mind, to see and tackle the causes as well as the symptoms, and to withstand the onslaught of distorted and partial truths from governments and corporations, escapist programming in the media, and soul-numbing myths of individualism and material progress. As we think more critically we can engage in social and political actions that are more effective in bringing about substantive and long-term societal change.

4 Engaging the religious and spiritual in sustainable actions.

Abrahamic religions, those most significant in the formation of Western thought and society, can be very patriarchal, hierarchical, and exclusionary (Wapner, 2003). Lynn White Jr. (1967) critiqued the anthropocentrism of Judeo-Christian religions, and their focus on interpretations that favoured salvation and human superiority which have associated these religions with ecological devastation. However debatable White's thesis, there is a need for dominant religions to reinterpret their religious stories in ways that address the current ecological challenges (see McFague, 1993; O'Murchu, 2000). By taking on the role of stewards, by seeing divine engagement in the ongoing creativity of nature, and by being "provocatively unorthodox—breaking the habit of complacency by living a provocative and relevant faith" (Coates, 2010), adherents to organized religion can address global issues like climate change. English (p. 30) refers to this as "creative engagement with the world and its needs."

Faith groups and wisdom traditions have established networks and a predisposition to explore moral, ethical, and justice issues. These networks can mobilize their members and others to both raise awareness and spearhead social actions to address the root causes of exploitation and climate change (see Lysack, 2010; OIKOS, 2010).

5 Living a life of integrity.

Acting in your immediate environment based on what you think needs to be done or said can be challenging, but it is one way each of us can, both personally and politically, illustrate daily examples of a sustainable lifestyle. Acting and speaking how you think a person should is a form of protest, and an affirmation of a way of life that supports human dignity. This is more than non-cooperation, it is a positive statement on how to build an alternative structure and professional practice (Schell, 2003). Such actions counter the negative stereotypes placed on environmentalists, by presenting a positive example of a sustainable lifestyle.

The challenge of an integrated life (Groen, Coholic, & Graham, p. 3) is to bring together personal and professional values and beliefs. Acting with integrity (when our actions are consistent with our values and beliefs) is possible when we strive to live a spiritual life, a life where our ultimate values and beliefs grow ever closer to those that govern our daily lives and actions. Living a life of meaning, regardless of our understanding of the divine, is a spiritual path.

The most effective area we can take individual action is in our own local communities and regions, where behaviour reflects progressive and substantive lifestyle changes and social activism. Local actions can restore habitats, decrease consumption and waste, and promote Earth-friendly activities such as community gardens and community-supported agriculture (buying local and supporting organic producers). They can serve social justice work, promote healthy communities, advocate for the use of fair trade products, and engage in local, provincial and federal politics. With such actions, it is possible to move toward "the higher-order possibilities of our human nature" (Korten, 2009, p. 91).

Spirituality is a process of transcendence that seeks to connect us with the Divine (however understood). As we continue forward on a spiritual path, we tend to move beyond dualism: there is less tension between emotional and cognitive, self and other, human and divine, and as these are reduced we are able to replace isolated, individual self-interest with a view of ourselves as intimately connected to all. This experience of interdependence, of being one with the rest of nature, is the foundation for a world view and social structure that promotes sustainability. To the extent that holistic spirituality becomes a positive attribute for an individual and societal world view, sustainability will follow as spirituality becomes a central element in the movement toward ecological and social justice.

References

Barker, J. (Producer). (1990). *The Business of Paradigms* [film]. Available from Charthouse International Learning Corporation, Burnsville, MN.

Beck, U. (1995). *Ecological enlightenment: Essays on the politics of the risk society.* Atlantic Highlands, NJ: Humanities Press.

Benyus, J. (1997). *Biomimicry: Innovation inspired in nature.* New York, NY: William Morrow.

Berger, R., & Kelly, J. (1993). Social work in the ecological crisis. *Social Work, 38*(5), 521–526.

Berry, T. (1988). *The dream of the Earth.* San Francisco, CA: Sierra Club.

Berry, T. (1999). *The great work: Our way into the future.* New York, NY: Bell Tower.

Besthorn, F. (1997). *Reconceptualizing social work's person-in-environment perspective: Explorations in radical environmental thought* (Doctoral dissertation, University of Kansas). ProQuest Dissertations and Theses database. (UMI No. 981157).

Besthorn, F. (2002). Expanding spiritual diversity in social work: Perspectives on the greening of spirituality. *Currents: New Scholarship in the Human Services, 1*(1). Retrieved from http://www.ucalgary.ca/currents/files/currents/v1n1_besthorn.pdf

Besthorn, F. (2003). Radical ecologisms: Insights for educating social workers in ecological activism and social justice. *Critical Social Work: An Interdisciplinary Journal Dedicated to Social Justice, 3*(1), 66–106. Retrieved from http://www.criticalsocialwork.com/CSW_2003_1.html

Besthorn, F., & Canda, E. R. (2002). Deep ecology for education and teaching in social work. *Journal of Teaching in Social Work, 22*(1), 79–101.

Brown, L. (1995). Ecopsychology and the environmental revolution: An environmental forward. In T. Roszak, M. Gomes, & A. Kanner (Eds.), *Ecopsychology: Restoring the Earth, healing the mind* (pp. xiii–xvi). San Francisco, CA: Sierra Club.

CANC (Climate Action Network Canada). (2009). Fossil Awards "bring it" to Canada [news release]. Retrieved from http://www.climateactionnetwork.ca/e/news/2009/release/index.php?WEBYEP_DI=11

Canda, E. R., & Furman, L. (2010). *Spiritual diversity in social work practice.* New York, NY: Oxford University Press.

Capra, F. (1982). *The Turning Point.* New York, NY: Simon and Schuster.

Chefurka, P. (2011). Home economicus, home ecologicus. *Mother Pelican: A Journal of Sustainable Human Development, 7*(3). Retrieved from http://www.pelicanweb.org/solisustv07n03page9.html

Christopher, M. (1999). An exploration of the "reflex" in reflexive modernity: The rational and prerational social causes of the affinity for ecological consciousness. *Organizations & Environment, 12*(4), 357–400.

Clark, M. (1989). *Ariadne's thread: The search for new modes of thinking.* New York, NY: St. Martin's Press.

Clinebell, H. (1996). *Ecotherapy: Healing ourselves, healing the Earth.* Minneapolis, MN: Fortress Press.

Coates, J. (2003). *Ecology and social work: Toward a new paradigm.* Halifax, NS: Fernwood Press.

Coates, J. (2005). Environmental crisis: Implications for social work. *Journal of Progressive Human Services 16*(1), 25–49.

Coates, N. (2010, August 10). Provocatively unorthodox [Web log post]. Retrieved from http://nicholascoates.blogspot.com/

Diamond, J. (2005). *Collapse: How societies choose to fail or succeed.* Toronto, ON: Viking.

Earley, J. (1997). *Transforming human culture.* Albany, NY: SUNY Press.

Eckersley, R. (1992). *Environmentalism and political theory: Toward an ecocentric approach.* Albany, NY: SUNY Press.

Einstein, A. (n.d.). Einstein quotes. Retrieved from http://www.einstein-quotes.com/index.html

Elgin, D. (2000). *Promise ahead: A vision of hope and action for humanity's future.* New York, NY: William Morrow.

Elshof, L. (2010). Changing worldviews to cope with a changing climate. In R. Irwin (Ed.), *Climate change and philosophy: Transformational possibilities* (pp. 75–108). New York, NY: Continuum Press.

English, L. (2012). For whose purposes: Examining the spirituality agenda in adult education. In J. Groen, D. Coholic, & J. R. Graham (Eds.), *Spirituality in social work and education: Theory, practice and dialogue.* Waterloo, ON: Wilfrid Laurier University Press.

Faver, C. (2009). Seeking our place in the web of life: Animals and human spirituality. *Journal of Religion and Spirituality in Social Work, 28*(4), 362–378.

Fein, S. (2010). Keys to a broken nation: The explosive potential of awakened youth. *Adbusters, 91.* Retrieved from https://www.adbusters.org/magazine/91/recipe revolution.html

Gladwin, T., Newbury, W., & Reiskin, E. (1997). Why is the northern elite mind biased against community, the environment and a sustainable future? In M. Bazerman & D. Messick (Eds.), *Environment, ethics and behavior* (pp. 234–274). San Francisco, CA: New Lexington Press.

Glavin T. (2006). *Sixth extinction: Journeys among the lost and left behind.* New York, NY: St. Martin's Press.

Godrej, D. (2001). *The NO-NONSENSE guide to climate change.* Toronto, ON: Between the Lines.

Goldsmith, E. (1998). *The way.* London, UK: Rider.

Gore, A. (2006). *An inconvenient truth. The planetary emergency of global warming and what we can do about it.* Emmaus, PA: Rodale.

Graham, J. R., and Shier, M. (2012). Religion and spirituality in social work academic settings. In J. Groen, D. Coholic, & J. R. Graham (Eds.), *Spirituality in social work and education: Theory, practice and dialogue.* Waterloo, ON: Wilfrid Laurier University Press.

Gray, M., Coates, J., & Yellow Bird, M. (2008). Introduction. In M. Gray, J. Coates, and M. Yellow Bird (Eds.), *Indigenous social work around the world: Towards culturally relevant education and practice* (pp. 1–12). Burlington, VT: Ashgate Press.

Green, A. (2010). Sacred evolution: A radical Jewish perspective on god and science. *Tikkun, 25*(2), 33. Retrieved from http://www.tikkun.org/article.php/mar2010green

Greenberg, P. (2010). *Four fish: The future of the last wild food.* New York, NY: Penguin.

Groen, J., Coholic, D., & Graham, J. R. (2012). Introduction. In J. Groen, D. Coholic, & J. R. Graham (Eds.), *Spirituality in social work and education: Theory, practice and dialogue.* Waterloo, ON: Wilfrid Laurier University Press.

Hamilton, C. (2003). *Growth fetish.* Crows Nest, Australia: Allen & Unwin.

Heath, Y., & Gifford, R. (2006). Free market ideology and environmental degradation: The case of belief in global climate change. *Environment and Behaviour, 38*(1), 48–71.

Hedges, C. (2009). *Empire of illusion: The end of literacy and the triumph of spectacle.* Toronto, ON: Random House.

Howard, P. (2008). Ecology, phenomenology, and culture: Developing a language for sustainability. *Diaspora, Indigenous and Minority Education, 2,* 302–310. doi: 10.1080/15595690802352788

Howe, D. (1994). Modernity, post-modernity and social work. *British Journal of Social Work, 24* (5), 513–532.

Hubbard, B. (1998). *Conscious evolution: Awakening our social potential.* Novato, CA: New World Library.

IPCC (Intergovernmental Panel on Climate Change). (2007). *Climate Change 2007: Synthesis Report.* Contribution of Working Groups I, II, and III to the fourth assessment report of the Intergovernmental Panel on Climate Change [Core Writing Team, R. K. Pachauri, & A. Reisinger (Eds.)]. Geneva, Switzerland: Author.

IPCC (2011). *IPCC Special Report on Renewable Energy Sources and Climate Change Mitigation.* Prepared by Working Group III of the Intergovernmental Panel on Climate Change [O. Edenhofer, R. Pichs-Madruga, Y. Sokona, K. Seyboth, P. Matschoss, S. Kadner, T. Zwickel, P. Eickemeier, G. Hansen, S. Schlömer, & C. von Stechow (Eds.)]. Cambridge, UK: Cambridge University Press, 1075 pp.

Irving, A. (1994). From image to simulcra: The modern/postmodern divide in social work. In A. Chambon & A. Irving (Eds.), *Essays on postmodernism and social work,* (pp. 19–32). Toronto, ON: Canadian Scholars' Press.

Jarman, M. (2007). *Climate change.* Halifax, NS: Fernwood Press.

Kelly, E. N., Short, J. S., Schindler, D. W., Hodson, P. V., Ma, M., Kwan, A. K., & Fortin, B. L. (2009). Oil sands development contributes polycyclic aromatic compounds to the Athabasca River and its tributaries. *Proceedings of the National Academy of Sciences, 106*(52), 22346–22351.

Kennedy, R., Jr. (2003, December 11). Crimes against nature. *Rolling Stone, 937,* 180–194.

Korten, D. (1995). *When corporations rule the world.* San Francisco, CA: Kumarian Press and Berrett-Koehler.

Korten, D. (2006). *The great turning: From empire to earth community.* San Francisco, CA: Kumarian Press and Berrett-Koehler.

Korten, D. (2009). *Agenda for a new economy: From phantom wealth to real wealth.* San Francisco, CA: Berrett-Koehler.

Lerner, M. (2003). Closed hearts, closed minds. *Tikkun, 18*(5), 7. Retrieved from http://www.tikkun.org/article.php/Lerner

Lertzman, R. (2008). The myth of apathy [Web log post]. *The Ecologist*. Retrieved from http://www.theecologist.org/blogs_and_comments/commentators/other_comments/269433/the_myth_of_apathy.html

Lifton, R. (1981). In a dark time. In R. Adams & S. Cullen, (Eds.), *The final epidemic: Physicians and scientists on nuclear war*. Chicago, IL: Education Foundation for Nuclear Science.

Livingston, J. (1994). *Rogue primate: An exploration of human domestication*. Toronto, ON: Key Porter Books.

Lovelock, J. (1979). *Gaia: A new look at life on Earth*. New York, NY: Oxford University Press.

Lysack, M. (2010). Environmental decline, loss, and biophilia: Fostering commitment in environmental citizenship. *Critical Social Work: An Interdisciplinary Journal Dedicated to Social Justice, 11*(3). Retrieved from http://www.uwindsor.ca/critical socialwork/environmental-decline-loss-and-biophilia-fostering-commitment-in -environmental-citizenship

Macy, J. (1989). Awakening to the ecological self. In J. Plant (Ed.), *Healing the wounds: The promise of ecofeminism* (pp. 210–211). Santa Cruz, CA: New Society Publishers.

Mary, N. (2008). *Social work in a sustainable world*. Chicago, IL: Lyceum Books.

May, E. (2006). *How to save the world in your spare time*. Toronto, ON: Key Porter Books.

McFague, S. (1993). *The body of God: An ecological theology*. Minneapolis, MN: Fortress Press.

Mezirow, J. (1978). Perspective transformation. *Adult Education, 28*(2), 100–110.

Mezirow, J. (1990). *Fostering critical reflection in adulthood*. San Francisco, CA: Jossey-Bass.

Montenegro, M., & Glavin, T. (2010) In defence of difference: Scientists offer new insight into what to protect of the world's rapidly vanishing languages, cultures, and species. *Seed Magazine*. Retrieved from http://seedmagazine.com/content/article/in_defense_of_difference/

Mullaly, B. (1997). *Structural social work: Ideology, theory and practice* (2nd ed.). Toronto, ON: Oxford University Press.

Naess, A. (1989). *Ecology, community and lifestyle* (D. Rothenberg, Trans. & Ed.). Cambridge University Press.

Nordhaus, T., & Shellenberger, M. (2007). *Break through: From the death of environmentalism to the politics of possibility*. Boston, MA: Houghton Mifflin.

Norgaard, K. (2006). "We don't really want to know": Environmental justice and socially organized denial of global warming in Norway. *Organization and Environment 19*, 347–370.

OIKOS. (2010). Retreats on climate change as a moral issue [Web page]. Calgary, Canada: OIKOS. Retrieved from http://www.ucalgary.ca/oikos/Retreat

O'Murchu, D. (1997). *Quantum theology: Spiritual implications of the new physics*. New York, NY: Crossroad Publishing.

O'Murchu, D. (2000). *Religion in exile: A spiritual homecoming*. New York, NY: Crossroad Publishing.

Orr, D. (2009). *Down to the wire*. Toronto, ON: Oxford University Press.

Rifkin, J. (2009). *The empathic civilization: The race to global consciousness in a world in crisis.* New York, NY: Tarcher/Penguin.

Rogers, R. (1994). *Nature and the crisis of modernity.* Montreal, QC: Black Rose.

Russell, P. (1998). *Waking up in time: Finding inner peace in times of accelerating change.* Novato, CA: Origin Press.

Sahtouris, E. (1998). *Conscious evolution: Awakening the power of our social potential.* Novato, CA: New World Library.

Scharmer, C. (2003). The blind spot of leadership: Presencing as a social technology of freedom. Retrieved from http://www.ottoscharmer.com/docs/articles/2003 _TheBlindSpot.pdf

Scharmer, C. (2009). The blind spot of economic thought: Seven acupuncture points for shifting to capitalism 3.0. Retrieved from http://www.ottoscharmer.com/docs/articles/2009_SevenAcupuncturePoints5.pdf

Schell, J. (2003). Power and cooperation. *Tikkun, 18*(5), 16–22. Retrieved from http://search.ebscohost.com/login.aspx?direct=true&db=tsh&AN=10720287&site=ehost-live&scope=site

Speth, J. G. (2008). *The bridge at the edge of the world: Capitalism, the environment, and crossing from crisis to sustainability.* New Haven, CT: Yale University Press.

Spretnak, C. (1997). *The resurgence of the real.* Don Mills, ON: Addison-Wesley.

Stutchbury, B. (2007). *Silence of the songbirds: How we are losing the world's songbirds and what we can do to save them.* Toronto, ON: HarperCollins.

Suzuki, D. (2010). Nature challenge [Web page]. *David Suzuki Foundation.* Retrieved from. http://www.davidsuzuki.org/what-you-can-do/nature-challenge/

Swimme, B., & Berry, T. (1992). *The universe story.* San Francisco, CA: Harper.

Wapner, P. (2003). Tikkun Environmentalism. *Tikkun, 18*(5), 42–45. Retrieved from http://search.ebscohost.com/login.aspx?direct=true&db=tsh&AN=08879982&site=ehost-live&scope=site

WCED (World Commission on Environment and Development). (1997). *Our common future.* New York, NY: Oxford University Press.

White, L., Jr. (1967, March). The historical roots of our ecologic crisis. *Science 155,* 37–67.

Wilber, K. (2007). *Integral spirituality: A startling new role for religion in the modern and postmodern world.* Boston, MA: Integral Books.

Zapf, M. K. (2009). *Social work and the environment: Understanding people and place.* Toronto, ON: Canadian Scholars' Press.

Chapter 5

Kindred Spirits? Challenges and Opportunities for the Faculties of Education and Social Work in the Emerging Teaching Focus on Spirituality

Janet Groen

Introduction

Recently, Arthur Zajonc (Palmer & Zajonc 2010) reflected on the need, as an academic, to overcome the divide between spirituality and higher education at both an institutional and individual level. At both levels, he stated that academics needed to find a way to an "undivided life where meaning and purpose are tightly interwoven with intellect and action, where compassion and care are infused with insight and knowledge" (2010, p. 56). Personally for Zajonc, such aspirations for a holistic and undivided life were already apparent in his college years. During his first few years as a student in physics, mathematics, and the Great Books, he struggled to find a connection between his coursework and his desire to find meaning and purpose in his life. Just as Zajonc was contemplating an end to his studies, he had a life-changing conversation with his physics professor. As they spoke about how to integrate meaning and purpose into the life of a scientist, Zajonc realized, "here was a person who had worked for forty years to knit together in his own fashion an undivided life philosophy that embraced an experiential, contemplative spirituality" (2010, p. 34). And so began his quest to live an integrated life as an academic, one that included a vision of spirituality in higher education reflected in the belief that spirituality and religion are not the same, but they may be interrelated (Tisdell, 2003). Spirituality is about being aware and honouring the wholeness and interconnectedness of all things through the mystery of a higher power. It is about seeking a sense of purpose and ultimately making meaning in one's life. Spirituality is always present in the learning environment. It is about how people construct knowledge through largely unconscious and symbolic processes (Tisdell, 2003, pp. 28–29). Spiritual development is movement toward greater authenticity. In addition, I believe that spirituality is about action and an outward response that challenges inequities, works toward social justice, and asks difficult and uncomfortable questions. "I am interested in a spirituality ... that does not tinker with the status quo, but ultimately calls us to stewardship as we challenge our economic assumptions and consumer culture" (Groen, 2004, p. 6).

As an academic immersed in adult learning and adult education, I resonate with Zajonc's desire to live an undivided life in which a holistic way of teaching and engaging in research is valued. While approaches that honour different ways of knowing, such as somatic, affective, and spiritual are gradually being accepted in pedagogical theory and included in coursework (Griffin, 1986; Dirkx, 1997; English, 2001; Miller, 2000; Tisdell, 2003), the overt presence of spirituality in teaching and research is still greeted with some caution and hesitation. Indeed, according to Dillard, Abdur-Rashid, and Tyson (2000), Tisdell (2000), Shahja-han (2005, 2009), and Palmer and Zajonc (2010), venturing into this arena as an academic can be risky business in a university culture that places emphasis on positivist research methods. "Academics may fear that their spirituality will be ridiculed within the confines of academe as an embodied practice or discourse" (Shahjahan, 2005, p. 295). However, I agree with Palmer's (2010) critique of the statement that spirituality and academics do not mix; he argued that reli-gion and spirituality are essential to our understanding of what it means to be human. Rather than focusing exclusively on an external, objective reality, higher education should be primarily helping students to practise deeper intellectual engagement. "Excluding religion and spirituality from serious study in secular settings is a stunning form of irrationality in itself. Religion and spirituality are among the major drivers of contemporary life" (Palmer, 2010, p. 47).

Despite the risky business of teaching and researching spirituality in secu-lar university settings, there are those of us working in the academy who have heeded the call of the undivided academic life by teaching courses that implicitly and/or explicitly incorporate spirituality, so our students can engage in a holistic education that takes them on both an outer and inner journey. A survey con-ducted by Duerr, Zajonc, and Dana (2003) was an early attempt at documenting such "academic programs and other initiatives in North American universities and colleges that incorporate transformative and spiritual elements of learning" (p. 177). As well, Fleming and Courtenay (2006) and Hunt and West (2007) conducted research that explored the connection between spirituality and the work of adult educators, including those who are faculty members in higher education settings. While these studies emphasized the value participants placed on living an undivided life, they highlighted the challenge of transferring this to their teaching and research agendas. In particular, Hunt and West (2007), two education academics in the United Kingdom, noted that participants in their seminar series focusing on the link between spirituality and lifelong learning experienced a disconnect between their aspirations for a holistic academic life and the reality they lived in. One academic participant raised the following concern: "I've a yearning to write more creatively, but higher education is an ever more difficult context—reminds me of the saying, 'sleep faster, we need the pillows!'" (p. 303). Another participant, inspired by engaging with other like-minded academics, made the following promise: "I also left feeling inspired to draw explicitly upon my spirituality and my teaching, rather than to hide it as something not 'valid' in academic/professional space" (Hunt & West, 2007, p. 303).

In this chapter, I contribute to the emerging discourse by presenting the voices of six full-time professors from the faculties of education and social work within the Canadian university context who are interested in teaching courses that address an aspect of spirituality as part of the core content. Through our dialogue, we had the opportunity to explore the hopes and challenges of striving to be an undivided academic. Specifically, we explored if and how our interest in integrating spirituality into our teaching practice emerged; how we understood spirituality and how this translated into our course content; and how spirituality was understood and valued by our respective students, faculties, universities, and disciplines.

Before I present the highlights of our dialogue, I briefly situate myself as an academic striving to live an undivided life, and present the approach I used to explore the experiences of other academics traveling on a similar path.

Divided to Undivided

Participating in a series of retreats at the Ignatius Jesuit Centre for Spirituality in Guelph, Ontario, began my shift toward to an undivided life. For more than a decade I had been cultivating my passion for teaching adults in a variety of roles and settings. As a staff development consultant for a Catholic school board, I was invited to participate in a leadership formation retreat series based upon Ignatian Spirituality. The root of this 450-year-old tradition comes from the Society of Jesus, usually referred to as the Jesuits, and was founded by a Basque soldier and low-level nobleman, Ignatius of Loyola. The link between this leadership program and Ignatian spirituality was my school board's wish to cultivate a specific approach to making critical and complex decisions at a particularly tumultuous time in its history: the process of discernment. "The sources of the Ignatian tradition are not for speculative contemplation or for academic discourse but for contemplative decision and action" (Veale, 2006, p. 148). While increasing my understanding about the power of discernment to make decisions at both a personal and organizational level was valuable, what caused the convergence between my deepening interest in adult learning processes and my spiritual journey were the ways we engaged in these exercises. Learning processes of storytelling, attentive and open listening, and dialogue were central to each of the retreat experiences. The idea that these approaches I valued so highly as an educator could be equated with spirituality was a revelation for me. At that time, my spiritual growth had stalled; no longer was I satisfied with the teachings of the church of my childhood and early adulthood. In hindsight, I now realize that I was struggling to move beyond an understanding of spirituality equated only with religion, even while I was seeking to "reclaim and reintegrate elements of strength from [my] childhood faith" (Fowler, 1981, p. 198). I wanted to connect to a broader notion of spirituality that underscored the centrality of my desire to pursue a meaningful life, to experience connectedness and community, and to challenge inequities and injustices evident in both my own workplace and a broader societal context.

The experiences I had at the Ignatian Jesuit Centre served as the catalyst for my return to doctoral studies and the focus of my dissertation on the role of adult educators in developing spirituality in the workplace (Groen, 2002). Over the past eight years, in my faculty role in Workplace and Adult Learning at the University of Calgary, I have continued to engage in research and teaching that links spirituality to adult learning both in formal and informal settings. Focusing specifically on teaching, I have had the opportunity to teach a course entitled Spirituality in the Workplace on an almost annual basis. I became aware that this was a unique opportunity while engaged in research (Groen, 2009) about the emerging focus of spirituality in business, education, and social work faculties in Canada. Within these faculties, I noted that there were just ten courses centring on spirituality, with six of those housed in the Faculty of Education at the University of Calgary. Therefore, I wanted to reflect upon and engage in dialogue with other colleagues across Canada interested in connecting spirituality to their coursework to contribute to an understanding of what it means to be an undivided and holistic academic.

The Process

Participants in this cross-faculty dialogue included six of the authors who contributed to this book divided between the faculties of education and social work. We divided into two smaller groups, ensuring that there was representation from both education and social work in order to explore reflexively our own personal experiences and understandings about teaching coursework that addresses some aspect of spirituality. Each dialogue, which occurred via teleconference, lasted sixty to ninety minutes, was recorded and retained by me. All participants reviewed and affirmed their representation in this chapter.

The approach of cross-faculty dialogue was chosen because it provided a comfortable framework in order to share our lived experiences of teaching in the arena of spirituality as opposed to examining in a more abstract and cognitive fashion our understandings about spirituality and its place within higher education. Moreover, dialogue, in providing such a space for multiple perspectives and stories to be shared, allowed for the possibility of deeper collective meanings

(Bohm, Factor, & Garrett, 1991) across our two faculties. Finally, I believed that the use of dialogue would provide a sacred space, offering congruence between the *topic* and the *process* of our conversation. "The heart of a spirited epistemology is respect for dialogue. Everything in your design moves toward the dialogue as a plant moves toward the sunlight" (Vella, 2000, p. 11).

Central to the process of dialogue was each person's ability to step back from their experiences and make meaning from them. "[In dialogue, we become] critically reflective; we also learn to speak about practice in a way that is authentic and consistent" (Brookfield, 1995, p. 45). Furthermore, we wished to listen deeply and openly to one another's experiences, ideas, and stories. English, Fenwick, and Parsons (2003) indicated that the starting place of such open listening is reverence for the other person. "It is grounded on a profound understanding that the other person is to be honoured and respected" (p. 83). In summary, dialogue facilitated the critical reflection process and invited each of us to share our reflections and to explore them collectively. In this way, through diversity of perspective, our experiences took on new meaning and provided us with the opportunity to uncover the wisdom and knowledge embedded in them.

Findings from Our Cross-Faculty Dialogue

Introducing My Colleagues

Education Faculty Members: Jack Miller, Professor in the Department of Curriculum, Teaching and Learning at the Ontario Institute for Studies in Education/University of Toronto, has been making connections between spirituality and education in his coursework for the past 25 years. The course Holistic Curriculum, launched in 1985, was his initial foray into the topic, and three years later he introduced a six-week component on meditation into the required coursework:

> I gave them a choice of different types of meditation so they could choose one that worked particularly well for them, and then over the six weeks, they gradually and hopefully worked up to 20 to 30 minutes a day. Since then, I've introduced meditation to 2,000 students.... At that time, meditation wasn't at the forefront. Now we hear about it everywhere.... It was a bit of risk at that time but it's been the most satisfying thing I've done as a teacher.

In 1998, Jack began teaching the course Spirituality and Education and "gave [students] a much broader choice where they would identify some kind of spiritual practice that they would do. Not necessarily meditation. Some of them would keep a journal or work on a relationship from a mindful or conscious kind of perspective."

Ian Winchester, Professor of History and Philosophy of Western Thought in the Faculty of Education at the University of Calgary, began to offer the course Mind and Spirituality several years ago. His course is one of several in the area of spirituality and education offered in this faculty. The catalyst for such a strong focus in this area was Dr. Tad Guzie, Professor of Religious Education and a well-known and respected Jesuit theologian. He began teaching the course Spirituality in a Postmodern Era in the mid-1990s and soon "had many students and many followers." It became the cornerstone of several other courses, such as Spirituality of Teaching Excellence, Spirituality of Inspired Leadership, and Spirituality, Culture and Education. When Tad Guzie died, Ian, who was Dean of the Faculty of Education at that time, stepped in and took the course on. "I called it Mind and Spirituality. It seems to me that the issues of mind and spirit have overlapped and intersected in Western and Eastern thought for thousands of years and in interesting ways."

Social Work Faculty Members: Susan Cadell, Associate Professor in Social Work and Director of the Manulife Centre for Healthy Living at Wilfrid Laurier University, indicated that "there's still a fair amount of stigma around social work and spirituality" in her context. Indeed, she faced the challenge of incorporating spirituality into either her research or her teaching early on in her academic career. "I did my Ph.D. and ended up doing research around HIV and AIDS bereavement, and had to kind of struggle to get spirituality included in that. It seemed rather obvious that it should be included, and so I spent a great deal of time trying to capture spirituality from a research point of view, quantitatively and qualitatively." Perceptions have not shifted significantly since she has taken the role of a faculty member. "I've had a colleagues approach [me] and whisper that they are interested in spirituality but do not feel able to air that in a meeting. So it's been kind of interesting thing to be, in a sense, 'out' and very public about my interests." Despite the limitations of her workplace, she has found a valuable collegial support network for her interest in connecting spirituality to social work research and practice. "Just after I graduated, I went to my first Canadian Society for Social Work and Spirituality Conference, which turned out to be the very first one ever, and so I got involved in the committee and have been a happily fulfilled member of that committee ever since."

John Coates, Professor in Social Work and Director of the School of Social Work at St. Thomas University, indicated his interest in spirituality converged with his academic life in the early 1990s when he was asked to develop and instruct a course on international policy issues. While engaged in research for this course, John determined one of emerging themes in the literature was an increasing interest in spirituality. "So I built that into the course, and then into my writing around environmental issues; my interest developed further and was probably most clearly expressed in my book, *Ecology and Social Work*" (Coates,

2003). John's engagement in spirituality and social work has been constant over most of the past two decades, and included assisting his friend and colleague Professor Brian Ouellette in evaluating a course entitled Spirituality and Social Work (for several years the only regularly offered social work course on spirituality at St. Thomas); co-founding, with three other colleagues, the Canadian Society for Spirituality and Social Work (CSSSW) in 2000; and helping to launch an annual local conference for students that explores how spirituality might inform social work practice.

> I think if students and social workers can look at their own lives and approach their professional practice from a place of spirituality and hope about what should be, they can create a desirable foundation for life and practice regardless of what the world says. Such a foundation provides a kind of endurance that is not present when one is primarily optimistic about change and repeatedly disappointed. (John)

Sarah Todd, an Associate Professor of Social Work at Carleton University for the past nine years, saw the connection between her work as an academic and spirituality early on. "My interest in spirituality came while I was at school ... spirituality was linked to the curriculum through service and that connection really sold me.... When I was a student at the Ontario Institute for Studies in Education, the community workers who I spoke to as part of my research had interesting connections and disconnections to spirituality that led us to do the work we do." Within her faculty, there is little focus on spirituality in the social work curriculum. While she is quick to acknowledge that a colleague does teach a course entitled Mindfulness and Social Work, it is not particularly focused on spirituality and social work. As a result, she is increasingly concerned that "when curriculums are getting squished and our schools are trying to be progressive and trying to establish priorities about what is most important, spirituality tends to slip off the page" (Sarah).

Why Spirituality?

Our wish to pursue spirituality in our teaching practice and research revealed a multifaceted understanding that valued interconnectedness with others and the universe, activism, and a quest for holism, particularly in our desire to move beyond the cognitive way of understanding and engaging the world typically manifested in university settings. As Ian pointed out,

> We're not permitted to look at ourselves in our own way, say, after the fashion of the Buddhists, which I would say is the first-person way. You look into yourself to try and discover what it is to be a human being, what the range of your

emotions are and how you can gain control of those if you wish to. How you can be a better person, and so on. But again, inwardly rather than looking outwardly.

Ian also revealed that he has always been interested in exploring a world that, from his perspective, is incredibly mysterious and can only be understood from a holistic vantage.

Jack's interest in holism and spirituality in education arose out of his own meditation practice:

> I had been meditating since 1974, so I had been meditating for fourteen years before I decided to bring it into my teaching. The main reason is that when we are talking about spirituality, it isn't enough to just talk about it.... I don't think we can just sit around a seminar table and discuss spirituality from a purely intellectual view. Again, I think we have to approach it holistically. Obviously the intellect is an important part of that, but if we leave out the other dimensions then I think it's a problem.

Susan pointed out that while spirituality has always been an important part of her life, she experienced convergence between her personal and professional life through her research. "For the past five years, a big part of my research life has been palliative care, and you can't do palliative care without including spirituality. So that's a big part of it as well." Susan indicated that incorporating spirituality into her practice is really a political statement against what is typically valued in the university setting, alluding once more to our quest for a holistic way of engaging in teaching and research.

> I've talked about coming out, because for me it was a political decision not to hide what I was interested in and what I thought was important. So yes, it's part of my goal to live that undivided life ... I remember years ago feeling the same way about feminism, that I was declaring myself because I didn't in some ways fit the stereotype, and so I wanted people to know that feminists were of all sizes and colours. So I've always spoken out about spirituality for the same kinds of reasons. I wasn't willing to hide anything. (Susan)

Finally, for both John and Sarah, the emphasis on interconnectedness was a central component of their understanding of spirituality. John's perspective on spirituality reflected his research on ecology and social work: "I come at spirituality from [what] I'm going to call a cosmological place, in the sense of the evolution of the earth as a sacred entity and humans having a place." Sarah's understanding of interconnectedness reflected the intertwining of social work and activism. "As spiritual beings, we are all interconnected and responsible for each other." Finally, returning to the collective concern we all have, that the emphasis of our curricula, and our faculties and universities, is becoming too instrumental and problem-based, Sarah and John see the necessity of instilling a deeper awareness and sense of meaning and purpose within their students situated in wisdom and an orientation "that as spiritual beings we are all interconnected and responsible for each other" (Sarah).

> I find that when the students get so focused on the issues that deal with social change, they frequently burn out. Stress and burnout can also [result] from the structure and realities of social work practice, if one does not have support and a personal/professional practice of self-care. A spiritual foundation and practice can help sustain and enrich our capacity for compassion and understanding, even when faced with trauma-filled lives and frequent crises that are a reality for so many of the people for whom we work. (John)

Spirituality and Coursework within Our Faculties

As we began contrasting and comparing the place of spirituality within the curriculum of our respective faculties and professions of education and social work, a common element for all of us was our students' desire to incorporate spirituality into their coursework. Indeed, Ian and I, colleagues in the same faculty of education, have noticed a consistent trend over the past decade; graduate courses that have the word "spirituality" in the title are quick to fill up, and those of us teaching them receive numerous requests from students to add extra spaces. "What we're seeing is that people [students] are coming to us, and we wouldn't have necessarily predicted this." (Ian). Jack also has a similar phenomenon within his faculty. "The courses that are offered in the area tend to be over-subscribed, and there are just a lot of students that are drawn to this area."

In other research I recently conducted with my colleague Dr. Jacob (Groen & Jacob, 2006), our exploration of graduate students' motivations and learning journeys within one of the spirituality and education courses offered at the University of Calgary revealed that they were looking for courses that held intrinsic interest, increased their self-awareness, and at the same time provided a change of pace from their more technical courses. For example, Karen, an elementary teacher, characterized her interest in the course in this way: "The most important thing for me was to take something that I felt a certain amount of passion toward … I think what I was looking for was a place to share, a place to talk about our lives.… " Then Beth, an adult educator, expressed a similar and complementary attraction to the course by noting it offered something she believed others lacked: "I think that there are other things that we need to think about as teachers, and I wasn't getting any of that in any of [my specialization] courses" (Groen & Jacob, 2006, p. 78).

Jack's reflection on the significant student interest in his course, Spirituality and Education, reflected students' pursuit of self-awareness, and their wish for community. "My classes are done in a circle—which becomes a healing circle where people are being present to one another; and that really is the beginning of a process and it's very gratifying to just sit with the students. By the end of the course, I've just sort of disappeared and it becomes its own organism."

Shifting to social work, it was the students' interest in spirituality that initially propelled John Coates' colleague Dr. Brian Ouellette, who passed away in 2005, to develop one of the few courses in Canada that explicitly linked spirituality to social work. According to Lwanga (2010), a doctoral student interested in Ouellette's pioneering work in spirituality and social work instruction, almost all the students who attended the undergraduate social work program at St. Thomas University chose to the take this course as one of their electives during the decade it was offered.

> The course enabled students to explore [the] spiritual perspective of social work through the exploration of the literature in areas of personal interest and creativity through term papers. Topics could range from social work practice and fundamentalism, [to] feminism and the welfare crisis; [students could research] spirituality and group practice or direct practice, social action, the workplace, global transformation, Native spirituality and Social Work, [or any] other topics based on a student's personal search. (Lwanga, 2010)

However, in 2006 the curriculum shifted in the undergraduate social work program, and without Professor Ouellette, Spirituality and Social Work was dropped as a regularly offered elective. "There are fewer electives now and those offered have a more applied focus—such as working with families, child welfare, mental health, and addictions. They are more problem-oriented or problem-focused" (John). The ending of this course reflects a larger Canadian trend in the field of social work; as John, Sarah, and Susan all indicated, there are very few, if any, courses that focus on spirituality because of the large number of courses the social work accreditation process requires. And yet they all agreed that many of their students still desire its inclusion in the curriculum. As Sarah explained, "I think the secularism of society has left students with a sense of emptiness, and I think that opens them up to searching and a curiosity about spirituality." John echoed this observation, and considered some of additional societal causes as to why students might be turning to coursework as a platform to explore meaning and purpose in their lives.

> I grew up in a strong religious tradition—there were religious schools, structures, and community groups that I became a part of, whereas my children have had a much less pervasive experience. They have strong relationships with their friends

and very supportive networks, but they don't engage in traditional organizations or with larger society in the same way. So I think that they are acting in a much more independent way. I think, as for many people in society today, this contributes to that search for meaning, because people themselves are more responsible for the answers they come up with and are less dependent on their churches, their doctors, and the authorities to inform their beliefs.

Our colleagues in social work do not believe that the removal of specific courses on spirituality and social work excuses faculty from infusing it within the existing social work curriculum. It is too important. As John indicated, "Many of [the students' future] clients will be members of a religious community, and it is important for social workers to be able to understand and to work with spirituality when it is expressed through a religion." Sarah also indicated how important it is to be respectful of "where clients are in terms of their spiritual faith and how one navigates that in an interview setting." John, Susan, and Sarah were each able to point to specific ways they incorporated spirituality into their curriculum. For example, Susan said,

We have a course here called Diversity, Marginalization and Oppression [developed] as a response to a need to represent diversity in the curriculum. That's a really logical place to have, as part of its discussion of diversity, a discussion on the diversity of religion, spiritual teachings, and points of view, but to my knowledge it is not always there in the classroom with the people who are teaching it here.

In his course on global policy, John introduces the "issue of the connectedness of all things; and I look at how our whole world, including humans, should have a sense of being part of the same system." In another course he teaches on the theory of social work, "we talk about Aboriginal approaches to social work, and there's a deep spiritual connection implicit in those Aboriginal approaches." Finally, Sarah made several connections between spirituality and her coursework.

In my community development course, spirituality is related to sustaining movements over time, how to cultivate hope with communities, and fostering a notion that change takes a long time. For example, I use my experience in Nicaragua as an example of how spirituality was used to sustain a movement. I also teach about sexuality, HIV, and AIDS, and [find] we are at an interesting point where we think about spirituality and religion.

Spirituality as a Research Focus within Our Faculties and the Profession

The varied levels of acceptance of coursework related to spirituality appeared to mirror the level of receptiveness for its inclusion into research within our respective faculties. While Susan, Sarah, and John are all able to find support through the Canadian Society for Social Work and Spirituality, Susan experienced resistance in her home faculty, and research on spirituality is perceived as peripheral in Sarah's department. For John, several social work faculty members at St. Thomas incorporate spirituality into their courses and their research. However, a number of CSSSW members and recent Ph.D. students have reported that they were actively discouraged from focusing their dissertations in the area of spirituality.

In many ways, while spirituality has made inroads back into social work, its acceptance from department to department varies quite a bit. Illustrating this point, Jack, Ian, and I are working in faculties hospitable to such explicit connections. For Jack,

> there are now a number of people who are moving into this area (research and teaching in spirituality).... My colleague Michel Ferrari is establishing a Centre for Wisdom Studies which includes several University of Toronto faculty. Of course there are some people who, again, don't feel comfortable, but the people who are doing (teaching and research in spirituality), I don't think that they need to hold back. That's been a very positive development here.

For Ian and me, it would be easy to just point to Tad Guzie as the catalyst for the inclusion of spirituality within our coursework and research agendas. However, Ian explained that this would not have occurred without a paradigm shift in our faculty of education. That shift was directly attributable to Ian's leadership as the Dean during the 1990s. As part of his mandate to transform the faculty, he made a fundamental change in the undergraduate teacher preparation program that moved it "away from the scientific paradigm, in the sense that everything must be in the third person and everything must be counted ... of course that seemed to me to lead rather naturally into the area of spirituality." On a structural level, Ian made the following changes in our faculty that are still in place today. "We departmentalized the faculty ... in order to make the faculty a unitary sort of faculty.... We minimized the importance of lectures ... and ended up in the conversational mode. Classes became small and intimate, and before we knew it, I would say that we had a very different sort of faculty." In turn, an increasing number of faculty members have created research agendas that explore spirituality within diverse educational contexts. However, both Ian and I are now standing at the cusp of change again, and wonder if current paradigm and structural shifts will support the inclusion of spirituality within our faculty's future teaching and research. At this time, it is too soon to tell.

While probing the level of hospitality in our respective faculties, we widened the net to include the broader professional field of education and social work, an area where we all feel some tensions. In schools, Jack has experienced varying degrees of reception to his work. "I do a lot of work with Catholic schools, and I do a workshop called Education and the Soul … when I broach that with public school people, they just back away." All of us felt that part of this caution was likely derived from a fear that the introduction of spirituality into education and social work might infringe on people's religious beliefs and understandings. "What one does is characteristically avoid the conversation, in so far as there is a religious connection with spirituality … whatever direction you take, people worry that you're going to offend somebody" (Ian).

Susan affirmed that her experience in the practice of social work was similar. "We purport to be about the person and the environment and [say we] do holistic assessments of people, but often our assessments of people's environments don't include any sense of spiritual and/or religious direction." Sarah concurred that this separation has occurred in the field, and suggested

> there is a lot of anxiety about some of the past and current social work that is carried out in the name of religion, and some of it comes into conflict with our notion of supporting people's self-determination, particularly in the areas of sexuality and reproduction.

Susan also pointed out "that our profession started with religious roots, and we've backed so far away from the early days of Christian charity that we've backed away from everything." John elaborated on the field's movement away and from spirituality:

> Social work, in its early efforts to be seen as a profession, became secularized and rational and gave decreasing attention to spirituality and religion. However, for social work in Canada, especially since 2000, religion and spirituality are increasingly part of social work discourse but are still far from being central.

Even though the field of social work has a long way to go, John, Sarah, and Susan all believe opening up more dialogue is critical.

> The profession needs to find ways to consider how our values and ethics are linked to ancient spiritual ways of knowing that have value, while also questioning spiritually based practice approaches that come into conflict with our social work values. The challenge is to remain in an engaged dialogue rather than separating in the way that we have. (Sarah)

Spirituality and the Broader University Context

An underlying theme to our dialogue was that we were the lucky or fortunate academics. "I think we're lucky in so many ways that we can work and do this work. What Parker Palmer talks about, the heart's reward—that inner feeling, that connection that we get—that's the satisfaction that we have that I don't think you get doing just purely intellectual work" (Jack). In acknowledging the position of privilege in incorporating spirituality into our research and teaching, we explored why we were the exception in the university, and not the norm. As Ian pointed out, "there is something of an irony that the university movement began as a movement that was connected with the church." Indeed, both Ian and Susan pointed out several universities in Canada that originated from various denominations.

Now "you might say that the university is disentangling itself from the church" and in turn, we are "not permitted to look at ourselves in our own way, say after the fashion of the Buddhists which I would say is the first-person way." Jack concurs, "I think that academic philosophy was symbolic of what happened in education. With the emphasis on analytic philosophy for so long, [the need to] address the 'big questions' in life was ignored."

However, we also acknowledged a possible and hopeful shift in our universities, as expressed by Jack. "At least some people at that level (senior university administration) are beginning to ask questions about what education is really about…. We need to start asking, what is the purpose of education?"

Concluding Thoughts

My hope in arranging dialogues with Ian, Susan, Jack, John, and Sarah was to create a space where we could share experiences and observations with other colleagues who believe that spirituality should be an important component of their lives as academics. In our dialogues, we explored how our interest in integrating spirituality into our teaching practice emerged; how we understood spirituality, and how this translated into our course content; and how spirituality was understood and valued by our respective students, faculties, universities and disciplines. I came into these dialogues focused on if and how spirituality was a basis for my colleagues' teaching and research. However, I am now left with a more expansive point of view, as our conversation widened to include students' perceptions and experiences and university contexts.

Regardless of whether there is an explicit focus on spirituality within course-work or not, many undergraduate and graduate students are interested in connecting spirituality to their studies. For those of us in education who offer courses related explicitly to spirituality, this is manifest in full class enrollments, with students being placed on waiting lists. For my colleagues in social work whose faculties do not offer such courses, students appreciate its inclusion within the existing coursework. This spiritual quest among our student population mirrors the findings of a recent study (Astin, Astin, & Lindholm, 2010) that found while religious engagement among students declines somewhat during undergraduate years, their spirituality shows significant growth. In particular, students who deliberately focused on their spiritual growth "include not only those who regularly engage in self-reflection or meditation but also those whose professors ... support students' spiritual development" (Astin et al., 2010, p. 48). Indeed, part of the motivation for many undergraduate students attending university is to reflect on meaning and purpose within their life; they hope that their experiences will help them gain self-understanding and awareness, and contribute to their spiritual growth. While this study focused on undergraduate students, I would venture a guess that this spiritual quest does not stop at their convocation ceremony. Indeed, many of our graduate students are on a similar spiritual quest, as they continue to explore questions of meaning and purpose in their personal and professional lives. Returning to the conversation between Zajonc and his physics professor—the student and the academic—I now realize that they were on the same spiritual quest to live undivided lives. So while my initial focus in our dialogues was to understand what it means to live an undivided academic life, it has expanded to include students in their pursuit to live undivided lives as well. Indeed, we must continue to take up the challenge of cultivating space within our classrooms where students can share their struggles and challenges. Shahjahan (2009) indicated

> we see that students are going through journeys that call many of their normalized perceptions into question ... spirituality is important in the process of teaching and learning for pedagogues who are challenging their students' normative thinking. (p. 130)

As we seek to support the undivided lives of our students by widening our pedagogical approaches beyond those that only favour the intellect to incorporate the physical, affective, and spiritual, there are varying levels of receptiveness within our faculties and universities. Indeed, as revealed by my colleagues in social work, recent accreditation adjustments have demanded an increase in courses that are problem-based and context-specific, leaving little time for varied instructional approaches and courses or content of a spiritual nature. At the University of Calgary, it was disappointing for Ian and me to find out that all of our graduate courses focusing on spirituality in education (e.g., Spirituality in the Workplace, Spirituality in a Postmodern Era) were no longer offered after the summer of 2011.

Turning to the research of spirituality in social work and education, I believe that there is reason to be hopeful. The majority of us noted hospitality for our research agendas in this area that can only increase with the Canadian Centre for Social Work and the Wisdom in Education Centre being established at OISE (the Ontario Institute for Studies in Education). And yet we continue to feel cautious as the discourse in some of our faculties and across all of our universities continues to question the validity of research that does not stay within the confines of intellectual engagement and a positivistic world view.

I believe that a response from those of us striving to live undivided academic lives is in order. As Shahjahan (2005) stated, we need to reclaim spirituality from the margins of academy. "We need dialogue so that we can address the question of spirituality in research from different social location and spiritual traditions. It is by looking at it from a prism of difference that we can address spirituality and pave a way for it to be at the center rather than at the periphery in the academy" (p. 703). As we chart a path for the future that has the potential to move us closer to the centre of the academy, we need to engage in ongoing critically reflective practice that English speaks of her chapter. We must continuously probe our motivations for introducing spirituality into our research and teaching, and be sensitive to the potential of acting exclusionary in our approaches. As well, we need to challenge the notion that spirituality in higher education simply means that we are creating caring and nurturing environments for our students and for one another. Critically reflective spirituality challenges us to deep intellectual engagement, so that we can delve into dimensions of power, oppression, and the ecological degradation of the planet.

While the dialogue that is the basis for this chapter is a beginning response to Shahjahan's challenge, it is just that, a beginning. Indeed, this dialogue leaves me with many questions. Even though we, in education and social work, are making connections between spirituality and our research and teaching, others might argue that this is only because we are both people-oriented professional faculties. Implicit in this assumption is the belief that spirituality does not fit into the discourse of other faculties, such as science and the humanities, and thus should remain on the university's margins. Therefore, I believe I must find connections in other faculties beyond social work and education and enter into dialogue with colleagues who are doing similar work. How is spirituality viewed in the humanities, the arts, and the sciences? Returning to the recent study by Astin et al. (2010) documenting an increasing student interest in spirituality, their quest was not relegated to social work and education. The wish for an undivided life is being expressed across our universities by both students and academics. The next step, of course, is to continue the dialogue across faculties, across universities, and with students as we seek to deepen our understanding of spirituality in higher education.

References

Astin, A., Astin, H., & Lindholm, J. (2010). *Cultivating the spirit: How college can enhance students' inner lives.* San Francisco, CA: Jossey-Bass.

Bohm, D., Factor, D., & Garrett, P. (1991). *Dialogue: A proposal* [Web page]. Retrieved from http://www.muc.de/~heuvel/dialogue/dialogue_proposal.html#3

Brookfield, S. D. (1995). *Becoming a critically reflective teacher.* San Francisco, CA: Jossey-Bass.

Coates, J. (2003). *Ecology and social work: Toward a new paradigm.* Halifax, NS: Fernwood Press.

Dillard, C. B., Abdur-Rashid, D., & Tyson, C. A. (2000). My soul is a witness: Affirming pedagogies of the spirit. *International Journal of Qualitative Studies in Education, 13*(5), 447–462.

Dirkx, J. (1997). Nurturing the soul in adult learning. *New Directions for Adult and Continuing Education, 74,* 79–88.

Duerr, J., Zajonc, A., & Dana, D. (2003). Survey of transformative and spiritual dimensions of higher education. *Journal of Transformative Education, 1*(3), 177–211.

English, L. (2001, June). *Global adult education, justice, and spirituality.* Paper presented at the Canadian Association for Studies in Adult Education Conference, Quebec City, QC.

English, L., Fenwick, T., & Parsons, J. (2003). *Spirituality of adult education and training.* Malabar, UK: Krieger.

Fleming J., & Courtenay, B. (2006). The role of spirituality in the practice of adult education leaders. *Adult Education Research Conference Proceedings* (pp. 124–129). Retrieved from http://www.adulterc.org/Proceedings/2006/Proceedings/FlemingCourtenay.pdf

Fowler, J. (1981). *Stages of faith: The psychology of human development and the quest for meaning.* San Francisco, CA: HarperCollins.

Griffin, V. (1986). Holistic learning/teaching in adult education: Would you play a one-string guitar? In T. Barer-Stein & J. Draper (Eds.), *The craft of teaching adults* (pp. 107–136). Toronto, ON: OISE Press.

Groen, J. (2002). *The experience and practice of adult educators in addressing the spiritual dimensions of the workplace* (Ed.D. dissertation, University of Toronto, ON).

Groen, J. (2004). The creation of soulful spaces: An exploration of the processes and the organizational context. *Organization Development Journal, 22*(3), 8–19.

Groen, J. (2009). Moving in from the fringes of the academy: Spirituality as an emerging focus in the Canadian professional faculties of business, education, and social work. *The Journal of Educational Thought, 43*(3), 223–244.

Groen, J., & Jacob, J. (2006). Spiritual transformation in a secular context: A qualitative research study of transformative learning in a higher education setting. *International Journal of Teaching and Learning in Higher Education, 18*(2), 75–88.

Hunt, C., & West, L. (2006). Engaging with spirit: Researching spirituality in adult learning. *Standing Conference on University Teaching and Research in the Education of Adults (SCUTREA) Proceedings,* Leeds, UK. Retrieved from http://www.leeds.ac.uk/bei/Conferences/Archive/conf_arch_default.html

Lwanga, C. (2010). Brian Ouellette: Canadian pioneer teacher on spirituality in social work. *Proceedings of the Fifth North American Conference on Spirituality and Social Work*, Calgary, AB. Retrieved from http://www.stu.ca/~spirituality/pdfs/Lwanga-text .pdf

Miller, J. (2000). *Education for the soul: Toward a spiritual curriculum*. Toronto, ON: OISE Press.

Palmer, P. (2010). Transforming teaching and learning in higher education: an interview with Parker J. Palmer. *Spirituality in Higher Education Newsletter, 5*(2), 1–9.

Palmer, P., & Zajonc, A. (2010). *The heart of higher education: A call to renewal*. San Francisco, CA: Jossey-Bass.

Shahjahan, R. (2005). Centering spirituality in the academy: Toward a transformative way of teaching and learning. *Journal of Transformative Education, 2*(3), 294–312.

Shahjahan, R. (2009). The role of spirituality in the anti-oppressive higher-education classroom. *Teaching in Higher Education, 14*(2), 121–131.

Tisdell, E. (2000). The spiritual dimension of adult development. *New Directions for Adult and Continuing Education, 84*(2), 87–95.

Tisdell, E. (2003). *Exploring spirituality and culture in adult and higher education*. San Francisco, CA: Jossey-Bass.

Veale, J. (2006). *Manifold gifts*. Oxford, UK: Way Publications.

Vella, J. (2000). A spirited epistemology: Honouring the adult learner. *New Directions for Adult and Continuing Education, 85*(2), 7–16.

Section Two

The Pedagogy of Spirituality in Higher Education

Against a university backdrop that places significant value on teaching strategies emphasizing the cognitive engagement and development of students, faculties of education and social work have begun to explore pedagogical approaches that incorporate spirituality in coursework, and to measure the implications of doing so. The varying levels of acceptance and ensuing tensions caused by including spirituality either implicitly or explicitly within these programs remind us that while we have begun to chart new territory, we are still affected by the wider university and academic culture.

In Section 2, Vokey (education) and Todd (social work) explore the tensions of increasing our pedagogical approaches to spirituality in higher education settings, and they offer supportive strategies to faculty who wish to take a more holistic approach for teaching and learning. Vokey argues that it is necessary to infuse spirituality into education and social work programs in order to cultivate professionals who are more caring and just. He outlines a curriculum framework that incorporates spirituality into our course content and processes of instruction. While Vokey acknowledges the challenges of incorporating broad understandings of morality, religion, and spirituality within such a framework, he believes a stance of openness expressed using dialogue and storytelling can offer the possibility of reaching across differences in its application.

Todd shifts the focus from the broader curriculum perspective to the front lines: her classroom. As she grapples with the inherent tensions of balancing the varied experiences and perceptions of religion and spiritualty students have in her class, she suggests that post-structural and critical approaches to pedagogy are useful and necessary. Indeed, as she works to create a classroom that cultivates competing discourses around spiritual and religious traditions, she is preparing her students to be practitioners who show respect and celebrate diversity to help create rich, diverse, and peaceful societies.

The final chapter on pedagogical approaches, written by Bohac Clarke, highlights a unique series of courses offered by the Faculty of Education at the University of Calgary. In particular, Bohac Clarke offers reflections on lessons she learned while teaching a graduate level spirituality course online, and advocates for the continued growth of spirituality as a legitimate and explicit subject within any faculty of education.

These three chapters that consider pedagogical approaches to incorporating spirituality into the social work and education classroom demonstrate the multiple ways we, as faculty members and teachers, can use more holistic ways of teaching and engaging our students. As we seek to broaden our approaches, we are responding to emerging research that indicates our students want to be taught as spiritual beings who are struggling with the meaning and purpose of their lives, and who wish to learn in other ways besides rational, objective, and cognitive approaches to the subject(s) at hand (Astin, Astin, & Lindholm, 2011).

Chapter 6

Spirituality and Professional Education: Contributions toward a Shared Curriculum Framework

Daniel Vokey

Introduction

Should universities and colleges preparing people for professions in education and social work devote time in their programs to understanding and promoting spirituality? From a Buddhist perspective (as I understand it), spirituality concerns all facets of life, and some measure of success in actualizing our spiritual potential is necessary to our individual and collective well-being (Vokey, 2005a). According to this view, teachings and practices that foster spiritual realization should be an integral part of educational initiatives across the lifespan, inside as well as outside formal institutions such as schools. Moreover, cultivating our spiritual potential is not a luxury that we can afford to forego when funds are tight or schedules are full. On the contrary, today, perhaps more than ever, we must understand and promote spiritual maturity in order to address the existential malaise that is partly responsible for the ecological, economic, political, and social breakdowns that are reaching crisis proportions across the globe. In making this claim, I am agreeing with those who maintain that attending to spirituality individually and collectively is a necessary part of a genuinely transformative praxis (Fernandes, 2003; Glassman, 1998; Gross, 1993; O'Sullivan, 1999).

Devoting time to understanding and promoting our spiritual potential is particularly important within professional education programs in order to assist faculty and students in becoming more just, caring, and effective helping professionals. One way spiritual maturity improves professional practice is through its relation to sound practical judgment. Individually and collectively, professionals must make decisions on issues with moral dimensions in order to fulfill their manifold responsibilities to clients, colleagues, employers, and society at large. Not least because of the complexity of contemporary social life, arriving at defensible decisions involves making sound practical judgments to interpret laws, principles, guidelines, precepts, and rules in a context-sensitive way (CASW, 2005; Nash, 2002; Trotman, 2008). Those responsible for programs of professional education should therefore undertake to help both prospective and practising professionals enhance their ability to make the sound decisions that are a key condition of responsible action. The capacity to know and do "the right thing at the right time" includes intuitive comprehension of the moral values at stake in particular situations (Vokey & Kerr, 2011). Intuition is necessary for sound judgment or discernment, because properly appreciating the force of moral considerations involves being profoundly moved by the right things, to the right degree. Moral values are apprehended when, for example, we are moved positively by acts of genuine kindness, generosity, courage, honesty, solidarity, and compassion; and negatively by acts of cruelty, greed, and willful ignorance. According to many traditions of virtue ethics both "Eastern" and "Western," becoming a person who is appropriately moved in particular situations is a process of unlearning habits of egocentric perception, feeling, thought, and action. From this, the conclusion follows that developing practical wisdom involves following a spiritual path, in Palmer's sense of a journey to connection with "something larger and more trustworthy than our egos" (1998, p. 6). This is one way in which spirituality and morality are intertwined: a topic I will return to as the chapter unfolds.

I find most faculty in professional education programs for teachers and social workers generally agree that, to be sound, professional judgment must be informed by considerations of social justice. Members of the helping professions who are familiar with the legacies of colonialism, racism, and other forms of systemic oppression will appreciate that fulfilling their professional responsibilities requires respectful attention to the cultural beliefs and practices of colleagues, students, and clients. In many cases, of course, religion and spirituality are inextricably woven into the fabric of a cultural context. On the West Coast, the location of my current academic work, the importance of various forms of spirituality to First Nations and other indigenous peoples is an important case in point. To exercise responsible judgment, then, members of the helping professions—and thus faculty and students in professional education programs—must work both on realizing their own spiritual potential and on gaining more understanding of how spirituality is practised and expressed in cultures and traditions besides their own.

Obstacles to Spirituality in Professional Education Programs

If understanding and promoting spiritual realization is important both to human well-being and to responsible professional practice, why is serious attention to these objectives so rare in the academy today? What are the prospects for greater attention to spirituality in professional education programs? I am encouraged by the growing number of initiatives being introduced by those scholar-practitioners, professional associations, academic societies, and educational institutions that are committed to re-integrating spiritual teachings and practices (such as contemplation) into higher education curricula.[1] At the same time, I am not optimistic that these initiatives will have sustainable effects on a significant scale unless advocates of spirituality also undertake two challenging philosophical and educational tasks. The first is to articulate and defend a cogent alternative to the mechanistic world view. Although scientifically long outdated, the mechanistic world view still influences what teaching and research objectives are given priority within the academy. An alternative world view is needed because spirituality plays no significant role within a world conceived in mechanistic terms, and unless we believe that we have a spiritual potential worth cultivating, we are not likely to make room for it in the curriculum.

Articulating a world view that gives spirituality its due is also a necessary aspect of legitimating knowledge claims grounded in contemplative spiritual experience along with other forms, so they will enjoy recognition alongside claims from the disciplines and fields of inquiry currently accepted within the academy. There has been excellent work published explaining how the objectivity and validity of spiritual investigations are comparable to other forms of inquiry (e.g., Smith, 1982); and why insights arising from personal experience should complement conclusions drawn from "third-person" research (Gyatso, 2005; Varela, 1999). Nevertheless, doctoral students and even tenured faculty continue to confide in me that they remain unwilling to include any reference to spirituality in their research proposals for fear they will not be funded. These reports (although anecdotal evidence only), along with the length of time it has taken to legitimate interpretive (or "qualitative") forms of inquiry as "real" research, suggest that much more epistemological and educational work remains to be done before the validity of spiritual insight will once again be recognized within the academy.

A related point is that clarifying proper norms, procedures, and practices for testing insights arising from spiritual experience should help eliminate—or at least reduce—the misconceptions that give rise to feelings of mistrust and even hostility toward religion and spirituality in the public sphere. One such misunderstanding I often encounter is the belief that religious commitment necessarily entails a dogmatic suspension of critical reflection, or "blind faith." Religious traditions, institutions, teachings, and practices should not be discredited simply because they are no more invulnerable to misinterpretation and corruption than any other human enterprise. Although great harm has been caused and continues to result from actions undertaken in the name of religion, I believe that this is the result of human frailty rather than any flaws intrinsic to religion per se. Regrettably, the history of science supplies plenty of examples to make an analogous case that great harm has been caused and continues to result when the norms intrinsic to the pursuit of scientific knowledge are misunderstood, or are compromised by competing and incompatible human interests, such as fortune and fame. This general point holds for both non-religious and religious forms of spirituality, for both are susceptible to distortion and decline when the pursuit of truth is compromised by various forms of bias (Lonergan, 1973).

The second philosophical and educational task facing advocates of spirituality in higher education arises from the challenges and opportunities presented by pluralism. As I use the term, "pluralism" refers both to the fact that citizens of liberal democracies such as Canada represent a wide variety of beliefs and backgrounds and to the moral principle of respect for cultural differences, understood broadly to include moral, religious, philosophical, and political commitments. In today's secular institutions, spirituality is no longer understood according to the traditional categories of a shared, institutionalized religion. Beliefs about how human spiritual potential is properly characterized and cultivated can vary considerably, according to the tradition or traditions—religious and otherwise— from which its advocates speak. Pluralism presents a problem when even those who agree on the importance of understanding and promoting spirituality do not agree on how (if at all) these goals should become part of professional education. But pluralism presents an opportunity when the different perspectives that people bring to the table are complementary to a significant degree. The corresponding task facing advocates is to reach some measure of shared understanding across and within moral traditions, religious and otherwise, about the variety of legitimate ways that human spiritual potential can be expressed, and about the legitimate ways the realization of that potential can be supported in the academy. Those sharing responsibility for a particular professional education program must work toward such a shared curriculum framework, not to eliminate all differences or even conflict between them, but to ensure they are not working at cross purposes. If my experience is any indication, even such a limited agreement would represent more of a shared understanding of spirituality than typically exists in secular institutions of higher education.

The process of seeking agreement across different perspectives on spiritual fulfillment will benefit from individual efforts to integrate teachings and practices from a range of traditions and disciplines.[2] However, such individual efforts cannot substitute for conversations among those sharing responsibility for particular professional programs.[3] When I propose that faculty come together to develop a shared curriculum framework, I imagine conversations similar to those involved in the faculty-wide process of redesigning the UBC teacher education programs that has been going on since 2006 under the leadership of Associate Dean Rita Irwin.[4] The process began with a small group of faculty meeting on a regular basis to reach an agreement both on the broad objectives of the new programs and the normative principles that would govern the pursuit of those aims. These were set forth in a document along with a rationale that made explicit many of the pedagogical, historical, psychological, sociological, moral, and political beliefs informing program design. Next, this "vision" was combined with an assessment of the human and material resources available to generate more detailed program outlines. Currently, departmental subcommittees are working on detailed course syllabi to further translate theory to practice. At each stage, agreements reached by committees are brought to the faculty as a whole for feedback before being formally approved by majority vote.[5]

Elsewhere, I have considered how a Buddhist understanding of spirituality might inform education in secular contexts (Vokey, 2005a). In this chapter, my intent is to share ideas that might facilitate the process of articulating an understanding of the nature and development of human spiritual potential substantive enough to inform curriculum design in professional education programs. Although some ideas I present are relevant to the epistemological tasks mentioned above, my suggestions are primarily concerned with the challenges and opportunities that pluralism presents to the goal of promoting spirituality in a secular age. In the first section, I say more about the kind of agreements that constitute a "curriculum framework," as I am using the term. Second, I consider how the shared assumptions informing specific spheres of collaborative activity are related to the sets of beliefs and priorities that constitute world views. Third, I describe the characteristics a curriculum framework for spirituality in professional education must possess to serve the intentions for which it is being developed. Fourth, I propose broad, heuristic definitions of key terms such as morality, religion, and spirituality to help avoid the conceptual confusion that can plague conversations across traditions and points of view. In the final section, I offer thoughts on the conditions in which a shared curriculum framework is likely to emerge from conversations among faculty representing different moral points of view.

World Views, Paradigms, and Curriculum Frameworks

Two kinds of relationships between belief and action are relevant to the project of reaching sufficient agreement across differences to enable collaboration in pursuit of educational ends. The first kind is the relationship that exists between world views and overall ways of life.[6] In the more narrow sense of the term, world views are sets of beliefs about existence: beliefs about the origin, history, and structure of the cosmos; the kinds of objects that exist in the world; and the nature of humans and their place in the world order. Relationships between the world views of individuals and that of their communities; between successive world views held by individuals or by communities; between a world view and individual or collective behaviour; and even between distinct beliefs within a world view are all complex. Speaking generally, however, a community's fundamental ontological assumptions both give shape to and are shaped by that group's attitudes toward the world, their broad interests, and their corresponding norms and priorities for living. These assumptions are given concrete expression in the group's actual practices over time. In other words, a "way of life" is the enactment of a social group's view of the norms and priorities that should inform individual and collective action, given what they assume to be true about the world and human nature.

The relationships between ontological beliefs and the attitudes, interests, norms, priorities, and practices of an overall way of life can be illustrated by the mechanistic world view mentioned in my introduction. A machine is its fundamental metaphor because the world is understood to consist of different parts defined by their functional relationships—how they fit or work together. Indeed, the mechanistic world view came to dominate European intellectual life in part because of the revolutionary success of Newton's theories in physics that described how the same laws govern both heavenly and earthly events. The mechanistic world view is materialistic, deterministic, reductionistic, and atomistic in the sense that all phenomena—including human thought and action—are understood to result from the interaction of discrete particles in absolute time and space according to universal and invariant laws. Based on this view, because phenomena are reducible to quantitative relationships among material particles, the qualities humans possess have no "objective" significance, but belong to the realm of merely "subjective" experience. A mechanistic universe has no inherent meaning or purpose, and is wholly indifferent, if not actually hostile, to human interests and desires. Accordingly, human interests and desires become the basis for the norms and priorities that direct and constrain human activity.

What overall way of life makes sense, given this view of the world? For those who believe that it has no inherent meaning or purpose, it makes sense to assume that the world, like a machine, exists to be used. Similarly, for those who believe that the world is indifferent or hostile to human intentions, it makes sense to try and bring it under control. In a mechanistic world, control is achieved through systematic experimentation that identifies the cause–effect relationships governing the interaction of various parts. Because it is assumed that all interaction is lawgoverned, it makes sense to attempt to maximize the satisfaction of human interests and desires by developing theoretical knowledge about all the domains of human experience. According to this view, it makes sense to assign priority to the application of theoretical and technical knowledge to social, political, and economic ends.

For the sake of brevity, I use the term "world view" in this chapter to refer to a social group's shared assumptions about "what is" as well as to its corresponding beliefs about the proper norms and priorities for human action that are explicitly professed or implicit in its ways of life. The second category of relationships between belief and action I must discuss are those between world views (in this broader sense of the term) on the one hand and, on the other, the sets of agreements that inform particular spheres of collaborative human activity. My point of departure here is Kuhn's (1962, 1977) account of paradigms in relation to communities of inquiry. In this context, the term "paradigm" refers to the set of mutually supporting beliefs, attitudes, interests, norms, priorities, and practices that distinguishes a particular community of systematic inquiry—whether philosophical, literary, historical, scientific, religious, moral, or otherwise—and provides the common ground that makes rational debate productive. The agreements shared by those operating within the same paradigm include what the aims of their discipline or field should be; what problems are significant; what theories are appropriate to addressing such problems; what heuristic models, images, and analogies are helpful in conceiving solutions; and what methods, standards, or criteria should be used in evaluating theories and claims (Laudan, 1977, pp. 78–93, 1984, pp. 68–69). The assumptions and commitments shared within a community of inquiry can be understood, to a certain extent, as the application of a world view to the disciplined search for knowledge. It is only reasonable to assume that how an individual or social group attempts to understand an environment (including themselves) is shaped by beliefs both about the kinds of things that exist in the world and the kinds of relationships that connect them. The mechanistic world view again provides a useful illustration because of its association with the positivistic paradigm of scientific research (Vokey, 2001b, pp. 90–92).

That a parallel set of relationships holds between world views and communities of educational practice is illustrated by Miller and Seller's description of distinct curriculum orientations. As they define it, a curriculum is "an explicitly and implicitly intentional set of interactions designed to facilitate learning and development and to impose meaning on experience" (1985, p. 3). Curriculum orientations are the specific sets of pedagogical and other assumptions that inform efforts to promote learning in particular contexts, such as the classrooms of K–12 public schools. Miller and Seller characterize distinct curriculum orientations as different sets of answers, explicitly affirmed or implicit in pedagogical practice, to these six questions:

> What should the aims of education be?
> What educational content is appropriate to achieving those objectives?
> What and how do learners contribute to their learning?
> What kinds of environments promote learning?
> What are the teacher's role and responsibilities?
> How should learning be evaluated? (Miller & Seller, 1985)

These or similar questions are one way that faculty who come together to develop a shared curriculum framework can focus their conversations. However, Miller and Seller's work is cited here more because of how they illustrate the links between (a) different sets of philosophical, psychological, and political commitments corresponding to different world views, and (b) fundamentally different ways of conceiving and pursuing educational ends (1985, pp. 5–9). They do so by identifying nine distinct curriculum orientations and describing how each represents one or another of three "major positions" on curriculum: Transmission, Transaction, and Transformation. I will review these three educational paradigms briefly because the differences between them help explain current conflicts over curriculum design in professional programs, and so point to the topics that might need to be discussed to reach agreement.

Transmission

> In the Transmission position, the function of education is to transmit facts, skills, and values to students. Specifically, this position stresses mastery of trad-itional school subjects through traditional teaching methodologies, particularly textbook learning (*subject orientation*); acquisition by students of basic skills and certain cultural values and mores that are necessary in order to function in society (*cultural transmission orientation*); and the application of a mechanistic view of human behaviour to curriculum planning, whereby student skills are developed through specific instructional strategies (*competency-based learning orientation*). (Miller & Seller, 1985, pp. 5–6; emphasis added)

Educators operating under these assumptions design curricula to "download" predefined sets of beliefs, skills, and attitudes in progressive segments to learners who, having no active role in setting learning objectives, require conditioning through a system of extrinsic punishments and rewards in order to be motivated to achieve curricular goals. Learning environments are organized bureaucratically to maximize efficiency and control quality of standardized outcomes.

It is not difficult to see links between this curriculum position and the elements of the mechanistic world view. It is a short step from materialism, determinism, reductionism, and atomism to behavioural psychology, in which learning is conceived as a process of conditioning, learners are passive, and moti-vation is extrinsic. When learners are seen as passive, it makes sense to conceive the goal of education in conservative terms; that is, passing on what is needed to reproduce and maintain a given social order or practice.

Transaction

> In the transaction position, the individual is seen as rational and capable of intelligent problem-solving. Education is viewed as a dialogue between the student and the curriculum in which the student reconstructs knowledge through the dialogue process. The central elements in the transaction position are an emphasis on curriculum strategies that facilitate problem solving (*cognitive process orientation*); application of problem-solving skills within social contexts in general and within the context of the democratic process (*democratic citizenship orientation*); and development of cognitive skills within the academic disciplines (*discipline orientation*). (Miller & Seller, 1985, pp. 6–7; emphasis added)

This way of conceiving educational ends and means makes sense within a naturalistic world view that attributes the existence of human intelligence and agency to their evolutionary advantages. Because learning is interactive, curriculum content must engage student interest by showing how what they learn is relevant to solving "real-life" problems. This constructivist position on curriculum fits well with liberal politics "in which there is general belief that rational intelligence can be used to improve the social environment" (Miller & Seller, 1985, pp. 7–8) and liberal morality, in which respect for people is based upon their capacity for rational autonomy.

Transformation

> The transformation meta-orientation focuses on personal and social change. It encompasses three specific orientations: teaching students skills that promote personal and social transformation (*humanistic* and *social change orientations*); a vision of social change as movement toward harmony with the environment rather than as an effort to exert control over it, and the attribution of a spiritual dimension to the environment, in which the ecological system is viewed with respect and reverence (*transpersonal orientation*). The paradigm for the transformation position is an ecologically interdependent conception of nature that emphasizes the interrelatedness of phenomena. (Miller & Seller, 1985, p. 8; emphasis added)

Perhaps the key educational difference between the transaction and transformation orientations to curriculum design is that the latter is concerned with emotion, aesthetic perception, and intuition as much as discursive reasoning. This makes sense within a non-dualistic view of the world where knowers are understood to be intimately related to the known (Palmer, 1998; cf. Miller & Seller, 1985, pp. 118–139). A commitment to personal transformation makes sense because human fulfillment is understood to be a matter of realizing one's interconnectedness with all. Similarly, a commitment to social transformation makes sense if one's well-being is tied up with that of others: "If, indeed, I am intimately related to all other beings, then I cannot ignore injustice to others" (Miller & Seller, 1985, p. 124).

The teachers and teacher candidates with whom I have discussed Miller and Seller's characterization of transmission, transaction, and transformation curriculum orientations have invariably remarked that choosing one need not entail rejecting all elements of the others, adding that it would be much easier to integrate particular transmission objectives within a transformation paradigm of education rather than the reverse. I mention this because members of the UBC Faculty of Education, when arguing over the merits of the proposed new B.Ed. programs, did not dispute the need for three kinds of pedagogical practices: (a) teaching content, so that teacher candidates would be familiar with, for example, the results of the latest psychological research into the characteristics of different kinds of learners; (b) coaching during problem-based learning activities, through which teacher candidates would learn the skills involved in finding answers to pedagogical questions on their own and in groups; and (c) facilitating personal reflection oriented to identify formation, through which teacher candidates would unlearn habits of perceiving, feeling, thinking, and acting that reinforce patterns of systemic discrimination in schools. However, there was (and remains) strong disagreement on the relative proportion of time that should be devoted to each objective within the new programs. These disagreements are often rooted in opposing assumptions on basic ontological and epistemological questions; for example, on the question of whether or not there is a universal, objective, tradition-free scientific method.

Kuhn's work on the paradigms that define distinct communities of inquiry was intended to challenge the view that scientific progress is linear and cumulative. Miller and Seller make explicit a range of different curriculum orientations and their underlying assumptions to help individual teachers ensure that their pedagogical means are consistent with educational ends. The curriculum orientations put forth by the two researchers also attempt to establish that both teaching and learning are aligned with teachers' fundamental beliefs about what is right, good, and true (1985, p. xi). Miller and Seller do not directly address the challenge of pluralism, and the connections they propose for the sake of illustration do not always capture the complexity of theory–practice relationships. At the same time, their work demonstrates the importance of attending to the assumptions people bring to education by illustrating the radically opposed approaches to curriculum design that can result from differences in world view. This point raises the question: How deep is it necessary or advisable to go into ontological, epistemological, psychological, religious, moral, and political issues in order to reach enough agreement on a curriculum framework to enable effective collaboration?

Those who seek cooperation on practical matters in pluralistic social contexts might wish to avoid raising contentious issues that can result in disagreements that are difficult to resolve. In some cases, similar priorities for action can be justified with reference to different world views, as when people with different moral, religious, philosophical, political, and cultural commitments are willing to endorse the same manifesto for ecological sustainability or the same declaration of human rights, for very different reasons. Conversely, identifying educational aims and principles broad enough to receive universal assent serves little purpose if disagreements reappear in the process of translating grand mission statements and abstract moral ideals into concrete courses and programs. The "How deep should we go?" question must remain open because we cannot predict what points of difference or disagreement need to be addressed among those sharing responsibility for professional education in a particular program, department, or school. The question can, however, be reformulated as general advice: Address differences in world view when, and to the extent, that doing so is necessary to enable meaningful collaboration.[7]

Characteristics of a Curriculum Framework for Spirituality in Professional Education

I believe that it is useful to begin the potentially difficult process of reaching agreement on a curriculum framework by identifying the characteristics it must possess to serve the intentions for which it is being developed. The task we are concerned with here is to reach a shared understanding of the variety of legitimate ways in which human spiritual potential can be expressed, and development of that potential can be fostered in the professional education programs offered within our pluralistic, secular institutions. I believe a curriculum framework adequate for this intention must meet the following criteria (and perhaps more; I do not assume that what follows is an exhaustive list):

To respect the various locations and perspectives of people in pluralistic social and institutional contexts, and to foster collaboration across difference, the curriculum framework must be inclusive. That is to say, its account of spirituality must, as much as possible, be one that people representing a wide range of moral, religious, philosophical, political, and cultural traditions can accept as right, good, and true in light of their fundamental convictions. Similarly, to reap the benefits of pluralism, a curriculum framework must be comprehensive: its account of human spiritual potential and legitimate forms of its expression must be rich, nuanced, and complex enough to allow for the integration of the experiences and insights that different perspectives afford.

To support spiritual development, the curriculum framework must be normative or prescriptive: education is not possible in any domain involving human judgment unless those judgments are open to correction (Boyd, 1989), and spirituality is no exception. Saying that a curriculum framework must be inclusive and comprehensive does not mean that "anything goes." A shared understanding of the nature and proper cultivation of human spiritual potential must strike a workable balance between embracing diversity in the name of inclusion on the one hand, and on the other, affirming a set of beliefs substantive enough to distinguish between what is and is not conducive to spiritual development within professional education. Moreover, to enable collaboration among faculty in secular, social, and institutional contexts, a curriculum framework must be non-dogmatic; there must be grounds for assessing what is and what is not conducive to spiritual development other than the authority of unquestioned custom and tradition.

To be socially just, a curriculum framework must be critical, in the sense of being informed about and sensitive to multiple forms of oppression. For example, to avoid reproducing historical patterns of subordination, an account of spirituality must honour feminist, indigenous, queer, non-Western, and other marginalized points of view. It cannot be simply assumed that spirituality is necessarily religious in the traditional sense, much less theistic, or that only humans have spiritual potential and intrinsic moral worth. Being critical also means avoiding the "individualistic bias" that frames and treats problems (e.g., forms of addiction) caused in significant part by inequitable economic, political, and social relationships (e.g., racism) as if they were simply symptoms of psychological pathologies or weaknesses of character for which an individual bears responsibility.

To be effective and credible, a curriculum framework must be internally consistent. Developing some measure of common understanding among those sharing responsibility for a professional education program defeats its purpose if they end up working at cross-purposes. The expectation of consistency also means that our understanding of the nature and cultivation of human spiritual potential cannot contradict beliefs about the world and human nature that are implicit in our other practices. It is for this reason that I believe we need to develop world views and corresponding philosophies of knowledge in which at least some conceptions of science and spirituality can both be affirmed without contradiction.

Morality, Religion, and Spirituality

One potential obstacle to success in agreement-oriented conversations within and across moral, religious, philosophical, political, and cultural traditions is the conceptual confusion that can result when the same word is used to mean different things.[8] For example, MacIntyre (1988) observed that disagreement over what kinds of employment equity initiatives are fair or not fair is unlikely to be resolved if the opposing parties in the dispute unwittingly use the same term to invoke competing conceptions of justice.[9] Conversely, I expect that collaborative efforts to develop a curriculum framework with the characteristics I have described will benefit if the participants can, in their conversations, use key terms such as morality, religion, and spirituality in more or less the same way. One strategy to avoid conceptual confusion is, of course, to stipulate what key terms mean when used in a particular context. This approach, while usually preferable to leaving the meaning of key terms unclear, can present another kind of obstacle to collaboration across traditions if the definition(s) brought to the table favour some perspectives over others. My suggestion in this case is to provide a measure of clarity while being inclusive. Without some significant overlap in their fundamental purposes, traditions cannot be rivals. Accordingly, stipulated definitions of key terms such as "morality" should be based upon the fundamental purpose or intention that competing traditions share. What, then, is the fundamental purpose that qualifies a tradition as moral?

A useful and defensible answer to this question can be extracted from MacIntyre's characterization of his own moral tradition in comparison to its two main competitors. When explaining Aristotle's distinction between intellectual and moral virtues, MacIntyre uses "moral" to mean something like pertaining to character (1984, p. 38). When describing his more Thomistic virtue ethics, MacIntyre uses "moral" to mean concerned with identifying and living the best human life (1984, p. 154; 1988, p. 115). While a somewhat broader sense of the term, "moral" in these contexts is still understood in a way that presupposes commitment to an Aristotelian or Thomistic teleological world view. In other places within his texts, however, MacIntyre refers to the anti-Aristotelian world views of "Encyclopaedia" (liberalism) and "Genealogy" as rival moral traditions. In such contexts, he is using moral with a third and much broader understanding of the term's meaning, which enables him to recognize other traditions as competitors to his own, although they articulate their perspectives using very different concepts (1990, p. 3).

In MacIntyre's characterization of teleological virtue ethics and its rivals, what is shared by traditions of inquiry and practice that makes them moral (in the broadest sense of the term) is a concern to establish norms and priorities for human life consistent with an accurate view of human nature and the world. In particular, different moral traditions elaborate on the practical implications of different beliefs directing human action that deliberative reason should play on the one hand, and pre-reflective interests, passions, and desires should play on the other (Vokey, 2001b, pp. 138–141). In pursuing this concern, moral philosophy contributes to the larger task of ensuring that the concepts we think with are well-suited to our purposes. Conversely, failure to achieve our purposes can signal a need for new conceptual and theoretical frameworks. For example, in scientific and other communities of inquiry, lack of progress on the problems they deem central to their discipline or field helps provide the conditions that precipitate a paradigmatic shift (Vokey, 2001b, pp. 52–54). I believe that the current reawakening of interest in spirituality inside and outside higher education can be understood as a response, at least in part, to a growing awareness of the connections between our social and ecological crises and the limitations of the mechanistic world view,[10] and corresponding hopes for the re-enchantment of the world.

What connects a set of basic assumptions about human nature with a social group's norms and priorities are narratives that concretely illustrate the ways of life that make sense within a given world view (Vokey, 2001b, pp. 257–263). Rival moral traditions—where "moral" is defined broadly to include religious, philosophical, political, and cultural traditions—are rivals because they enact competing stories about the challenges and opportunities of human life: they describe what those limitations and potentials are, and how the obstacles to realizing the most desirable of human possibilities can be overcome. MacIntyre makes a similar point when he observes that different moral theories and philosophies can be distinguished according to their particular narrative structures.

> In moral enquiry we are always concerned with the question: what *type* of enacted narrative would be the embodiment, in the actions and transactions of actual social life, of this particular theory? For until we have answered this question about a moral theory we do not know what that theory in fact amounts to; we do not as yet understand it adequately. And in our moral lives we are engaged in enacting our own narrative, so revealing implicitly, and sometimes also explicitly, the not-always coherent theoretical stance presupposed by that enactment. Hence differences between rival moral theories are always in key part differences in the corresponding narrative. (MacIntyre, 1990, p. 80; cf. 1984, p. 23)

For example, when it is assumed that humans are born with an innate nature or *telos* that is their highest good to achieve, life stories have the narrative structure of a quest. When life is conceived on the model of a quest, the significance of the decisions and actions of individuals and social groups lies in whether they move closer to, or further away from, the final goal of human life. Moral traditions might have very different beliefs about which ways of life are conducive to human fulfillment, and which are not (conceived, perhaps, as *eudaimonia*, redemption, enlightenment, or self-actualization) and still have more in common with each other than with world views in which the notion of a final end plays no significant role.

Different kinds of narratives fulfill different functions in establishing, elaborating, criticizing, and renewing world views and ways of life. For our purposes, what is important is that narrative structure provides a helpful and defensible way to distinguish religious from other kinds of moral traditions. In Slater's

(1978) examination of meaning and change in religious traditions, narratives of the limitations and potentials of human life are religious by virtue of their transcendent end. At the core of every religious tradition, functioning as its central symbol, is a person, text, or event that portrays the way of life through which (or in which) the fundamental oppositions plaguing human existence can be (or are) transcended, reconciled, or overcome (Slater, 1978, p. 58). The central symbol points the way to a future that will be radically different from the current experience of human existence, providing an image of hope for the realization of a better world. In Slater's analysis, familiar examples of central symbols include "Jesus the Christ, Gautama the Buddha, the Torah in Judaism, the Qur'an in Islam, the Veda in India, the Sage in China, Socrates the Lover of Wisdom, and Mao the True Comrade" (1978, p. 34). However, he also emphasized that, to qualify as religious, visions of a "new age" and the paths toward its realization need not be otherworldly. Examples of a transcendent end in Slater's sense of the term would include at least some images of a post-patriarchal, post-capitalist, post-colonial, and post-anthropocentric world order.[11]

In Slater's analysis, the common purpose or shared intention that makes moral traditions religious (in addition, perhaps, to being a philosophical, political, and cultural tradition) is overcoming a tension, conflict, and opposition so fundamental to human experience that its resolution is either the key to, or equivalent of, realizing the most desirable human possibilities.[12] Why is this important? My hope is that defining religion with reference to the notion of transcendent ends might remove barriers to communication between people representing different moral traditions (theistic versus non-theistic traditions in particular) by highlighting similarities of structure and intent between the different educational initiatives and social movements that seek radical change. For example, it is not unusual for those committed to social and ecological justice to assert the necessity of transformative learning: "Transformative learning involves experiencing a deep, structural shift in the basic premises of thought, feelings, and actions. It is a shift in consciousness that dramatically and permanently alters our way of being in the world" (O'Sullivan, Morrell, & O'Connor, 2002, p. xvii). In other contexts and traditions, similar arguments would be made for the necessity of conversion (Lonergan, 1973). Thus, agreement across moral traditions on a curriculum framework might be found by focusing upon the kinds of transformations that each aspires to effect.

In this context, I propose that spirituality be understood or experienced as a path, where the student enacts a personal, embodied understanding of the theories, teachings, stories, images, symbols, practices, institutions, and exemplars of one or more particular moral traditions. Each tradition represents a particular view of the way or ways of life that makes sense, given their assumptions about human nature and the world. Commitment to any moral tradition, thus broadly defined, involves a spiritual path, again understood in very broad terms. Religious forms of spirituality can be distinguished from non-religious according to whether or not the teachings and practices of the moral tradition in question are oriented toward the achievement of a transcendent end.

Defining spirituality in this way is meant to be inclusive, and welcomes a wide range of perspectives to the table to discuss what it could mean to foster spiritual maturity within professional programs. As noted above, however, to inform educational practice, a shared understanding of the nature and cultivation of human spiritual potential must be substantive enough to be prescriptive. We cannot assume that all forms of spirituality must be embraced: George Lucas was not the first to show how fear can make us vulnerable to the seductive force of the "dark side," which presents domination through aggression as the path to salvation. The example of MacIntyre's arguments for the rational superiority of Thomistic over competing moral traditions suggests that a broad definition should support and enable rather than substitute for comparisons between the more particular ways in which spirituality is understood within different ways of life. Recognizing the sometimes radically different perspectives that people bring to education must progress from appreciating to assessing their comparative strengths and limitations. Affirming some lowest common denominator is no stable solution to the juxtaposition of opposing world views.

Current interest in the benefits of mindfulness meditation (Sanskrit: *shamatha*, Tibetan: *shiné*) illustrates the educational importance of considering the very specific ways spirituality is understood within particular traditions and world views. When the object of mindfulness meditation is breathing (*ānāpānasaati*), the instructions are simple: maintain a wakeful posture and return attention to breathing as often as we notice it has strayed. On occasion, when practising *shamatha*, we are suddenly aware that we have become so engrossed in reliving past events or inhabiting imagined futures that we have completely forgotten our intention to be mindful. The instruction for such occasions is to gently and patiently label the whole excursion into discursiveness as "thinking" without judging the thoughts as good or bad, and then simply come back to the breath. Following the instruction to gently return attention to breathing creates a "space" of relaxation in which we can witness internal dialogues without being held captive by them. In other words, by interrupting them, we can gain perspective on our habitual patterns of feeling and thinking by learning to dis-identify with the products of our discursive mind. A related benefit of this practice is some measure of stability and clarity of mind: the ability to hold attention on the object of our choice, which might be a sequence of physical sensations such as breathing, an artefact such as a candle flame or picture, an image produced by our imagination, or an idea held in thought.

When reduced to a set of instructions, contemplative practices such as mindfulness meditation can be introduced within a variety of educational and therapeutic contexts. Whether or not they have moral benefit or promote spiritual insight very much depends, however, upon both the intention and the view of the practitioner in following the instructions. Like the strength and flexibility developed through physical exercise, the strength and clarity of mind cultivated through meditation can be put to a variety of larger purposes, which can be morally/spiritually positive, negative, or neutral. Accordingly, in Mahāyāna Buddhist and similar "wisdom traditions," meditation practices such as *shamatha* are integrated within a complex pedagogical process that addresses the physical, emotional, intellectual, imaginative, intuitive, volitional, and "unconditioned" or transcendent aspects of human experience. Most importantly, for example, walking the Mahāyāna path properly involves a commitment to observing ethical precepts governing "body, speech, and mind." It might also involve some or all of painting *thankhas*, executing calligraphies, memorizing precepts, visualizing mandalas, repeating mantras, reciting texts, engaging in dialectical debate, composing spontaneous songs of realization, or simply resting in the clear light of unconditioned awareness (Vokey, 2007). The general point is that, to be part of a curriculum that promotes genuine spirituality, contemplative practices must be informed by some specific understanding of the nature of human spiritual potential and the means of its realization. As a Buddhist, even defining spirituality as a journey to connect with something larger and more trustworthy than our egos does not go far enough, because designing a curriculum requires getting down to specifics about (i) what is meant by ego, (ii) what it might mean to realize egolessness, (iii) why one might undertake to do so, and (iv) what is involved in the process (Vokey, 2001b, pp. 214–217).

Process Notes on Developing a Shared Curriculum Framework

I have argued that advocates of returning spirituality to higher education must reach some measure of shared understanding across various traditions of legitimate ways human spiritual potential can be expressed and development of that potential can be supported in the academy. Seeking understanding across traditions and perspectives is challenging; more so is the process of seeking sufficient agreement to enable effective collaboration. Even if those who shared responsibility for a professional education program, department, or school came together to develop the kind of curriculum framework I am recommending, there is no guarantee that they would reconcile their differences. What might improve their chances of success?

MacIntyre asserts, and I agree, that there is no standpoint from which to engage in argument, discussion, or debate except one that is internal to a community of inquiry, defined by shared standards and procedures for assessing the intelligibility and validity of the claims and commitments that are the concern. To become a full member of such a community, we must gain whatever historical knowledge, practical experience, and theoretical understanding we need to participate in the debates through which standards and procedures of assessment are tested, revised, or replaced. Similarly, to clearly represent a particular understanding of the nature and cultivation of human spiritual potential to others, we must be deeply rooted in the corresponding tradition (Walker, 1987). This demands a personal engagement that, while remaining non-dogmatic, goes beyond simply reading the texts of a tradition, as there are limits to what one can learn about a culture from the outside.[13] Similarly, to find or develop common ground with people representing other perspectives, we must be willing to try to meet and understand them on their own terms (Vokey, 2001, pp. 57–61), and this might require leaving familiar territory to walk a mile in their shoes.

The key role that stories play in connecting world views and ways of life has two major implications for this discussion. Kuhn (1962) observed that, while some elements of a shared paradigm of inquiry take the form of explicitly formulated beliefs, other assumptions integral to that paradigm are embodied in images, models, metaphors, and exemplars, including narrative accounts of pivotal events. Initiation into particular communities of inquiry thus involves a process, not only of absorbing facts and arguments but also of subliminally learning to see in new ways. Tacit knowledge is essential to moral development as well: recent empirical research reports that the range of capabilities involved in sound judgment and responsible action are acquired through the process of becoming a full member of one or more healthy communities—and corresponding traditions—dedicated to the cultivation of practical wisdom (Vokey & Kerr, 2011). It is through participation in such a community's ways of life that an individual develops perceptual, affective, intuitive, deliberative, volitional, and communicative competencies of mature moral agency, thanks in significant part to the guidance provided by the words and deeds of the individuals esteemed as exemplars within that group (Vokey, 2001b, pp. 261–273). Stories are the heart of moral traditions because, by portraying the actions of exemplary characters we identify with and wish to emulate, stories shape how we see and feel as well as how we think.[14]

Not surprisingly, then, images, models, and metaphors play an important role in shaping educational practice.[15] This suggests that those undertaking to develop a shared curriculum framework for spiritual education might fruitfully wait to begin debating the pros and cons of their pedagogical, psychological, sociological, and political theoretical commitments until after they have shared the stories about the imagined futures inspiring their work. In my experience, a group of instructors, supervisors, administrators, and other staff forms a genuine educational community, to the extent they have complementary visions about the ultimate purposes of education. I find support for this view in the accounts of educational leadership that stress the importance of building community by identifying shared moral commitments, and then consistently "walking the talk" in day-to-day activities.

The relationship between morality, religion, and spirituality I have sketched above suggests that common cause exists between those who advocate attention to spirituality in higher education and those who wish to return character education to the academy. Because both projects must address the challenges and opportunities of pluralism, I expect both are more likely to succeed if advocates of each learn from the experiences and reflections of the other. A recent collection of essays debating the prospect of renewed attention to moral education in American colleges and universities makes it clear that the obstacles to this project are not just philosophical, but involve a cultural context of systemic inequality with regard to cultural and economic capital (Kiss & Euben, 2010). Advocates of spirituality must also confront political contexts and institutional structures that more often tend to reward a focus on "production," one aspect of the growing influence of neo-liberal economic priorities upon higher education (Davidson-Harden, 2010). The conclusion I draw from such observations is that advocates must come together, not only to develop a shared curriculum framework but also to contemplate what changes in reward structures and work habits might be required to create institutional environments aligned with spiritual values.

In contexts of conflict we cannot assume, of course, that beauty, truth, goodness, and justice are all on our side. I have learned to begin the courses I teach in professional ethics at UBC by acknowledging that the class is meeting on the traditional, ancestral, and unceded territories of the Musqueum and Coast Salish First Nations. I do so not only to follow protocol as an expression of respect but also to initiate a discussion within the class of the ways in which our geographical, historical, social, and intellectual locations are never politically neutral. Morality, religion, and spirituality are challenging topics not least because of the tension, hostility, and distrust resulting from ongoing processes of colonization and other forms of conflict. For this project, as in my courses, I have no easy solutions to offer and no way to guarantee a "safe environment" for dialogue across difference. I do expect that, in most educational contexts, the stories we tell to develop shared understanding must acknowledge and address the conflicts of the past while also looking forward to new possibilities. In this regard, my aspiration is to learn from those who recognize oppression, and then interrupt, resist, and remove relations of domination without resorting to aggression.

Conclusion

In this chapter I proposed that, in order to exercise responsible judgment, members of the helping professions as well as faculty and students in professional education programs must work both on realizing their own spiritual potential and on gaining a better understanding of how spirituality is practised and expressed in cultures and traditions other than their own. I also proposed that, to overcome the challenges posed to spiritual education by skepticism and pluralism, those sharing responsibility for professional education programs should develop a shared curriculum framework, addressing differences in world view when doing so is necessary to enable meaningful collaboration. I considered what characteristics such a curriculum framework must possess; I suggested broad, inclusive definitions of key terms such as morality, religion, and spirituality; and I described some conditions conducive to success in agreement-oriented conversations among people representing different points of view.

To link this discussion to other work on spirituality in higher education, I would like to conclude with two additional points. First, a curriculum framework should reap the benefits of methodological as well as cultural pluralism, integrating insights from careful scholarship and reflective practice in every relevant discipline and field. Part of the process of developing new paradigms of professional education will be assessing different candidates for a meta-framework (such as Wilber's integral theory) that can integrate multi- and trans-disciplinary research results. Second, given the obstacles to reaching agreement across traditions and paradigms, efforts to develop a shared framework will require participants to bring open hearts and minds to the conversation. This underlines the importance that, as advocates of spirituality, we remain committed to our own contemplative and devotional practices, and to bringing an awake, curious, and compassionate awareness to all our activities in the academy.

Notes

1 Examples of institutions in Canada with educational initiatives incorporating attention to spiritual development include the Canadian Research Institute of Spirituality and Healing (http://www.crish.org/index.html) and the Transformative Learning Centre at OISE/UT (http://tlc.oise.utoronto.ca/). For up-to-date information on spirituality in US higher education, see the reports and publications available from the Center for the Contemplative Mind in Society (http://www.contemplativemind.org/programs/academic/reports.html).

2 One example recently brought to my attention is *Essential spirituality* by Walsh (1999). The permeability of disciplinary boundaries among others characteristic of postmodernity is conducive to such integrative work. The following biography illustrates this trend: "Doug Duncan is a Canadian-born Dharma teacher, residing in Kyoto, Japan. His principal teacher, Ven. Namgyal Rinpoche, was a Westerner with roots in both Theravada and Vajrayana Buddhism. Doug Sensei's ... talks draw on diverse sources, including:

Dzogchen practice, Jungian psychology, recent findings in neuroscience as well as Sufi, Taoist, Zen and Western Mystery traditions" (http://www.muditabc.org/).

3   For the sake of brevity, henceforth I will refer to those who share responsibility for a professional program as its faculty, understood in this context to include the non-faculty staff and practising professionals who typically are equally important to the successful delivery of a program.

4   For a schedule of this process, go to http://teach.educ.ubc.ca/resources/faculty-resources/create/schedule.html

5   For example, see (http://teach.educ.ubc.ca/resources/pdfs/CREATE_Faculty_Meeting_Sept2009.pdf).

6   The material that follows builds upon work previously published, simplifying some points and elaborating others. For a more detailed presentation along with references to relevant research, please refer to Vokey (2001b, pp. 87ff).

7   Egan (1999; see also Blenkinsop & Egan, 2009) has long argued that K–12 school curricula will continue to have, at best, mixed results so long as they keep trying to implement three incompatible visions of education's purpose: to socialize children to perform well in society; to teach them to think critically; and to support them in realizing their unique, individual potential.

8   The same holds true for empirical research: it is difficult to compare results across different studies of (for example) intuition, when the same word is used to refer to different phenomena (Vokey & Kerr, 2011).

9   Plato's *Republic* suggests that concern over competing conceptions of justice dates back to the early days of Western philosophy.

10 The website for the new film about Gregory Bateson and his work offers this summary of his concern: "The major problems in the world are the result of the difference between how nature works and the way people think" (http://www.anecologyofmind.com).

11 Over the course of its history, a tradition's central symbol can be reinterpreted in stories that use secondary symbols to unpack its implications for the norms and priorities of human life in some particular historical context. In one time and place, for example, the implications of affirming Jesus as Christ might be elaborated through stories of Jesus as the Good Shepherd. As social or personal conditions change, new possibilities are revealed through stories of Jesus as King, Judge, Rabbi, Healer, or Lord (Slater, 1978, p. 44). While these stories can portray very different ways of life, each in its own way centres on the redemptive power of God represented by Jesus as Messiah. Slater thus illustrates how, through re-interpretation of its central symbol in successive narratives, adherents of a religious tradition can provide for both continuity of identity and adaptation to change.

12 Swimme and Berry's *The Universe Story* illustrates the way in which moral perspectives are often rooted in binary oppositions. In this text, they envision the future in terms of

> the tension between the Entrepreneur and the Ecologist, between those who would continue their plundering, and those who would truly preserve the natural world, between the mechanistic and the organic, between the world as a collection of objects and the world as a communion of subjects, between the anthropocentric and the biocentric norms of reality and value.

13 The value of integrating "first-person" experience of contemplative practices with "third-person" study is affirmed in a variety of contemporary academic initiatives such as the 2010 Mind & Life Summer Research Institute at the Garrison Institute, Garrison, New York, June 14–20, 2010, discussed in *Education, Developmental Neuroscience and Contemplative Practices: Questions, Challenges, and Opportunities* (http://www.mindandlife.org/sri10.ml.summer.institute.html); cf. Naropa University 2008.

14 These characters need not, of course, be human (Archibald, 2008).
15 Email messages sent by the Dean of Education at UBC, Jon Shapiro, conclude with a quote from William Butler Yeats: "Education is not the filling of a pail, but the lighting of a fire."

References

Archibald, J. (2008). *Indigenous storywork: Educating the heart, mind, body, and spirit.* Vancouver, BC: UBC Press.

Bateson, Nora. (n.d.). *An ecology of mind: A daughter's portrait of Gregory Bateson* [Web page]. Retrieved from http://www.anecologyofmind.com/thefilm/

Blenkinsop, S., & Egan, K. (2009). Three "big ideas" and environmental education. In M. McKenzie, P. Hart, H. Bai, & B. Jickling (Eds.), *Fields of green: Restorying culture, environment, and education* (pp. 85–93). Cresskill, NJ: Hampton Press.

Boyd, D. (1989). Moral education, objectively speaking. In J. Giarelli (Ed.), *Philosophy of education 1988* (pp. 83–100). Normal, IL: Philosophy of Education Society.

CASW (Canadian Association of Social Workers). (2005). *Guidelines for ethical practice.* Retrieved from http://www.casw-acts.ca/practice/guidelines_e.pdf

Davidson-Harden, A. (2010). Interrogating the university as an engine of capitalism: Neoliberalism and academic 'raison d'état.' *Policy Futures in Education, 8*(5), 575–587.

Egan, K. (1999). Education's three old ideas, and a better idea. *Journal of Curriculum Studies, 31*(3), 257–267.

Fernandes, L. (2003). *Transforming feminist practice: Non-violence, social justice, and the possibilities of a spiritualized feminism.* San Francisco, CA: Aunt Lute Books.

Glassman, B. (1998). *Bearing witness: A Zen master's lessons in making peace.* New York, NY: Bell Tower.

Gross, R. M. (1993). *Buddhism after patriarchy: A feminist history, analysis, and reconstruction of Buddhism.* New York, NY: SUNY.

Gyatso, T. (His Holiness the XIV Dalai Lama). (2005). *The universe in a single atom: The convergence of science and spirituality.* New York, NY: Morgan Road Books.

Kiss, E., & Euben, J. P. (2010). *Debating moral education: Rethinking the role of the modern university.* Durham, NC: Duke University Press.

Kuhn, T. (1962). *The structure of scientific revolutions.* Chicago: University of Chicago Press.

Kuhn, T. (1977). *The essential tension: Selected studies in scientific tradition and change.* Chicago: University of Chicago Press.

Laudan, L. (1977). *Progress and its problems: Toward a theory of scientific growth.* Berkeley, CA: University of California Press.

Laudan, L. (1984). *Science and values: The aims of science and their role in scientific debate.* Berkeley, CA: University of California Press.

Lonergan, B. J. (1973). *Method in theology* (2nd ed). London, UK: Dartman, Longman, and Todd.

MacIntyre, A. (1984). *After virtue.* Notre Dame, IN: University of Notre Dame Press.

MacIntyre, A. (1988.) *Whose justice? Which rationality?* Notre Dame, IN: University of Notre Dame Press.

MacIntyre, A. (1990). *Three rival versions of moral inquiry: Encyclopaedia, genealogy, and tradition.* Notre Dame, IN: University of Notre Dame Press.

Miller, J. P., & Seller, W. (1985). *Curriculum: Perspectives and practices.* New York, NY: Longman.

Mind and Life Institute. (2010). *Education, developmental neuroscience and contemplative practices: Questions, challenges, and opportunities* [Web page]. Retrieved from http://www.mindandlife.org/research-initiatives/sri/sri10/

Naropa University. (2008). *Contemplative Education* [Web page]. Retrieved from http://www.naropa.edu/conted

Nash, R. (2002). *"Real World" ethics: Frameworks for educators and human service professionals* (2nd ed.). New York, NY: Teachers' College Press.

O'Sullivan, E. V. (1999). *Transformative learning: Educational vision for the 21st century.* Toronto: University of Toronto Press.

O'Sullivan, E. V., Morrell, A., & O'Connor, M. A. (2002). *Expanding the boundaries of transformative learning.* New York, NY: Palgrave.

Palmer, Parker. (1998). *The courage to teach: Exploring the inner landscape of a teacher's life.* San Francisco, CA: Jossey-Bass.

Slater, P. (1978). *The dynamics of religion.* San Francisco, CA: Harper & Row.

Smith, H. (1982). *Beyond the post-modern mind.* New York, NY: Crossroad.

Swimme, B., & Berry, T. (1994). *The universe story: From the primordial flaring-forth to the ecozoic era.* San Francisco, CA: HarperCollins.

Trotman, D. (2008). Liberating the wise educator: Cultivating professional judgment in educational practice. In A. Craft, G. Gardner, & G. Claxton (Eds.), *Creativity, wisdom, and trusteeship: Exploring the role of education* (pp. 158–166). Thousand Oaks, CA: Corwin Press.

Varela, F. J. (1999). *Ethical know-how: Action, wisdom, and cognition.* Palo Alto, CA: Stanford University Press.

Vokey, D. (2001a). Longing to connect: Spirituality in public schools. *Paideusis: The Journal of the Canadian Philosophy of Education Society, 13*(2), 23–41.

Vokey, D. (2001b). *Moral discourse in a pluralistic world.* Notre Dame, IN: University of Notre Dame Press.

Vokey, D. (2005a). Spirituality and educational leadership: A Shambhala Buddhist view. In C. Shields, M. Edwards, & A. Sayani (Eds.), *Inspiring practice: Spirituality and educational leadership* (pp. 87–99). Philadelphia, PA: Pro-Active Press.

Vokey, D. (2005b). Teaching professional ethics to educators: Assessing the "multiple ethical languages" approach. In K. Howe (Ed.), *Philosophy of Education 2005* (pp. 125–133). Urbana, IL: Philosophy of Education Society.

Vokey, D. (2007). Hearing, contemplating, meditating: In search of the transformative integration of heart and mind. In C. Eppert & H. Wang (Eds.), *Cross-cultural studies in curriculum: Eastern thought, educational insights* (pp. 287–312). New York, NY: Lawrence Erlbaum Associates.

Vokey, D., & Kerr, J. (2011). Intuition and professional judgment: Can we teach *moral discernment?* In L. Bondi, D. Carr, C. Clark, & C. Clegg (Eds.), *Towards professional wisdom: Practical deliberation in the "people professions."* London, UK: Ashgate.

Daniel Vokey

Walker, S. (Ed.). (1987). *Speaking of silence: Christians and Buddhists on the contemplative way*. New York, NY: Paulist Press.

Walsh, Roger. (1999). *Essential spirituality: The 7 central practices to awaken heart and mind*. New York, NY: John Wiley & Sons.

Chapter 7

The Ties That Bind and Unwind: Spirituality in the Secular Social Work Classroom

Sarah Todd

The issues of spirituality and religion are never neutral in a social work classroom. While many have used spirituality as a more inclusive term than religion (Canda & Furman, 2010), it still presents some troubling challenges within the context of secular education. For some students, their positive experiences with religious communities or spiritual knowledge have proved foundational for their turn toward social work. For others, their negative experiences or disengagement from religion or spiritual ways of knowing may ground their commitment to a secular social work. These negative experiences are often associated with religion, but tend to spill into discussions of spirituality, as the concepts are not entirely distinct. There is a spectrum of experiences beyond antipathy and attachment to religion or spirituality. They intersect in the university classroom, with its own history and expectations, leaving social work professors caught between frustration over a lack of positive discussion about spirituality and religion, and expectation that secular social work remains clearly separated from the sacred.

The ways in which social work practitioners and students make sense of their religious or spiritual motives has long been an interest of mine. For me, the historical and contemporary intimacy between religious and spiritual experiences and participation in secular social work practices suggests that attempts to divide the sacred from the secular are misleading and unhelpful (Todd, 2007). While I have found this rethinking of the secular/sacred divide helpful for practice, I have struggled with understanding what it means in the university-based social work classroom (see Todd & Coholic, 2007). The disparate voices around spirituality and religion, and the intensity of emotion that accompanies discussions in these areas, are often difficult to negotiate. As an educator, I find myself attempting to create a liminal space in the classroom; one where religion can be seen as having contradictory histories, meanings, and effects, and spirituality can be considered relevant to most of our lives, even vital, but also troubling in its own way. Such a space is not without its own tensions and difficulties. I worry about the turn to spirituality and its individualistic, internal orientation; in my view, it is a self-reflective, thoughtful practice that does not necessarily speak to social action. I agree with Wiebe's critique that our favouring of spirituality over religion is incongruent with our concern for creating social justice (Wiebe, in press). While possibly avoiding some of the institutional problems of religion, the turn to spirituality tends to ignore the important work that religious institutions have done, for instance, to challenge poverty and advocate for the environment (Wiebe, in press; Skillen, 2004; Lernoux, 1982). In addition, there seems to be a new pressure in social work to understand the self and others as spiritual beings, which in my experience does not always speak to students' ways of understanding themselves. Finally, I am concerned that many discussions about spirituality are still deeply embedded in cognitive ways of knowing as opposed to taking up those emotions and sensations outside of intellectual and rational debate. While intellectually interesting, such discussions do not necessarily provide students with the skills to negotiate the multiple experiences of religion and spirituality they will have with themselves, colleagues, and clients.

In this chapter I seek to unpack how attachments to and disconnections from religion and spirituality shape both the social work classroom and the possibilities and limits of various responses from social work educators. I work to establish a liminal space between some students' antipathy toward spirituality and religion, and others' attachment to the very same set of practices and beliefs. My interest in fostering spaces between the sacred and secular in social work classrooms intensified after a student requested a meeting with me following the first lecture I gave in an interviewing class. As part of my introduction, I explained my practice background, which involved work both in an abortion clinic and a community-based HIV/AIDS centre. This narrative is often read by students to situate me within a certain liberal progressive politic dominated by secularism. In the meeting that followed this class, the student identified herself as a Muslim, and as someone who found it difficult to negotiate her religious beliefs around abortion and homosexuality with her participation in the school of social work. Her religious beliefs were important to her, yet she experienced them as conflicting with the social work she was being taught in university. She seemed to articulate compassion, but used the language of "sin" to characterize persons who have abortions or engage in same-sex relations. She identified herself as engaging in sinful activities all the time, so this was not necessarily a position of superiority, but one of strained tolerance, not acceptance or celebration. In addition, she described previous conflicts with educators and students who had suggested that her religious beliefs meant she couldn't be a social worker. Her primary concern was that my belief system would not allow space for her and her belief system in the class. I found myself in a conundrum. On one level, I understood her religious beliefs to be in conflict with core tenets of the Canadian Association of Social Workers (CASW) Code of Ethics and the mission statement of our school of social work, but the fact that she was struggling to find ways to craft a coherent moral space for a progressive practice that was not entirely incongruent with her religious values suggested to me that encouraging her to remain on that path might be more fruitful than staking out a space of exclusion. I also wondered whether there was an important space in the profession for workers engaging in this type of struggle. Maybe they could engage more effectively with some of the clients I find challenging.

It was a difficult conversation. I asked her to question some of her strategies for resolution that included referring clients to other social workers. Was it really possible to do this respectfully? And was it not possible that her perspectives would make disclosure, a precursor for referral, unlikely? We discussed how the professional code of ethics supersedes the religious and political beliefs we both held, requiring us to think carefully about how we negotiate personal beliefs in our professional practice. In the end, we agreed that there was space for her in the classroom, and that we could engage in dialogue with each other and the other students. I tried to encourage her to continue questioning and challenging herself. At the same time, this conversation significantly shifted how I taught the interviewing course, particularly how I used the idea of non-judgment in the classroom and how I presented social work professional ethics. As a result, I now increasingly speak about the various ways we use judgment and to what ends, rather than creating an image of social work as a practice of being non-judgmental. I also tend to talk about ethics in more strategic, situated terms. By doing so, I attempt to move away from the idea that social workers are a particular type of person, and consider instead the idea that social workers think, feel, and act in particular ways to achieve particular outcomes. In this way, I hope to create a more inclusive kind of social worker, one for whom the process and outcomes are particularly important.

This experience also pushed me to reflect further upon my own ambivalence with respect to spirituality and social work in the classroom. Growing up, I had both positive and negative experiences with Christianity. In my church community and through the religious component of my education, I learned about my responsibility to those who are more vulnerable than me, and it was in these spaces that I gained a sense of my commitment to social justice as a deep, binding moral obligation. However, in my teens I accompanied some friends to a summer camp where, for a short period of time, I encountered a religious community with members who seemed to exhibit problematic aspects, such as moral judgment of others borne of a belief in the exclusive righteousness of themselves and their chosen way of life. I rapidly abandoned this community, and became increasingly suspicious of those who explicitly identified with religious or spiritual movements. In particular, I have always been challenged in my practice when encountering people who hold strong religious views about the sinfulness of abortion and homosexuality. When I encountered women seeking abortions who also held strong pro-life/anti-abortion opinions, I found it a challenge to remain supportive to them. I remain discomfited by those who hold religiously conservative views, and they continue to present a challenge to me in my pedagogy. I am not sure that this discomfort is altogether different from the unease some students feel when working with those who have accessed abortion services or who identify as gay, bisexual, or lesbian.

As an adult, I continue to understand myself as a spiritual being, but have not remained active in any religious community for more than a brief period of time. In my work as a social worker and subsequently as an educator, I see the important role that spirituality and religion can play in people's lives, but I also see its dangers and exclusions. In my research, I have spoken to practitioners across the spectrum of belief about how their spirituality influences their secular practice. I remain firmly committed to social work as a secular practice, but think that there needs to be space to make sense of and experience the ways in which the sacred shapes and reshapes secularity. I use the term "sacred" to include both religion and spirituality, as I believe both are relevant to secular practice. Also, it is important to me that students have some awareness of and responsibility for those clients for whom religious belief is central in their day-to-day lives. I see spirituality as offering another way of making meaning, and I think we need to honour the multiple ways we make sense of our individual lives, our communities, and our profession. At the same time, this is not limitless. It seems disingenuous to suggest that social work embraces all views and value systems. We do not; there are limits, and we need to carefully consider how we regulate and maintain them. There are a great many views that we do not tolerate, and I am not sure that this is problematic. Tensions emerge because we tend to present the profession's values as natural and all-inclusive, and they are not. In part, this tendency has caused me to reflect on how I previously located social work as progressive as opposed to having a particular ideological home. These days, I tend to locate the profession not as progressive, but steeped in certain political and religious traditions. The issue then, for me and my students, is to consider whether there is a fit between one's professional identity and code and one's personal, spiritual, moral, and political beliefs.

I understand institutional religion as having an important historical and contemporary role to play in achieving social justice. I see religious communities and institutions that are active in social justice movements as instrumental in creating social change, and have trouble imagining other contemporary institutions having a similar effect. These religious groups are able to reach a broad range of people efficiently, and often have resources that are rarely available to other activist and community-based groups. Religious institutions have been centrally important in human rights struggles (such as the civil rights movement), environmental protection, and anti-poverty work. For instance, the Aga Khan Foundation is instrumental in justice-oriented development work around the world, and Kairos is an ecumenical group that has worked tirelessly for human rights, economic justice, ecological rights, and the rights of indigenous people across the globe.

Others have suggested that only those with a keen enthusiasm for spirituality should attempt teach it within the classroom (Henry & Beaty, 2008). However, I am not convinced that there is no room for those of us who want to make more tentative, cautious moves to contribute to these discussions. In particular, I think we might offer some ideas about how one can speak to the centrality of spirituality and religion as it relates to social work practice, accounting for its complexity and multiplicity while also maintaining a critical voice. My experience suggests that all social work educators will have to grapple with these issues, as they are ever present in the diversity of our social work classrooms. This multiplicity is marked not only by Canadian-based religious and spiritual diversity but also by the perspectives that international students bring to our classrooms.

I also situate myself within feminist post-structuralism (Butler & Scott, 1992), which is a perspective that focuses on plurality and diversity rather than universalism (Furman, 2002). From this perspective, I am interested in how the discourses of spirituality, the university, and social work intersect, disconnect, disrupt, and reinforce one another. I am interested in teaching students to evaluate ideals and standards of assessment on how the world is and how it should be, but to remain aware of how universal truths tend to get messy and less certain when considered in context. So I am particularly interested in how the subjectivities of students and professors are shaped through participation in a university and professional practice that is firmly entrenched in the secular, yet haunted (as I will discuss below) by a history and a personal presence of the sacred.[1] In addition, this perspective lets me consider spirituality as another key way of making meaning, particularly understanding that social work is never just a rational practice, that it exceeds our rational ways of knowing. One of these excesses is spiritual in nature.

In the following sections, I outline the histories and expectations that shape the terrain of the university-based social work classroom. I argue that it is these institutional and personal histories and expectations that form the foundation upon which we attempt to negotiate an ambivalent space between the secular and the sacred. I address how we are situated as educators and students in this dynamic, and then speak more specifically about possibilities for reshaping the social work classroom to increase the discursive space for a nuanced understanding of the sacred and the secular in contemporary professional education. This is not a space without conflict, which is, I suspect, one of the greatest challenges to integration within the social work program, since the classroom is increasingly being reconstituted using the neo-liberal model of student as consumer and professor as service provider, offering a product that must meet consumer demands (Brulé, 2004). The pressure to ensure that the consumer/student is satisfied tends to orient the classroom toward a more palatable, less discomforting pedagogical practice. This makes it difficult to deal with contentious issues such as spirituality.

Spirituality in Social Work

The roots of North American social work are firmly embedded in religious and spiritual notions of responsibility toward those who are vulnerable in society. This is evidenced in the Aboriginal societies that existed long before the English and French arrived, and in the settler societies that brought religious and spiritual beliefs focused on the responsibility to one another (Graham, Coholic, & Coates, 2007). This is both a celebrated and a troubling history, as many so-called helpful interventions by religious community members and institutions often imposed deeply moralistic views on immigrants, people living in poverty, and—most devastatingly—Aboriginal persons. The perspectives of many within religious institutions were used to justify a significant amount of investigation, regulation, and destruction of various peoples' ways of life and even, in some cases, life itself (Margolin, 1997; Graham, Coholic, & Coates, 2007). At the same time, the social gospel movement was a context that supported a great deal of activism, in which primarily middle-class women advocated for changes to the handling of garbage and sewage, the establishment of public health clinics and playgrounds, public education for the poor, and other equalizing changes in society (Stebner, 1997). Many of these women felt their commitments to social justice and challenging inequality were rooted in their spiritual and religious beliefs (Stebner, 1997; Otters, 2009).

The spiritual/religious roots of social work began to change dramatically through the early part of the twentieth century, as the power of religious institutions was gradually eclipsed by the gospel of science. Social work strove to be seen as a secular quasi-science, a profession based on objectivity and standardization (Margolin, 1997). In previous works, I have argued that this secularization was incomplete; spirituality and religion remain at play in the background of social work, shaping the world views of practitioners and clients, and informing the values, morals, and ethics upon which social work is predicated (Todd, 2005; see also Otters, 2009; Canda & Furman, 2010).

The relationships between religion, spirituality, and social work have, at alternative moments, been more conservative or classically liberal. Those who adhere to the religiously dogmatic elements of the profession have recently argued against their own marginalization within a social work profession that now understands itself as progressive. They have asked that the profession accommodate their beliefs about, for example, abortion, marriage, and sexual orientation (Hodge, 2003, 2005; Spano, 2007). However, there has also been a long tradition of adherents to liberation theology, environmental spirituality, and Aboriginal spirituality that have pressed the profession for a broader understanding of social justice and a commitment to social activism (Coates, 2003; Bruyere, 2007; Este, 2007). In addition, many religious institutions (some of which are conservative) in Canada remain at the forefront of anti-poverty service and activism across this country (Wiebe, forthcoming). These include local, religiously funded and run organizations such as the Good Shepherd Centres (Catholic Church), Wesley Urban Ministries (United Church), and the Salvation Army. These organizations have a variety of positions with respect to service and activism, some more charity-driven, others more activist and overtly political.

Recently, the historical and contemporary relevance of religion and spirituality to social work has gained ground. Social work is guided—indeed governed—by explicit values, morals, and codes of ethics (Graham, Coholic, & Coates, 2007). The profession and its educational discipline show a high "commitment to moral and ethical reflection and action" (Canda & Furman, 2010, p. 32). These commitments, argue Canda and Furman, "imply a stance of compassion with a transpersonal, that is egotism-transcending orientation—a profound and challenging spiritual ideal" (2010, p. 33). This type of analysis has challenged the more traditional (and purely secular) discussions of social work values and ethics.

Today, interest in religion and spirituality takes many forms, but of particular relevance to this discussion is the profession's efforts to understand, at least at an academic level, why spiritual and religious beliefs are important to understand how people make sense of their lives, cope with problems, or make decisions (Canda & Furman, 2010; Letendre, Nelson-Becker, & Kreider, 2005; Beres, 2004). This coincides with an awareness of the sheer breadth of spiritual and religious beliefs that exist in our communities. As a result, there have been increasing calls for social workers to develop spiritual and religious competencies in order to practice effectively (Furness & Gilligan, 2010). Others take a less structured approach to considering how spirituality shapes approaches to practice, instead suggesting a more personal, reflective focus to our work (Beres, 2004). This presents an interesting challenge to those of us who educate in secular schools of social work. Many social work educators are struggling to bring spirituality into the classroom in ways that are inclusive, yet not relativistic, and in a manner that can capture spirituality not as a series of contained pieces of rational logic, but as an alternative way of making sense of life and its challenges. This history of social work and the sacred shapes the contemporary classroom in a number of contradictory ways. The recitation of the problematic ways religious values have shaped professional practice, while important, tends to foster a sense of hostility toward religion and, at the very least, suggests an incompatibility between secular social work and religion. It sets up a dichotomous terrain in which the religious past is regarded as old-fashioned, conservative, judgmental, and dangerous in contrast to the non-judgmental, progressive nature of contemporary social work. Yet this history should, I contend, also highlight the ways in which there is an alignment between many religious and spiritual values, particularly the ethics and values of the social work profession.

Spirituality in Higher Education

The discourse of the university is itself fragmented; still dominated by liberal secularism, but disrupted by critical theory and those advocating for the inclusion of spirituality in the curriculum. Like social work, the idea and practice of the university itself has always been intimately entwined with religious institutions. In Canada, many universities evolved with an arts college and theological seminary (Harris, 1976). The goals of these institutions was to educate clergymen, and for many of the earliest colleges, to educate citizenry in the British tradition (in contrast to the republican tradition of the United States; Harris, 1976). This legacy continues to shape the contemporary university. As Emberley argues,

> However remote the lives of Socrates and Christ may appear from the daily enterprise of teaching and learning in university classrooms, the symbols of their lives still constitute the major forms of students' intellectual and spiritual searches. And the tension between them is, in great part, the source of the alternative positions put forward whenever reforms and restatements of the university's essential mission are undertaken....These symbols come down to us through distinctly mediaeval cross-fertilization of Near and Far Eastern Judaic and Hellenic ideas, and became associated with the thirteenth-century doctrines of scholastic philosophers. However, it would be reducing severely the richness and suggestive quality of these symbols to believe they are narrowly "Western" or "Christian-Platonic." One might say, instead, that these two primals contain a vast range of meaning, and that vital threads present at the origins of the "West" are always available to be unearthed and used for their restorative possibilities. (1996, p. 32)

Despite being haunted by the spiritual and religious, most Canadian universities continue to imagine themselves as bastions of liberal education, focusing largely on rational debate and objective knowledge. This approach to education has been challenged for excluding emotions, empathy, connection, and education for action in the world (e.g., work, knowledge production, and service). There has been significant pressure from critical theorists to expand our notion of a liberal education in order to prepare students for a much broader civic engagement in both public and private spheres (Mulcahy, 2009). This is where much of the critical pedagogy that influences social work education emerged and gained a foothold.

In the past, higher education was associated with at least five purposes:

1 To prepare students to understand, conduct, or apply research of various kinds
2 To instruct students in the rational traditions and academic disciplines associated with literal or advanced learning
3 To provide vocational training that will enable students to enter the workforce, earn a living, and engage in productive and satisfying labour
4 To initiate students into the study of substantive visions of the good, and
5 To foster the dispositions and skills required for democratic citizenship. (Alexander, 2007, p. 251)

Social work is valued in higher education as vocational training, but our pedagogy is simultaneously geared toward fostering the skills for democratic citizenship. While contemporary neo-liberal philosophy and the resulting managerial trend in education pressures schools to create efficient workers (Brulé, 2004; Lewis, 2008; Milz, 2005; Smith, 2004), many social work educators also strive to teach students to consider themselves as critical thinking subjects within a nation-state. Such a subject position requires skills in critical analysis and reflection.

In addition to the challenges posed by critical theorists, there is also another, mostly American debate that has opened up deliberations regarding the nature of university education, influencing growing discussions about the place of spirituality in post-secondary education. There is some concern that the lack of common ground within secular universities has people turning increasingly to religious communities to uncover the morals, values, and ethics that are integral to living in a modern society (Zajonc, 2003; Henry & Beaty, 2008). A number of writers have suggested that

> if students bring a religious tradition to university, they should have the opportunity to challenge or re-evaluate previous commitments, either to reaffirm or reject them for new ones. And, if students have not come from such spiritual backgrounds, it is the university's obligation to provide opportunities to discover or create them. That an institution professes no tie to a particular spiritual tradition does not relieve it of the obligation to assist students in exploring and eventually making in an appropriate way spiritual and moral commitments. (Alexander, 2007, p. 260)

These authors are not necessarily advocating for a return to religious education in the university, but instead suggest a variety of ways to rethink the project of knowledge-making. Some, like Zajonc (2003), advocate for knowledge production that includes contemplative methods in which cognitive spirituality enhances our understanding of the world. Alexander (2007) also notes,

> To the extent that higher education should be concerned with the preparation of democratic citizens, and insofar as education in spirituality involves initiation into study of traditions of thought and practice focused on how one should live, then institutions of higher learning should seek to promote the exploration of intelligent spiritual traditions that seek to balance the common or universal with the distinctive or particular. Education in intelligent spirituality, in other words, has a significant role to play in the creation of democratic citizens and so deserves an important place in higher education. (p. 251)

While these debates are quite provocative within discussions of higher education in general, they have particular implications for social work education, which already spends a significant amount of time encouraging students to reflect upon the morals and values they bring to their practice and the ethics of the profession itself. The struggle, I think, is how to introduce this discussion without students ending up in tidy spaces where liberal progressive values are imposed. It is possible, I believe, to work toward highlighting the messiness and complexity of values in practice by demanding a cautious, situated place in which one's morals and values are respected, but are seen as simultaneously helpful and problematic.

Approaches to the Classroom

As outlined in the previous sections, the history and contemporary context of the profession of social work and the university creates an interesting set of contradictions that educators need to consider when working with students who are strongly attached to particular notions of religion and spirituality, and those who are more comfortable with a purely secular education (as well as those whose notions of spirituality and religion conflict with others in the class). I have noted that the secular university context tends to consider spirituality and religion as peripheral to academic thought and debate, or at the very least, that any discussion in this area will be "intellectual" in nature. The profession of social work also sets up a number of contradictory expectations. On one level, the profession establishes itself as fully inclusive of all diversity, thereby suggesting that there will be space to discuss a broad range of religious and spiritual beliefs and values. As many of its values align closely with spiritual and religious values, social work can be quite appealing to those students who have a strong attachment to a religious tradition or spiritual beliefs. At the same time, there is a sense that contemporary social work takes a dim view of its religious roots, and that religious beliefs that deviate from the professional code of ethics constitute untenable violations of profession. There also remains a residual pressure to construct social work as a science fully distinct from other ways of knowing, as evidenced through the current popularity of evidenced-based approaches to practice.

I tend to agree with Otters (2009), who stated that, "Social work socialization, at its best, offers students a way to access the larger world of meaning and belief, relationally through professors, field supervisors, and others, who as role models embody these values and ethics" (2009, p. 9). In the abstract this sounds achievable, but on the ground it is often a journey full of conflict. The problems that I have encountered in the classroom take a number of common forms: (1) complaints that the curriculum does not make sufficient space for discussion of and reflection on spirituality; (2) complaints that the ideological terrain of progressive social work education discourages discussion about certain religious and spiritual beliefs that may come into conflict with the professional code of ethics; (3) concerns that the vast majority of references to religion are with respect to religious institutions' problematic role in relation to vulnerable populations; and (4) secular students' frustration with the views expressed by students from conservative religious communities and with religion and spiritual beliefs being part of the curriculum.

Many others have written about the importance of including spirituality in the classroom and ways to go about doing so (Coholic, 2003, 2006; Letendre et al., 2005; Ai, 2002; Rothman, 2009; Sheffield & Openshaw, 2009). I hope to discuss here specifically how these projects might be thought of, particularly in the context of diverse commitments to religion and spirituality in the classroom. My discussion will focus on courses that are not specifically about spirituality and social work. I think very different pedagogical approaches are needed, depending on whether students are choosing to participate in a spirituality-focused course or they are taking a required course in which it would be reasonable to expect that spirituality might be present. In many schools, the pressure to offer a wide range of courses on a variety of topics combines with declining numbers of faculty and increasing numbers of students. As a result, spirituality does not always get a course of its own, and is integrated (along with many other topics) into the general courses of the curriculum. It is this context that has grabbed my attention over the past few years, as the school where I teach does not offer particular courses on spirituality and social work (though more recently, an elective on mindfulness approaches to social work has been offered) and thus the pressure to integrate it into a wide range of other courses has increased.

I contend that post-structural and critical approaches to pedagogy are useful in thinking through these tensions. Wright (2000, 2007) has written a number of interesting texts integrating critical pedagogy with spirituality. Although he focuses on educating children, his work has some helpful insights for application when educating adults. While post-structural cautions about universal truths are helpful in a post-colonial world where we are increasingly aware of how the truths of the powerful tend to justify the oppression of the weak, it is also clear, as Wright points out, that there is no neutral ground, and that post-structural moves to question various truths are moves within the ongoing search for truth (2000, 2007). Thus, Wright encourages us to think of a critical spirituality in which ideals of classic liberalism—peace, dignity, freedom, tolerance, and solidarity—are the moral ground upon which the classroom rests. But to achieve these values, students and professors must engage thoughtfully with their beliefs. Beliefs and truths are understood as being valuable, contested, and situated. This approach is, I think, nicely compatible with the ideals of social work pedagogy discussed above.

Wright (2000) thus argues for an educational space that is simultaneously focused on nurture and critique. He challenges educators to create space for engagement and reflection, but to also demand intellectual rigour. The social work classroom can be imagined as a space where we encourage students to reflect upon, and when necessary, struggle with their beliefs and values, but where opinion and anecdote do not provide sound enough terrain for a thorough examination. Students need to reflect more deeply and analytically, thinking through the context and implications of their ideas.

Wright's notion of a critical spiritual education attempts to bridge the exclusive–inclusive divide by "attending to the universality of our shared spiritual quest and the integrity of the particular spiritual traditions in which this quest is pursued. This requires a rich, multidimensional presentation of spirituality that does not hesitate to embrace controversy" (Wright, 2000, p. 103). While the arguments for the universality of spirituality are convincing, it is important to remain aware that some students in social work do not understand themselves as spiritual beings, and find somewhat oppressive the contemporary notion that we are all spiritual. There have been a number of students who have provided me with sharp reminders that this is the case. This reality challenges educators to find a way to speak about spirituality that encompasses a broad experience, but one that is not so mandatorily inclusive as to dilute opportunities for debate and cause some students to resist the idea entirely. It seems possible for some students to understand a search for meaning and truth as solely a rational exercise. At the same time, the social work classroom cannot be fully inclusive. At various moments, different students will feel more or less marginalized, but what is important is providing a space to consider the implications of such beliefs and what that means for our profession. Rather than maintaining the veneer of inclusivity, we need to begin to grapple with how to respond to those who feel tenuous and dislocated.

The challenge in social work is how to facilitate debates around spiritual and religious beliefs that encourage critical reflection while not denying their value, but exploring them within the context of the field's professional values. Wright and many social work educators draw on Freire's (1971) notion of conscientization; teaching, through role modelling, a practice of continual questioning that helps students to train themselves to question the ideologies that determine their lives. This type of approach to spiritual education is helpfully illustrated in Letendre et al.'s (2005) work on negotiating spirituality and religion in the social work classroom. Specifically, the authors illustrate a practice of questioning that, if deployed in the classroom, may encourage all students to reflect critically on their value systems, and where they experience discomfort while not being excluded or disrespected in practice. The questions that Letendre and her colleagues ask students to think through situations that might arise in practice and decide how they will deal with them. This model of an active engagement and proactive dialogue is integral to opening spaces for thoughtful debate, but it is a tricky practice, particularly when deployed in classrooms where there is a minority of students who hold onto religious or spiritual beliefs and a large group of supposedly progressive, secular social work students. In the following section, I attempt to suggest some ideas for moving through these difficult spaces, not toward resolution or compromise, but just to show that there is a way forward.

Negotiating Ambivalence

Opening up spaces for those with disparate views to debate, discuss, and learn from one another in the university is clearly instrumental to creating a rich learning environment. Such discussions tend to offer more learning than lecturing on a topic. There are a number of disruptions that seem particularly important to make visible when trying to carve a space between the secular and the sacred. First, it seems vital that those who understand themselves as progressive and secular have an opportunity to understand how their belief systems are built on borrowed knowledge, much of it coming from ancient religious and spiritual wisdom (see Emberley, 1996). Also, when viewpoints are presented as progressive by juxtaposing them against conservative religions, these perspectives need to be complicated.

The problem is not only that religious and spiritual views are silenced in the social work classroom but also that information on so-called conservative religious beliefs and values is sometimes presented from an unchallenged liberal and secular perspective. The notion that social work values are intrinsically liberal (and progressive) secular values is made to seem natural and unquestionable (Fram & Miller-Cribbs, 2008, p. 893). This makes it difficult for students to engage in social work learning in an open climate for inquiry and professional growth, which should be the main goal of our work.

Such a framing of religion needs to be unpacked, and the multi-layered histories and present practices of institutional religions need to be made visible. Also, the notion that progressive and conservative, in relation to religious and spiritual views, are always coherent, knowable, and inflexible needs to be rethought. The values and ethics of the social work profession are not easily categorized as drawing solely upon progressive or conservative discourses. The struggle is not only about becoming more inclusive and respectful but also has to be about framing tensions in ways that speak to social work values and ethics rather than disparaging religious groups. As Fram and Miller-Cribbs (2008) argue, such a re-interpretation of the material will hopefully elicit less defensiveness and instead provide an opportunity for students to think through their political and religious values in light of social work values and professional knowledge (which, in itself, needs to be seen as evolving through debate and discussion). For example, it is not that self-determination is necessarily progressive, but when placed in the context of abortion or queer sexuality, it becomes so. Moving in this direction opens up the possibility for us as educators to develop a greater understanding of how students integrate various belief systems and ways of knowing themselves and one another. What we encourage is a way of understanding the self that does not always have to be protectively in opposition, magnifying and stigmatizing difference, which makes our own complexities more manageable (Fram & Miller-Cribbs, 2008). The opportunity to learn about one another provides important grounds for considering how social workers might relate to clients who are significantly different from themselves.

This is not an easy transition for those educators who imagine themselves and their profession to be progressive. It requires challenging their own reactions to difficult beliefs and values, and critically engaging with their professional values or ethics. Again, this process would be invaluable to students, who are more likely to encounter clients whose beliefs conflict with their professional values than people with progressive beliefs.

What to Do with the Presence or Absence of Spirituality

The constraints of 12-week courses present an ongoing problem for those of us teaching in social work. It never seems to offer enough time to cover the issues that resonate with students and the profession. One strategy that I have used to attempt to create a more inclusive curriculum is to think of each class in terms of layering. While there is an overarching theme for a class, and thus a focus, I insert case studies, exercises, films, or video clips to layer on other topics. When embedding sub-themes into the class, I try to create presences where there were absences, the kind of presence that allows students to see content as central, without necessarily having it taken up explicitly. This type of layering also helps to account for the different interests of different groups of students.

For some years I have embedded case studies that examine spirituality, and they have become a jumping-off point for lengthy discussions; other times the case study is only read in terms of its relevance to the central theme, and spirituality remains on the periphery.

The most challenging aspect of this kind of layering is attempting to avoid stereotypes and offering the topic in a number of different ways. So for instance, with spirituality and religion, over the years I have tried to layer them sometimes as a positive strength, and at other times as a challenge. We may, for example, consider how religious organizations are often some of the very few groups offering food and shelter to the poor. These offers are problematic in that they are charitable, and in encouraging the practice of one person being obligated to thank another, the sense that food and shelter should be a basic human right for everyone is lost. At the same time, secular society hasn't been willing or able to organize an alternative. These "charitable" spaces are equally important for the formation of communities that often get involved with activism. In this way, we can critically explore the notion of community as a space for pre-figurative politics, for belonging and activism, and social regulation and exclusion. Community can be explored in terms of the secular or the sacred. Depending upon the particular group of students, the issues of religion and spirituality may emerge as more or less important. My hope is that even when such discussions do not unfold into full-scale explorations of a topic, students can see an opening into a space for themselves, where they can connect their experiences and values with the curriculum.

Over the years, it has become clear to me that our classrooms offer an important space for people who have felt marginalized throughout their lives to be recognized and re-valued. For some of these students, a professor's attempt to articulate institutional problems as having multiple perspectives can feel like abandonment. This is another delicate balancing act. For those students for whom schools of social work are a space to recover and re-establish oneself after harmful experiences in various institutions, the shift toward understanding institutional religion as having multiple effects is important, even if difficult to grasp. These types of shifts require educators to work carefully with students to help them develop skills for negotiating discomfort. Educators must remain engaged and curious even when their sense of self is under threat.

It seems that one of the most interesting and helpful places to take up spirituality and religion in the secular classroom is during discussions of ethics (Ai, 2002; Coholic, 2006; Sheffield & Openshaw, 2009). In particular, my teaching on ethics focuses less on the social work code itself (though it is introduced as a helpful starting text) and more on how we muddle through difficult moments. Ethical dilemmas in social work are less about reading the code and more about negotiating the competing and often impossible demands of the contexts we practice in (Weinberg, 2010). This suggests that the process of understanding where our values, morals, and ethics have emerged and to understand these in context and critically reflect on them is important. Banks (2006) argues that "if we accept the embeddedness of ethics in social work practice, then it is important to study how certain ethical beliefs and qualities of character are constructed and performed"(as cited in Weinberg, 2010, p. xv). There is great similarity between the ethical guidelines of social work and those offered by religious and spiritual traditions. They include respect, responsibility, integrity, and concern for the welfare of others. As outlined earlier, the values of both the university and the profession are rooted in spiritual, religious, and contemplative traditions, thus spending some time examining the richness of those contributions offers an opportunity to celebrate spirituality and religion.

The performance and construction of these values and ethics are also important to understand. What does it actually mean to be part of a religious community whose values conflict with one's professional values? What are the various ways that social workers manage and perform such contradictions? Do these spaces of tension offer important wisdom for social work? These are areas that need further research so that they can be effectively drawn on in social work education. We have very little information on what these disconnections actually mean in practice.

Conclusions

As those in education grapple with expanding a notion of liberal education to include spirituality, social work is in an interesting place to both enrich such debates and learn from them. It is a discipline that is already creating a certain kind of civic engagement, one that is deeply concerned with injustice, the most vulnerable, and our responsibility treat one another with dignity and respect. This engagement is being negotiated on neo-liberal terrain oriented far more to consumer and managerial priorities. Despite the contextual challenges, we are already at the forefront of imagining democratic space that is based on strong notions of common values, morals, and ethics. We are also in a space of struggle, as we negotiate in our classrooms with religious, spiritual, and secular values that challenge these notions. We already consider what happens when such values conflict and how we can both challenge them and make our classrooms inclusive. It seems vital that discussions of spirituality and religion are part of this process, as they provide a historical and contemporary knowledge that helps to challenge the neo-liberal valuing of education, social work, and life.

The presence of discussions, reflections, and engagement with spirituality in social work classrooms is key to facilitating our students' engagement with and reflection upon their own moral frameworks. Such discussions help us understand some of the foundations of social work's moral framework and the resulting code of ethics. Finally, these discussions help students understand, navigate, and reflect upon the multiple spiritual and religious beliefs in society and how those create congruent and conflicting moral frameworks for making sense of our world. All three aspects seem vital not only to educating citizens in contemporary societies but more specifically professionals who hold significant amounts of authority.

Creating liminal spaces separating students who adhere strongly to religious traditions or spiritual knowledge from those who want to invest in a secular profession is a task filled with tension that will not easily evaporate from the classroom. The competing discourses social work education rests upon will ensure that expectations conflict and are challenging to negotiate, but doing so is the core of social work practice: respecting, celebrating, and learning from difference so that we can create rich, diverse, peaceful societies.

Notes

1 I use the term "sacred" to include both religion and spirituality. I do not want to rely solely on notions of spirituality that tend to be understood as outside or beyond religion. The term sacred is hopefully able to embrace both the institution of religion and individual spirituality.

References

Ai, A. L. (2002). Integrating spirituality into professional education: A challenging but feasible task. *Journal of Teaching in Social Work, 22*(1–2), 103–130.

Alexander, H. A. (2007). Spirituality and citizenship in higher education. In D. Bridges, R. Juceviciene, T. McLaughlin Jucevicius, & J. Stankeviciute (Eds.), *Higher education and national development: Universities and societies in transition* (pp. 250–278). London, UK: Routledge.

Banks, S. (2006). *Ethics and values in social work* (3rd Ed.). New York, NY: Palgrave Macmillan.

Beres, L. (2004). A reflective journey: Spirituality and postmodern practice. *Currents: New Scholarship in the Human Services, 3*(1). Retrieved from www.ucalgary.ca/currents/

Brulé, E. (2004). Going to market: Neo-liberalism and the social construction of the university student as an autonomous consumer. In M. Reimer (Ed.), *Inside corporate U: Women in the academy speak out* (pp. 247–264). Toronto, ON: Sumach Press.

Bruyere, G. (2007). Making circles: Renewing First Nations ways of helping. In J. Coates, J. Graham, & B. Swartzentruber (with Brian Ouellette) (Eds.), *Spirituality and social work: Selected Canadian readings* (pp. 259-272. Toronto, ON: Canadian Scholars' Press.

Butler, J., & Scott, J. (1992) *Feminists theorize the political.* New York, NY: Routledge.

Canda, E., & Furman, L. (2010). *Spiritual diversity in social work practice* (2nd Ed.). New York, NY: Oxford University Press.

Coates, J. (2003). *Ecology and social work: Toward a new paradigm.* Halifax, NS: Fernwood Publishing.

Coholic, D. (2003). Student and educator viewpoints in incorporating spirituality in social work pedagogy: An overview and discussion of research findings. *Currents: New Scholarship in the Human Services, 2*(2). Retrieved from www.ucalgary.ca/files/currents/v2n2_coholic.pdf

Coholic, D. (2006). Spirituality in social work pedagogy, a Canadian perspective. *Journal of Teaching in Social Work, 26*(3–4), 197–217.

Emberley, P. (1996). *Zero tolerance: Hot-button politics in Canada's universities.* Toronto, ON: Penguin.

Este, D. (2007). Black churches in Canada: Vehicles for fostering community development in African-Canadian communities—A historical analysis. In J. Coates, J. Graham, B. Swartzentruber (with Brian Ouellette) (Eds.), *Spirituality and social work: Selected Canadian readings* (pp. 299–322). Toronto, ON: Canadian Scholars' Press.

Fram, M. S., & Miller-Cribbs, J. (2008). Liberal and conservative in social work education: Exploring student experiences. *Social Work Education, 27*(8), 883–897.

Freire, P. (1971). *Pedagogy of the oppressed.* New York, NY: Continuum Press.

Furman, G. (Ed.). (2002). *School as community: From promise to practice.* New York, NY: SUNY Press.

Furness, S., & Gilligan, P. (2010). *Religion, belief and social work: Making a difference.* Bristol, UK: Policy Press.

Graham, J., Coholic, D., & Coates, J. (2007) Spirituality as a guiding construct in the development of Canadian social work: Past and present considerations. In J. Coates, J. Graham, B. Swartzentruber (with Brian Ouellette) (Eds.), *Spirituality and social work: Selected Canadian readings* (pp. 23–46). Toronto, ON: Canadian Scholars' Press.

Harris, R. (1976). *A history of higher education in Canada, 1663–1960.* University of Toronto Press.

Henry, D., & Beaty, M. (2008). *The schooled heart: Moral formation in American higher education.* Waco, TX: Baylor University Press.

Hodge, D. R. (2003). The challenge of spiritual diversity: Can social work facilitate an inclusive environment? *Families in Society, 84,* 348–358.

Hodge, D. R. (2005). Epistemological frameworks, homosexuality and religion: How people of faith understand the intersection between homosexuality and religion. *Social Work, 50,* 207–218.

Horton, M., & Freire, P. (1990). *We make the road by walking.* Philadelphia, PA: Temple University Press.

Lernoux, P. (1982). *Cry of the people: The struggle for human rights in Latin America. The Catholic Church in conflict with U.S. policy.* New York, NY: Penguin Books.

Letendre, J., Nelson-Becker, H., & Kreider, J. (2005). Teaching spirituality in the classroom: Building compassionate and non-judgmental conversations with students. *Reflections, 11*(3), 8–19.

Lewis, M. (2008). Public good or private value: A critique of the commodification of knowledge in higher education—a Canadian perspective. In J. Canaan

& W. Shumar (Eds.), *Structure and agency in the neoliberal university* (pp. 45–66). New York, NY: Routledge.

Margolin, L. (1997). *Under the cover of kindness: The invention of social work.* Charlottesville, VA: University of Virginia Press.

Milz, S. (2005). Canadian university Inc., and the role of Canadian criticism. *Review of Education, Pedagogy, and Cultural Studies, 27*, 127–139.

Mulcahy, D. G. (2009). Energizing liberal education. *College Quarterly, 12*(1). Retrieved from http://www.collegequarterly.ca/2009-vol12-num01-winter/mulcahy.html

Otters, R. (2009). Following in Jane Addams' footsteps. *Journal of Social Work Values and Ethics, 6*(3). Retrieved from http://socialworker.com/jswve

Rothman, J. (2009). Spirituality: What we can teach and how we can teach it. *Journal of Religion and spirituality in Social Work: Social Thought, 28*, 161–184.

Sheffield, S., & Openshaw, L. (2009, October). Integrating principles of spirituality into the social work classroom. Paper presented at the North American Association of Christians in Social Work (NACSW) Convention, Indianapolis, IN.

Skillen, J. (2004). *In pursuit of justice: Christian democratic exploration.* Washington, DC: Rowman and Littlefield.

Smith, D. (2004). Despoiling professional autonomy: A woman's perspective. In M. Reimer (Ed.), *Inside corporate U: Women in the academy speak out* (pp. 31–42). Toronto, ON: Sumach Press.

Spano, R. (2007). What is sacred when personal and professional values collide? *Journal of Social Work Values and Ethics, 4*(3). Retrieved from www.socialworker.com/jswve

Stebner, E. (1997). *The women of Hull House: A study in spirituality, vocation and friendship.* New York, NY: SUNY Press.

Todd, S. (2007). Feminist community organizing: The spectre of the sacred and the secular. In J. Coates, J. Graham, & B. Swartzentruber (with B. Ouellette) (Eds.), *Spirituality and social work: Selected Canadian readings* (pp. 161–174). Toronto, ON: Canadian Scholars' Press.

Todd, S., & Coholic, D. (2007). Christian fundamentalism and anti-oppressive social work pedagogy. *Journal of Teaching in Social Work, 27*(3–4), 5–25.

Weinberg, M. (2010). The social construction of social work ethics: Politicizing and broadening the lens. *Journal of Progressive Human Services, 21*, 32–44.

Wiebe, M. (in press). [Title]. *Canadian Social Work Review.*

Wright, A. (2000). *Spirituality and education.* London, UK: Routledge.

Wright, A. (2007). *Critical religious education: Multiculturalism and the pursuit of truth.* Cardiff: University of Wales Press.

Zajonc, A. (2003). Spirituality in higher education: Overcoming the divide. *Liberal Education, 1*, 50–58. Retrieved from www.arthurzajonc.org/uploads/Spirituality%20in%20Higher%20Ed%20AACU%20compressed.pdf

Chapter 8

Engaging the Noosphere: An Integral Approach to Teaching Spirituality Online

Veronika Bohac Clarke

Introduction

Spirituality has been the subject of several face-to-face and online graduate courses in the Faculty of Education at the University of Calgary for a number of years. The venture into explicit focus on spirituality was initiated by Dr. Tad Guzie, a Jungian scholar who made a connection between Jung's theory and spirituality in his teaching. Tad developed the first course on spirituality offered by the Faculty of Education, which he titled Spirituality in a Postmodern Age. I often attended Tad's class, and we had many conversations about teaching spirituality. In this course, Tad used *A Theory of Everything*, a book by Ken Wilber (2000), because he admired the author's comprehensive approach to human development. Tad corresponded with Ken until his untimely death from cancer. Before he died, Tad passed his course on to me, and I was glad for all the discussions we had had on the subject of teaching. There were a number of other professors who subsequently began to offer spirituality courses. These courses continue to be very well attended by teachers and administrators from both public and separate school systems, as well as educators from post-secondary institutions. I have been teaching the course Spirituality in a Postmodern Age for ten years now. The organizing framework for the course has been and continues to be Wilber's integral model (1999); I will discuss its application in detail later in this chapter.

Since the course is explicitly about spirituality, I do not share some of the challenges discussed by Vokey and Todd, two contributing authors in this book, who teach about spirituality as a part of broader-based courses. The students in my spirituality courses constitute a self-selected group. Most of the students are already self-reflective and analytical. Many do or have practised yoga or meditation to some degree. In this sense, they already have various degrees of personal awareness of their spirituality when they begin the course. Those who have not had prior experience with spirituality at the beginning of the course, and elected to take the course out of genuine curiosity—as opposed to having an agenda of "disproving spirituality"—have demonstrated increased awareness of different ways of knowing their world.

The approach to facilitating various ways of knowing in this course is a combination of information, analysis, practice, and integration. Students acquire and discuss information from various textual and online sources. Students learn about states of consciousness using Wilber's analysis of transpersonal psychology. Practice includes various types of meditation exercises, in which the students engage systematically at home. Integration is facilitated by the application of the integral model to their overall experiences and learning.

Is a course on spirituality a practical investment, or a personal luxury? Based on my students' comments, it appears that a graduate course on spirituality has direct applicability to their personal development and utility for their work as teachers, in spite of its seemingly esoteric subject matter.

The purpose of this chapter is to reflect on the lessons I have learned from ten years of teaching a graduate level spirituality course online, and to consider the implications of using an integral model of spirituality to foster the growth of new perspectives on learners and learning. In the first section, I will review theoretical issues and advocate for the continued evolution of spirituality as a legitimate subject, concluding with a description of approaches to teaching spirituality that particularly support the inclusion of experiential learning. In the second section, I will introduce and explain a theoretical framework which embraces, contextualizes, and accounts for connections between spirituality and new developments in the sciences, consciousness studies, and technology-mediated creativity in learning. In the final section, I will advocate for the legitimate inclusion of speculation about human potential, as well as for the systematic study of spiritual training and understanding the power of the mind in future courses. I will conclude with the example of Teilhard de Chardin and noosphere, his positive vision of human spiritual evolution, and describe the role that technology could play in engaging learners creatively and experientially.

Teaching Spirituality: Theoretical and Practical Considerations in Current Context

At this point, my personal working definition of spirituality is: intuition about, or experience of transpersonal consciousness and non-dual reality, used to inform a person's world view and behaviour toward self, others, and nature. The study of spirituality, from my perspective, is defined as *work* toward transpersonal literacy through acquisition of knowledge and through practice. The important point here is that spirituality, in the sense that I use it, includes and transcends humanist notions of compassion, social justice, and awareness of the interconnectedness of all human beings, to arrive at a world view that defines consciousness beyond that which is ordinarily felt and understood by individual human beings. This level of consciousness, described as "non-dual" consciousness in Buddhist terms (Wilber 2006) is also increasingly being referred to as participation in the "field of potentialities" by quantum physicists (Wolf, 1999; Bohm, 1990). The definitions of mind, matter, and existence that are provided by some physicists tend to approximate the language of mystics:

> And now, according to quantum physics, there is a third reality.... I think of this third reality as a bridge between the world of the mind and the world of matter. Having attributes of both, it is a paradoxical and magical reality.... [T]he laws of cause and effect manifest. The only problem is that it isn't objects that are following those laws, ... but ghosts!... In modern usage, they are called "quantum wave functions." (Wolf, 1989, pp. 185–186)

The term "spirituality" continues to be problematic in academic settings, because it is laden with connotations and ambiguity. It appears to be used as an umbrella term for a multitude of practices, world views, interpretations of traditions, and individual understandings (Boone et al., 2010). Spirituality can, but certainly need not be, associated with religion. Drawing on quantum physics and the Kabbalah, physicist Wolf derived the following definitions:

> spirit: the vibrations of nothing
> soul: the reflection of spirit at nodes of time
> matter: the reflection of spirit at nodes of space
> self: the reflection of soul in matter (1999, p. 271)

In the Spirituality in a Postmodern Age course, the term "spirituality" is defined from a postmodern perspective of looking beyond traditional, structural, and cultural divisions. Peeling away the contextual layers reveals important commonalities among these perspectives. A perusal of literature from most major wisdom traditions invariably yields strikingly similar themes, particularly from the teachings of mystics. Aldous Huxley used Gottfried Leibniz's term "perennial philosophy" to refer to these themes, and outlined the common spiritual meeting ground that they map out (Bohac Clarke, 2002). In this sense, the perennial philosophy, as a fundamental set of principles underlying spiritual teaching, is an intuitive, interpretive tool for understanding the perspectives of the texts. The perennial philosophy is not without its critics, of course. From a Christian perspective, Helminiak (1998) explains that the perennial philosophy contravenes Christian dogma:

> Wilber supports his argument that "all the world is really Brahman," by citing words attributed to Christ in the *Gospel of St. Thomas*.... But this gospel is not in the Christian canon. Why not? ... Indeed, the *Gospel of St. Thomas* is Gnostic. As

such, its thought follows the same basic position as Wilber's perennial philosophy, as Hinduism, neo-Platonism, and all Great-Chain-of-Being philosophies. But the basic incompatibility between such philosophies and Christianity needs to be noted, and Wilber's gross misrepresentation of Christianity needs to be flagged. (p. 280)

The perennial philosophy, which Wilber uses in a transreligious sense of spirituality, is thus drawn right back into a religious context. Other criticisms come from contemporary arguments of scholars and philosophers and are analytical in nature. For example, Beauregard and O'Leary (2007) explore the contrasting views of "perennialists," which stem from mystic experience and validate a common mystic (non-dual) consciousness, and constructivists who deny any commonality in mystic experiences owing to the intervention of cultural conditioning and assumptions. It seems apparent in the constructivist position that those who make these arguments have not had the personal experience of a mystic state.

Confusion and perhaps tolerant carelessness may be other reasons why, even today, in spite of the explanations of "perennialists," the term "spirituality" continues to have connotations with religion in the general understanding and usage of the term. The confusion may be augmented by the postmodern explosion of New Age perspectives and practices, some of which are genuinely based on perennial philosophy, while others are indeed based on superficial readings of traditional teaching and assumptions that "pre-rational" and "trans-rational" spirituality are the same thing (Wilber, 2006).

Spirituality also tends to provoke a strong negative reaction (Dawkins, 1976) from the established scientific community, often mediated by their mistrust of religion. Ironically, early philosophers and mystics were often also scientists and mathematicians, and both mystics and scientists were persecuted and executed as "heretics" throughout history (for example, Hypatia in 415, Giordano Bruno in 1600). Even scientists who take a very comprehensive view of human evolution tend to reduce spirituality to some version of genetic determinism (E. Wilson, 1998), or offer a more tempered support of the scientific method which recognizes complexity and allows for the possibility of creativity, but which nevertheless dismisses the importance of the interior aspects of the development of human consciousness (Davies, 2004). However, a rapidly growing number of current writers, both philosophers (Wilber, 2006) and scientists (Wolf, 1989, 1999; Swimme & Berry, 1992; Lipton, 2008; LeShan, 2003; Beauregard & O'Leary, 2007; Kaufman, 2008), argue that spirituality and science need not be mutually exclusive, and new findings reported by quantum physicists seem to corroborate some of the world views of the mystics.

The interaction of mind, brain, "person," and spirituality with its subjective and undefinable nature is variously discussed, disputed, and dismissed in debates among neuroscientists, neuropsychologists, and philosophers (de Waal, 2009; Damasio, 1999; Bennett, Dennett, Hacker & Searle, 2007; Dennett, 1998, 2003). The Dalai Lama believes that a rigorous application of phenomenological "bracketing" can provide a scientific description of individual consciousness, and evidence for non-ordinary states and their effects on mind and body:

> Biology, for instance, has made tremendous advances in giving us a scientific understanding of life and its various forms and constituents, despite the fact that the conceptual and philosophical question of what life is remains open. Likewise, the remarkable feats of physics (especially in quantum mechanics) have been achieved without a clear answer to the question "What is reality?" and while many conceptual issues pertaining to their interpretation remain unresolved. (Gyatso, 2005, p. 160)

The Dalai Lama suggests that, rather than deny the subjectivity of consciousness, researchers should be trained in a rigorous methodology of first-person empiricism as a legitimate scientific methodology:

> In training ourselves to take conscience itself as the object of first-person investigation, we must first stabilize the mind. The experience of attending to the mere present is a very helpful practice. The focus of this practice is a sustained training to cultivate the ability to hold the mind undistractedly on the immediate, subjective experience of consciousness. (Gyatso, 2005, p. 160)

The study of the types of "spiritual" experiences that can be apprehended has been the focus of "transpersonal psychology" (Wilber, 2000; Combs, 2002; Helminiak, 1998). Spiritual experiences are often described by individuals as events of cognitive dissonance that gave rise to the intuition of a transpersonal consciousness. In this sense, one might suggest a term such as "transpersonal knowing" as a more legitimate replacement for "spirituality"; however, as Vokey pointed out in his chapter, the term "spirituality" has also been used to describe phenomena other than simply knowing, as the term can encompass several phenomena (Grof, 1993; LeShan, 2003). Therefore, before embarking on the task of teaching spirituality, we need to unpack and clarify the term spirituality from an applied perspective as well.

Can Spirituality Be Taught?

Teilhard de Chardin, much maligned and discredited by both Church and Science, has been rehabilitated by New Age proponents, who use his most recognizable statement, that people are spiritual beings having a physical experience, as their mantra (this is evident after a quick perusal of any number of New Age books currently on the market). Can remembering one's spiritual origins—"in-spiration"—be akin to connecting with or participating in the "common ground" of the Kosmos, Christian God as Spirit, the Brahman, divine ground, Bohm's field of potentialities, et cetera? The ongoing mind-body-"person"-spirit debates among philosophers and scientists are also present in the personal quests that "ordinary people" make in pursuit of spiritual development. In my spirituality course, students raise such questions as: What's beyond the self, beyond the personal consciousness? Can spirituality, in the sense of experiencing oneself in a transpersonal consciousness, be taught, or only taught about? Is there such a thing as transpersonal literacy? Why do we have to get out of our heads in order to experience Spirit or the bigger picture of our existence—or at least an expanded picture of our own consciousness? These questions cannot be reduced to interactions between chemicals in the brain. Kaufman (2008), LeShan (2003), and Pearce (2004) use the idea of a unified field to explain the mystics' descriptions of "dissolution of the self" in some greater (non-dual) reality. Bohm used the principles of quantum theory and the field, to explain the relationship between the mind, the brain, and the mystics' "divine ground" in complex but reassuringly scientific terms:

> This approach is based on the causal interpretation of the quantum theory, in which an electron, for example, is regarded as an inseparable union of a particle and a field. This field has, however, some new properties that can be seen to be the main sources of the differences between the quantum theory and the classical (Newtonian) theory. These new properties suggest that the field may be regarded as containing objective and active information, and that the activity of this information is similar in certain key ways to the activity of information in our ordinary subjective experience. The analogy between mind and matter is thus fairly close. This analogy leads to the proposal of the general outlines of a new theory of mind, matter, and their relationship, in which the basic notion is participation rather than interaction. Although the theory can be developed mathematically in more detail, the main emphasis here is to show qualitatively how it provides a way of thinking that does not divide mind from matter, and thus leads to a more coherent understanding of such questions than is possible in the common dualistic and reductionistic approaches. These ideas may be relevant to connectionist theories and might perhaps suggest new directions for their development. (Bohm, 1990, p. 271)

Wilber describes a range of non-ordinary states, from sleep and dreaming, to the non-dual states of consciousness that people have experienced throughout recorded history (2006). Anyone can access these states, whether through deliberate training, or spontaneous "accidents." Access does not depend on age or maturity; in fact, small children are particularly adept at entering these states, until they are convinced by helpful adults that such experiences are nonsense, a fanciful flight of imagination, or "just a dream," and ultimately are reassured that what they are experiencing is not real. Access can be considerably more difficult for adults who have lived with the conviction that such states and experiences do not exist, except as a mental disorder or a byproduct of overindulgence in spicy food too close to bedtime, consumption of illicit drugs, or work-related stress (LeShan, 2003).

While some individuals can access even the non-dual states of consciousness spontaneously or with relative ease, everyone has the innate ability to achieve this state, with various degrees of effort. In the Western world of competition and stress, the "serenity" necessary for the simple task of sitting still, clearing one's mind, and remaining alert but not thinking thoughts, is difficult to achieve (Combs, 2002; Brown, 1983).

Can spirituality be taught? Spirituality as "transpersonal literacy" can, and has been taught for millennia, although the impact of its practice on the body and brain has not been studied seriously until relatively recently. As the Dalai Lama recounts (Gyatso, 2005) when scientists conducted systematic testing of trained Buddhist monks during meditation, they were amazed at how those results changed the accepted scientific parameters of human brain functioning.

From the personal accounts of spiritual leaders such as Mother Teresa or the Dalai Lama, and from survivors of "near-death experiences," the same message comes through: Beyond the measurable external indicators, spiritual practice can help students gain far greater working knowledge of their mind and conscious-ness, and an intimate awareness of the interconnectedness of our world, than environmental data, scientific theories, or the politically correct presentation of our world by the media.

Ultimately, a growing percentage of the populace of the Western world is engaged in spiritual activities and experiences, regardless of whether or not scientists consider the mind real. One need only to peruse a local bookstore to see the evidence of this interest represented by plethora of books on spirituality, meditation, lucid dreaming, out-of-body experiences, yoga, and so on. One is reminded of the old saying, "the dogs bark, but the caravan moves on."

Should Spirituality Be Taught in a Twenty-first Century Secular Curriculum?

The students in my graduate course in spirituality are teachers who generally work in the K–12 system. The topic of the course therefore contains another level of relevance, beyond the personal focus. Given today's turbulent political climate and natural as well as man-made environmental disasters around the globe, it is clearly important to prepare our teachers with the skills and understanding to teach their pupils inclusive and compassionate attitudes both toward people around the globe (who appear in our classrooms in increasing numbers) and toward the natural environment. With the emphasis on interdependence that is included in many current spiritual teaching approaches (Buddhist or shamanic derivatives), such challenging goals can be approached with an increased expectation of success.

The development of a course on spirituality requires the teacher to have a broad knowledge base, as well as openness to creative ways of engaging students in this type of material. Clearly, the integral model is helpful in preparing a holistic and coherent program both for K–12 and post-secondary education. I discussed the application of the model in this context in another article (Bohac Clarke, 2002). The question remains, however, whether the effort of preparing teachers in this specialized area is warranted. Given the current and future policy directions of Alberta's Ministry of Education, an integrally taught course on spirituality may be a requirement rather than an interesting option.

The Current Educational Context in Alberta, Canada

After extensive community consultations around the province, Alberta Education—the provincial government ministry responsible for K–12 education in this Canadian province—released a policy document that delineates the direction for all aspects of education over the next 20 years. The plan, titled *Inspiring Education* (Alberta Education, 2010), outlines radical changes to the teaching and learning process. Within this document, one of the three stated goals of education is "ethical citizenship." Comments from citizens are featured throughout the report: "When I think of learning in 20 years, I hope that education will have responded to children in a whole way, including their physical, emotional, and spiritual well-being as well as their academic needs" (Alberta Education, 2010, p. 6).

How can teachers be prepared for the comprehensive task of teaching the whole person? While teachers are prepared to teach academic subjects and physical education, it is far less clear as to how well they are prepared to respond to pupils' emotional and spiritual needs.

The subject of spirituality does not come under discussion in public schools until the high school grades, where pupils study literature and discuss themes that resonate with their own personal development. Familiarity with the issues around spirituality would give teachers the language, understanding, and ready examples for responding to pupils' questions and validating their experiences and needs related to spirituality.

From the feedback given to me by teachers who have taken my graduate course on spirituality over the years, it is clear that those individuals who are interested in and seek out spiritual practices, consider them a valid need and an important source of wisdom. My doctoral student McKinnon (2009) conducted research with teachers who consistently pursue spiritual practices for personal development and healing. A surprising finding from McKinnon's study was the sense of isolation that these teachers reported regarding their spiritual practice. The teachers reported a lack of community and support in the school for discussing such politically sensitive topics as spirituality. There was no safe space for them to share their experiences and reflections, as spirituality was often officially regarded as suspect and politically incorrect.

The teachers reported a need to critically analyze their spiritual experiences, and to reflect on and clarify their perspectives on life, in conversation with colleagues. They felt unsupported in their search for meaningful dialogue and feedback. Conversely, in my spirituality courses students were actively involved and valued the opportunities to honestly exchange personal views on spirituality with fellow students in a safe and respectful setting.

Discussions about spirituality can be emotionally charged. One strength of a course is that it can be a setting specifically designed for inclusive discussion. The subject matter, such as compassion or interconnectedness of people and ideas, tends to invite participants to model the values they are discussing. The students in this course, in their role as schoolteachers, also need to know how to model compassion and inclusion, and how to explain these perspectives "factually" (Kernochan, McCormick, & White 2007).

Is there a "Teachable" Spiritual Curriculum?

Although students need to know about the ideas passed down through millennia about spiritual practices and experiences, this constitutes only the first step—background preparation. Students do need to critically analyze various schools of thought about spirituality, and the postmodern context encourages analysis, as do contemporary teachers of Buddhism, for example. However, once armed with comprehensive background preparation, students need to engage in practice, in order to fully understand the concepts as well as themselves. Aldous Huxley, in reviewing the teaching of ancient spiritual leaders, noted,

> A philosopher who is content merely to know about the ultimate Reality—theoretically and by hearsay—is compared by Buddha to a herdsman of other men's cows. Mohammed uses an even homelier barnyard metaphor. For him, the philosopher who has not realized his metaphysics is just an ass bearing a load of books. Christian, Hindu, and Taoist teachers wrote no less emphatically about the absurd pretensions of mere learning and analytical reasoning. (1944, p. 15)

What types of results are generally expected in a program of spiritual practices? Formal spiritual teaching programs, which were and are traditionally offered in monasteries to students wholly dedicated to the study of spiritual practices, as well as guru or master-led programs, generally are quite integral in nature, addressing all four quadrants of the integral model—from individual mind work, to a community of practice, to the learning of rules and rituals, and to the learning of body control. Contemporary Western programs usually focus primarily on aspects of yoga and meditation (LeShan, 1974).

The products of the learning in the Western contemporary context include the development of physical skills and their impact on the body, and the development of mental skills and their impact on the mind. The two sets of skills cannot be easily classified in separate categories, since their effects are synergistic. For example, the practice of yoga initially yields observable physical results from internal massage of the glands, improved posture and breathing that lead to better overall health and stress reduction. Most yoga classes also include meditation which, if practised consistently, leads to increased mental clarity and decreased stress. If the meditation is combined with coherent instruction in accessing transpersonal states of consciousness, then the internal learning leads to the expansion of conscious awareness, which in turn leads to observable changes in behaviour and attitudes, including the ability to attain and maintain equanimity, and authentic compassionate treatment of others.

Meditation, usually using visualization or other focusing techniques, has been practised and studied in elementary schools for some years. A notable proponent of meditation in public institutions, Kabat-Zinn, observed increased on-task focus in elementary school pupils, as well as a general improvement in behaviour and student interaction (2003). My doctoral student Ross, who completed his dissertation on the use of meditation and biofeedback in a high school population in the summer of 2011, recorded various instances where meditation had a beneficial effect on the manner in which participants faced challenges in their daily lives.

Once students participating in a spiritual curriculum gain increased awareness of the mental and physical experiences associated with meditation, they are better able to understand the symbolism of texts from various mystery traditions located in specific times and cultures. In applying these experiences to K–12 classrooms in a broad-based spiritual component of the public school curriculum (Buchanan & Hyde, 2008), great care clearly must be taken while discussing religious scriptures, as pupils' personal beliefs could become entangled with the subject. The current popularity of Buddhist teaching in Western cultures may be in part due to its presentation—with the separation of philosophy from the mystery and religious aspects of Buddhism. The current popular books on Buddhist practices are geared to the eclectic Western reader. The presentation of ideas is logical, the approach to explanations is analytical, and the fundamental principles are often discussed as Buddhist psychology (Kornfield, 2009).

For this reason, the books on Buddhist spiritual practices are more accessible to the contemporary reader than, for example, the Kabbalah or Christian mystic practices and exercises. Aboriginal shamanic practices also require understanding that is not readily accessible to the average urban reader.

Spiritual practices are ultimately aimed at some sort of personal transformation, though the types of expectations range considerably from the monastic to the graduate course settings. The transformation is dependent on the student's perseverance—it may be a modest change, such as stress reduction through an altered attitude, or a fundamental shift in world view, brought about by direct non-dual experience. Are such shifts and insights legitimate "products," and can they be measured? This question will be the focus of conversation in the next section, as we examine actual experiences of teaching spirituality in an academic setting.

Teaching Online

Having taught spirituality in both face-to-face and online courses, I conclude that teaching spirituality integrally online has not been markedly different or more difficult than teaching face-to-face. As Vokey discussed in his chapter, the need for establishing a safe classroom environment is paramount in order to foster the authentic and respectful exchange of ideas about spirituality, whether face-to-face or online. Each type of class has its own mode of establishing connectedness. In both cases, it is entirely possible to establish a safe, intimate, and authentic space for shared conversation and personal risk-taking. The initial responsibility for shaping the class ethos rests, of course, with the instructor. It must be clear from the outset that the classroom will be at once inclusive and exclusive. The students must feel assured that all voices will be heard respectfully, and that this particular class differs from "regular" classes in that its specific ethos is characterized by cooperation and creativity, as opposed to competition, and instructor and grade-centred work.

How can this be achieved during 13 weeks in a regular semester, or 3 weeks in a summer semester online? The instructor must take the initial risk to be authentic, open, personal, and scrupulously fair-minded. The initial "classroom tone" is set with the instructor's "profile," which is posted before the course begins. This tone is then reinforced by the instructor's reactions to questions and encouragement of critical analysis by students, whether this is focused on the assigned textbook or on the content presented by the instructor. From the very beginning of the course, the instructor must look for opportunities to demonstrate authenticity. This can be challenging, because the instructor is deliberately vulnerable. Even within a self-selected group, there can be a great range of belief systems represented—I have encountered a complete spectrum, from fundamentalist New Age proponents, to Wiccans, Muslims, Christians, Buddhists, agnostics, and fundamentalist science proponents. Nevertheless, the instructor's authentic behaviour is essential to building a safe community. Once the initial measure of trust is established, the community tends to form fairly quickly, partly because of the focus of the class and partly because of the need of many participants to share and compare their spiritual experiences and theories with interested others.

After a critical measure of trust and mutual respect is established, the real work of the course can begin. Examining spirituality from the integral frame-work perspective necessarily involves self-reflection and cultivating an "all quadrant" awareness about one's life. In the UL (interior subjective) quadrant specifically, the course must provide opportunities for analysis of current or past transpersonal experiences.

In addition to analysis, active participation in various types of meditation provides opportunities for inner experiences that lead to awareness and possibly the embodiment of different ways of knowing. At the very least, these types of exercises should allow students to become better acquainted with the ways in which their minds work. From my experience, active participation needs to take place individually as well as communally. The individual work is done by each student alone, as "homework." This is followed by a discussion of students' experiences in class—both in the form of postings on discussion forums and orally during synchronous audio sessions.

It is also useful to lead the students through at least one comprehensive guided visualization session during a synchronous audio class. Thus far I have used only my voice, and Tibetan Singing Bowls where appropriate. This simple approach of speaking directly "to the minds" of the students seems to create a sense of intimacy. The experience of meditating together also creates a surpris-ingly strong sense of connection among class members, as do their comments on homework and general discussion. Students' comments about which methods did not work for them are just as useful as the sharing of meditative insights, and should be encouraged. Undoubtedly, students are engaged, but is this a "real" course? This is a question that Vokey grappled with in his chapter: how can we structure a spirituality course into a "proper" course, with objectives and assessment criteria?

To structure spirituality curriculum with a focus on transpersonal literacy into a legitimate course requires the use of a solid theoretical framework, such as the integral model, clear objectives that provide themes and topics, identi-fication and availability of content from wisdom traditions, a systematic and progressive set of meditation exercises, and a solid theme-based infrastructure for class discussion. There must be opportunity to critically analyze all aspects of the course. In order to allow for an authentic flow of ideas and creativity, grade assessment in this course is structured on a contract basis. Each grade requires a predetermined set of assignments and activities, which does not merely entail the addition of more assignments for each higher grade, but also ensures that the layering of assignments across grades is done thematically, purposefully and coherently. By giving students the opportunity to fulfill the course contract to achieve the grade of their choice, the competition between them is greatly reduced, as is the tendency to write the assignments "for the instructor" instead of for the optimal learning value to the student. The predictability of the contract structure alleviates stress and puts control over learning into the hands of the students. Invariably, students feel accountable to one another and to themselves, and take ownership of their learning in very personal and creative ways.

Lessons from the Field

Every time I teach the spirituality course, about one-third of the students indicate they are searching for a spiritually active and supportive community of fellow educators. Their stories are very similar to those that McKinnon (2009) encountered in his doctoral research. The students have eventful personal and professional lives, yet often they come to this course feeling very much alone in their search for spiritual meaning. Other students report that they took the course with the intention of reconnecting with the meaningful life they led before they began dedicating most of their energy to their organizations and to full-time membership in the consumer society.

Vokey and Todd speak about the difficult terrain of risk-taking and openness, particularly in culturally and religiously mixed classes. Both the instructor and the students take risks in these situations. First, the instructor takes the risk of encouraging personal expressions of values, and the attendant emotional outpouring that can follow. Within the community of the class, students begin to take risks not only in terms of expressing their opinions and questioning their fellow course participants and instructor but also in terms of revealing more about themselves and the large questions in their lives. It is here that "spirituality" as transpersonal literacy becomes an "applied science." As students become more public in their self reflections, other class members share information, advice, and resources such as books and websites.

One important lesson I have learned over the years of teaching this course is to be very explicit in the course description, and state clearly what the course is and is not about. Some students who are attracted to this course already possess strong views, sometimes approaching certainty, about the correctness of their spiritual perspectives, be they religious or scientific. It is very important to ensure from the beginning of the course that students are aware they will not be engaged in proving or disproving the legitimacy of spirituality or a particular brand of spirituality. Emotional investment and personal validation need to be balanced by a conscious effort to keep an open mind and to listen and engage with fellow participants' views attentively and respectfully. This is an area where the instructor must use the utmost tact to intervene when the discussion loses focus and direction, and at the same time guard against imposing "right answers" (unless the interpretation or understanding of the theoretical framework used in the course is incorrect).

Every year, the discussion postings document noteworthy examples of students broadening their world views and stepping out from their initial sense of certainty. For some, there are also examples of a very evident and often dramatic process of personal development. These amazing changes notwithstanding, a practical curricular question voiced by Vokey remains: Do personal transformation and developmental insights 'count' as learning products? A practical answer might be that such transformative effects are a hoped-for byproduct of completing the practice component and reflecting critically on the theoretical and applied content of the course. Clearly, personal transformation is difficult to assess objectively. This is also an area where the instructor must navigate a fine line between coaching and psychological counselling. Todd's discussion of teaching practice and the obligation to train morally responsible practitioners underlines this point.

Teaching Integrally

As Vokey stated in the introduction to his chapter, "teachings and practices that foster spiritual realization should be an integral part of educational initiatives across the lifespan, inside as well as outside formal institutions such as schools" (p. 97). Teaching integrally includes teaching content as well as skills and application. The content needs to be contextualized and interpreted from all four quadrants, its meaning analyzed from various developmental levels. Placed in the big picture, spiritual writing, whether historical or current, can be understood from a developmental perspective as embedded in its historical and cultural context, rather than as theory exported into our current world view. In addition to cognitive understanding from a third-person perspective, the skills and practice add a first-person understanding, while class discussion adds a second-person understanding.

A postmodern approach to spirituality requires a framework that is capable of holding together different approaches to and interpretations of spirituality. The framework must also be capable of pointing to and accommodating expansions of existing theories. R. A. Wilson suggested in his book, *Quantum Psychology* (1993), that theoretical models actually represent the way our minds work and the degree to which we can explain our current reality. In his teaching and writing, Wilson deliberately used an approach he called "Guerrilla Ontology," bringing to bear seemingly disparate and unrelated perspectives on the issue under study, in order to unbalance the students' unquestioning acceptance of current theory and official perspective on the issue. In his insistent reminder that students should hold every theory only "for now," Wilson tried to caution against the false sense of security that early closure brings, thus echoing Nietzsche's famous observation, "we live as if we know."

Discussion: Understanding the Integral Framework for Current Realities and Future Possibilities

Is it a road map which allows the individual to develop their own architecture of consciousness and transcend their current level?
(J. K. Donlevy, personal communication, June 2012)

Applying Wilber's Model: Holding "Broad Spectrum Spirituality" together Coherently

One of the challenges in teaching spirituality is to find a respectable conceptual framework, as Vokey already cautioned in his chapter. The theoretical framework holding together the content, analysis, and practice of my spirituality course is Wilber's integral model (1999, 2000, 2006). Wilber's work, however, is not without controversy. Academics in particular are vocal and sometimes vicious critics, though a sizable portion of the criticism seems to be directed at Wilber himself, rather than at his model. Wilber's personal Buddhist-based spirituality is particularly stringently criticized as confounding the clarity of his model. (Visser, 2003; Helminiak, 1998).

McIntosh (2007), who wrote a balanced review of the theorizing of notable integral thinkers, offers his own critique of Wilber's model, and with one amendment finds the model stands up well to critical analysis. McIntosh based his assessment of Wilber's model on the same criteria that he applied throughout his meta-analysis of integral theorizing, as well as on his own experience of working with the model for ten years. His particular critique concerns Wilber's definition of the lower-right quadrant.

Some of the criticisms levelled against Wilber's model focus on the fact that it is a meta-analysis and that it is based on developmental theory, both of which are currently out of fashion with postmodern deconstructivist thinking. Education in the Western world is nevertheless based on developmental models. Developmental theory is not likely to be discarded in the near future, particularly as it does not appear to be inimical to new perspectives on learning, such as pupil engagement and pupil co-creation of knowledge with teachers. In spite of the decreased popularity of meta-models, a coherent framework such as the integral model is needed in education, to organize and put into relational perspective the growing number of theories vying for the attention of curriculum planners.

Unfortunately, teachers are generally introduced to new theories and approaches piecemeal, without a coherent big picture to help orient them.

One strength of the integral model is its ability to account for key developmental stages and provide parameters for individual and societal development. The model is dynamic and capable of identifying complex relationships. It has the capacity to specifically identify the interior context (terrain) as a fundamental component in human development, and provide organizing parameters for its study. This interior component will continue to gain importance in education, as it is implicated in the nature of student engagement and creativity in the pursuit of co-creation of knowledge in the classroom.

I will offer a brief description of the integral model, and show why it is useful and appropriate for my spirituality course specifically.

Wilber (1999, 2000, 2006) has been working on an integral model of human development for many years, and continues to see it as work in progress. Wilber did a meta-analysis of all major aspects of Western culture in the areas of philosophy, individual and social development, and science recorded in history (and available to the Western reader). His model is on the surface very simple— by tracing two basic human perceptions: inside and outside, and singular and plural—he was able to show that human development can be placed in four categories based on their perspectives. The four perspectives are a combination of inside-outside, singular-plural, which are mapped out as four quadrants of a square. The model is often referred to as a map, and the quadrants are named and identified according to their geographic directions; UL (upper left), UR (upper right), LL (lower left), and LR (lower right). Each quadrant contains two zones. Since the model can only be addressed in a very brief form here, I have described the quadrants and their zones using key words:

I—Upper Left (UL): The interior of the individual, "intentional," first-person perspective; the subjective aspect of consciousness; mind; individual awareness; personal and transpersonal psychology; the self-conscious self; the self-reflective self; character; values; spirituality; personal experience of emotions; personal experience of art, music, and literature; qualia; impact of meditation on states of consciousness. Examples—Zone 1: being inside your head, actually doing the meditating or thinking; Zone 2: being inside your head, watching yourself meditating or thinking.

IT—Upper Right (UR): The exterior of the individual, "behavioural," third-person perspective (e.g., the brain is studied as "it" not as "I"); these are objective or exterior correlates of interior states of consciousness; objective, empirical accounts of scientific facts about the individual organism; observable and measurable individual characteristics, such as the impact of meditation on behaviour and academic performance. Examples—Zone 3: engaging the physiological process of burning calories by running on a treadmill; Zone 4: watching the instruments attached to your body that measure the amount of heat you produce.

WE—Lower Left (LL): Interior (inside of) the collective, "cultural," second-person perspective; inter-subjective communications; group values; world views and ethics that are shared by any group of individuals; group norms that define inter-subjective (group-defined) meaning-making; a cultural understanding of "us" and "others," and the rules of engagement: competition, compassion, cooperation, et cetera. Examples—Zone 1: being inside of the group relating to other group members (in the staff room, at a family reunion, etc.); Zone 2: being inside the group and watching yourself and others relating to other group members ("playing the game").

ITS—Lower Right (LR): Exterior (outside of) the collective, "social," third-person perspective; inter-objective mechanisms for coexistence and development of living systems; social systems such as institutions, geopolitical formations, forces of production; political and religious systems; Examples—Zone 3: fulfilling the job description as a member of an organization or system; Zone 4: conducting a policy analysis or assessment of that organization or system.

While it is not my intention here to explain the model in detail, I will add that there are within it additional distinctions beyond the simple use of the four quadrants. I will refer to some of them briefly in the discussion of the model's application. To reiterate, each quadrant represents a specific perspective on human life and development. Wilber analyzed theories of human development from all four perspectives and synthesized them into developmental levels. Within all four quadrants, individual or group development proceeds (as defined by developmental theory) in sequential steps, so that advancement to the next developmental level happens after the previous one has been assimilated, rather than skipping over developmental steps. Wilber describes this process with the characteristic phrase, "transcend and include."

Wilber mapped out a progression of developmental levels within each quadrant, and suggested two distinct overall tiers of development, where a fundamental shift in perspective would result in a developmental leap from tier one to tier two. For ease of use, he assigned each level a colour as a shorthand descriptor of the developmental characteristics. Thus, the red level can be characterized as a "might is right" survival mentality, while green is a "global cooperative" mentality. Wilber identified developmental "lines" (capacities or intelligences) running through each quadrant and level. For example, in the individual "Upper" quadrants, such lines include cognitive, emotional, kinesthetic, interpersonal, moral, and so on. Developmental models pertaining to the UL quadrant, such as Fowler's "Stages of Faith" (Fowler & Keen, 1980) correspond very accurately to the levels described by Wilber.

This model, though it appears highly abstract when viewed in full detail, can be surprisingly helpful to practitioners when it is used to put their complex contexts into perspective. For example, even a cursory application of the model to schools shows us that a classroom is experienced by students subjectively "in their heads," objectively as measured by each student's performance on tests, inter-subjectively as each classroom develops its own culture over time, and inter-objectively as the discipline in the classroom is compared to school policy requirements. One of the frequent issues for educators, for example, is that while the students, parents, and the school community (and, indeed government policy-makers) require teachers to provide a holistic education, meaning "all quadrants," what students and schools are usually assessed on is proficiency in the Right-Hand quadrants—the scientific knowledge and its application to current social institutions and systems. What is missing is the "untestable" Left-Hand quadrant "stuff," which is nevertheless mentioned prominently in all mission statements at each level of the education system as an essential component of preparing future citizens.

To summarize, I have attempted to provide a very brief explanation of the conceptual model that I use in the spirituality course, and to demonstrate the model's capacity to address a wide range of individual and social situations. This model is particularly useful in this course because it contains a detailed description of human development in the individual interior (UL) quadrant, including states of consciousness.

The currently popular and cutting-edge complexity theory, which has been adopted in various disciplines far beyond its mathematical subject of origin, is very compatible with the integral model, both in terms of the developmental levels and in terms of the recognition of the interactions within and between contexts (Kaufman, 2008). As is the case with complexity theory, there is a certain predicitve capacity inherent in the integral model.

In its "big picture" application, integral theory takes us beyond the insular world of individual conditioning, beliefs, and cultural programming by placing these within larger societal and historical contexts. Human development, shown concurrently side-by-side in all four quadrants, can show the struggle for meaning under various conditions. While it is not the model's function to convince those who use it about the acceptability of other people's beliefs, it does increase understanding of why they ended up with the conclusions they hold.

Simply put, integral theory can at once provide a way of perceiving the world, and point to situations or developmental issues that need to be understood within a specific context under study. Students can study the UL in depth, while at the same time continuing to be aware of how this quadrant interacts with the others. The "content" of each developmental stage in the UL can be examined and put into perspective in relation to its inter-subjective and objective contexts.

Final Thoughts: Rehabilitating the Noosphere and Speculating about the Future: Theoretical and Practical Possibilities for Learning and Being

Wilber's idea of spiral development (rather than a straight-line progress), continuing until every society masters all the developmental levels and a leap to "second tier" or higher order integration becomes possible, is very compatible with Teilhard de Chardin's concept of Noosphere. Like Wilber, Teilhard de Chardin was another thinker who suffered vicious attacks from academics throughout his scholarly career. He did not have Wilber's model to anchor and contextualize his ideas, however, so he was dismissed as a priestly dreamer who should not meddle in science. Currently, Teilhard de Chardin is being rehabilitated in popular culture as a visionary who, among other things, "predicted" the development of the Internet. His ideas are also valued by some integral thinkers (Combs, 2002).

Teilhard de Chardin's Dream

Teilhard de Chardin (1955) had a very hopeful vision for human development, provided humanity did not self-destruct before ultimately reaching Wilber's second tier. A similarly positive outlook was proposed by Pearce (2004), assuming humanity managed to develop beyond what he calls "fear-based programming." Lipton and Bhaerman (2009) are equally confident, based on the new advancements in the science of epigenetics, that human development is far less determined by genes and heredity, and far more amenable to the influences of the human mind consciously participating with the world.

In contrast with Pearce (2004), who saw the use of technology in schools as problematic, Teilhard de Chardin's hopeful vision saw technology as a catalyst for the development, rather than the destruction of human spirit. He envisioned second-tier development to be mental-spiritual, integrated, and global. This mental-spiritual network, which he called the Noosphere, would grow through Noosphere, would grow through and exist beyond the biosphere. It is easy to see how the Internet could be interpreted in popular culture as the beginning of Noosphere; however, Teilhard de Chardin's vision aimed considerably beyond that. He postulated that humanity's evolutionary imperative would eventually force a fundamental change in world view, from competition to cooperation; only then would technology be used to sustain the biosphere and thus allow people around the globe to focus on mental development. What would a change from a Darwinian jungle (Lipton & Bhaerman, 2009) to collaborative motivation look like? We cannot totally imagine, even from the most developed level of "green" reality today, what second-tier development or higher-order complexity could look like on a global scale. Seeds of imaginative thinking are being sown however, seemingly randomly and with the help of technology, in ways that are widely accessible and engaging to the general populace. An intriguing example is the film *Inception*, which deals with the use of lucid dreaming in a way that is related to Teilhard de Chardin's notion of mind work and Noosphere.

In this final section of the chapter, I would like to engage in some speculation about the future of human development, or perhaps uncovering of consciousness, and the implications for the role of transpersonal literacy in education.

Technology as well as the instant availability and use of communications have facilitated an explosion and rapid dissemination of knowledge, which keeps educators busy adding more new truths to the curriculum while pushing yesterday's high school content into the junior high schools. Engaging in speculation about possibilities is an indulgence that few public school teachers can afford for themselves, let alone their pupils. Given that speculating about possibilities is a natural expression of human creativity, pupils tend to find their own opportunities to dream and create outside of school, on their computers.

Perceptive teachers will recognize that this "new way" represents a fundamental shift in world view, and not merely technological savvy. There is a growing scholarly interest in youth culture in general, and young people's approach to learning through the use of technology in particular (Ito, 2009). Given the current emphasis on student achievement testing as the primary indicator of quality in western education systems, there is a danger that teachers might just change existing class assignments into multimedia formats, with no consideration of their pupils' new ways of learning.

> If the paradigm for learning in old media is a notion of direct transfer, the question that interests us most is "what does a theory of learning look like for collective, social, and participatory media?" To get at that question, we believe it is necessary to understand the epistemological foundations of social and collective participation, to understand how people are learning in the social context of new media. In doing so, we examine learning in the context of three frames: knowing, making and playing.... What may be most important to understand is that each of these dimensions of learning are in the process of evolving in response to the demands of the 21st century. In a world of flux, knowing, making, and playing emerge as critical components of becoming. (Thomas & Seely Brown, 2009, p. 3)

Integral Framework and the Really Big Picture

Playing with ideas, regardless of whether they are proven or provable, has the practical benefit enabling us to step out of prescribed roles or perspectives—and into our zone 2—which allows us to check out our accepted/traditional/taken-for-granted mindsets and assumptions. In this section, I will indulge in "what if" thinking about possible future uses of the integral model and its relation to complexity theory and human development.

I have already mentioned the complementarity of the integral model framework and complexity theory. Both suggest the possibility of a learning leap into a fundamentally higher order of coherence, organization, interconnectedness, and functioning. Wilber's "second tier" of human development corresponds to this higher-order complexity. As is the case with the integral model, stages of complexity can be seen in the small picture of teachers' lives as well.

In the big picture, the role of technology on the planetary scale of human evolution can be traced through the evolving levels in all quadrants. Commonly used terms such as "digital native" and "digital immigrant" attest to the pervasive and powerful influence of technology on human development. On a societal scale, individual quadrants, beginning with the technological inventions of the (upper right) UR which are quickly seized upon by the imagination of the UL, are evolving much faster than the collective quadrants of LL and LR, which tend toward preserving equilibrium. While individually, technology can act as a chaotic attractor stimulating revolutionary developmental growth, collectively, technology is currently used by existing social systems to curtail it. Populations in the Western world live under constantly increasing surveillance, though it may appear to be benign—from flush monitors on toilets in private residences, to cell-phone-based tracking systems "to keep up with friends," security cameras in public places and buildings, data mining on Facebook and other social media, and restrictions on personal choices such as the use of herbal food supplements and energy drinks, to name just a few examples—technology seems to be in the service of the right-hand quadrants.

How is spirituality implicated in these changes? Technology can be directed to the left hand quadrants to search for spiritual learning and community building. The Internet has facilitated the exchange and proliferation of spirituality-related information around the globe, as can be seen in even a cursory search using Google or any other popular search engine. New Age books have been translated into many languages, and meditation music and videos abound on disks and websites. Such a proliferation of information requires some discernment on the part of the searcher. Since many of the searchers are teenagers, the need for teachers with some degree of transpersonal literacy becomes evident.

What kinds of developmental strides are possible when spiritually and technologically literate teachers co-create knowledge with spiritually curious and technologically creative pupils? If Teilhard de Chardin and Wilber are correct, then teachers would be well advised to keep current with transpersonal and technological literacy skills, and with developments in popular culture, especially youth culture.

Why is this discussion relevant to a graduate course on spirituality? It seems to me that an occasional assault on the minds of educators by means of "guerrilla ontology" creates spaces for broader views of developmental potential, and more imaginative approaches to the implementation and harnessing of different ways of knowing. Graduate students continue to be interested in taking spirituality courses in the Faculty of Education partly for personal growth, and partly because, as schoolteachers, they feel the pressure and professional responsibility to keep up with the needs of the "new learners" that populate their classrooms. While the new learners require their teachers to be fluent and creative in the technology-mediated learning environment, beyond this basic need they also require the teachers to facilitate their spiritual and ethical development as global citizens (Tiri, Tallent-Runnels, & Nokelainen, 2005; Kernochan et al., 2007; King 2010).

I conclude with one more reference to the conversation I had with my colleague about the course on spirituality and its possible impact:

> So, if I understand this correctly, curiosity leads the student to the course, and the course provides the tools to do the work of spiritual development. The invitation to do the work does not come from the professor but from the student's own interior. I imagine it as standing in front of a lake. If the student chooses to pick up the tools and enter the lake, she will learn to swim in the water and emerge changed, perhaps unafraid, transcending her current level of consciousness, perhaps entering the Noosphere. (J. K. Donlevy, personal communication, June 2012)

References

Alberta Education. (2010). *Inspiring Education*. Edmonton, AB: Government of Alberta.

Beauregard, M., & O'Leary, D. (2007). *The spiritual brain: A neuroscientist's case for the existence of the soul*. New York, NY: HarperOne.

Bennett M., Dennett, D., Hacker, P., & Searle, J. (2007). *Neuroscience & philosophy: Brain, mind & language*. New York, NY: Columbia University Press.

Bohac Clarke, V. (2002). In search of school spirit: The cloud of unknowing in public education. *International Electronic Journal for Leadership in Learning, 6*(10). Retrieved from http://www.ucalgary.ca/iejll/bohac_clarke

Bohm, D. (1990). A new theory of the relationship of mind and matter. *Philosophical Psychology, 3*(2), 271–286.

Boone, M., Fite, K., & Reardon, R. F. (2010). The spiritual dispositions of emerging teachers: A preliminary study. *Journal of Thought, 45*(3–4).

Brown, B. S. (1983). *Supermind: The ultimate energy*. New York, NY: Bantam.

Buchanan, M. T., & Hyde, B. (2008) Learning beyond the surface: Engaging the cognitive, affective and spiritual dimensions within the curriculum. *International Journal of Children's Spirituality, 13*(4), 309–320.

Combs, A. (2002). *The radiance of being*. St. Paul, MN: Paragon House.

Damasio, A. (1999). *The feeling of what happens: Body, emotion and the making of consciousness*. London, UK: Heinemann.

Davies, P. (2004). *The cosmic blueprint*. Philadelphia, PA: Templeton Foundation Press.

Dawkins, R. (1976). *The selfish gene*. New York, NY: Oxford University Press.

Dennett, D. C. (1998). *Brainchildren*. Cambridge, MA: MIT Press/A Bradford Book.

Dennett, D. C. (2003). *Freedom evolves*. New York, NY: Penguin Books.

de Waal, Frans. (2009). *The age of empathy: Nature's lessons for a kinder society*. New York, NY: Harmony Books.

Fowler, J., & Keen, S. (1980). *Life maps: Conversations on the journey of faith*. Waco, TX: Word Books.

Grof, Stanislav. (1993). *The holotropic mind: The three levels of human consciousness and how they shape our lives*. San Francisco, CA: Harper.

Gyatso, T. (His Holiness the XIV Dalai Lama). (2005). *The universe in a single atom: The convergence of science and spirituality*. New York, NY: Morgan Road Books.

Helminiak, D. (1998). *Religion and the human sciences: An approach via spirituality*. New York, NY: SUNY Press.

Huxley, A. (1944). Introduction. In *The Song of God: Bhagavad Gita* (S. Prabhavananda & C. Isherwood, Trans., pp. 11–22). New York, NY: Mentor Books/New American Library.

Ito, M. (2009). *Hanging out, messing around, and geeking out: Kids living and learning with new media*. Cambridge, MA: MIT Press.

Kabat-Zinn, J. (2003), Mindfulness-based interventions in context: Past, present, and future. *Clinical Psychology: Science and Practice, 10*(2): 144–156.

Kaufman, S. A. (2008). *Reinventing the sacred: The science of complexity and the emergence of a natural divinity*. New York, NY: Basic Books.

Kernochan, R. A., McCormick D. W., & White, J. A. (2007). Spirituality and the management teacher: Reflections of three Buddhists on compassion, mindfulness, and selflessness in the classroom. *Journal of Management Inquiry, 16*, 61.

King, U. (2010). Earthing spiritual literacy: How to link spiritual development and education to a new Earth consciousness? *Journal of Beliefs & Values, 31*(3), 245–260.

Kornfield, J. (2009). *The wise heart: A guide to the universal teachings of Buddhist psychology*. New York, NY: Bantam Books.

LeShan, L. (1974). *How to meditate: A guide to self-discovery*. New York, NY: Bantam Books.

LeShan, L. (2003). *The medium, the mystic, and the physicist: Toward a general theory of the paranormal*. New York, NY: Helios Press.

Lipton, B. H. (2008). *The biology of belief: Unleashing the power of consciousness, matter and miracles*. New York, NY: Hay House.

Lipton, B. H., & Bhaerman, S. (2009). *Spontaneous evolution: Our positive future (and a way to get there from here)*. New York, NY: Hay House.

McIntosh, S. (2007). *Integral consciousness and the future of evolution*. St. Paul, MN: Paragon House.

McKinnon, D. (2009). *Uncovering and understanding the spirituality and personal wholeness of school educators*. (Unpublished doctoral dissertation, University of Calgary, Alberta).

Pearce, J. C. (2004). *The biology of transcendence: A blueprint of the human spirit*. Rochester, NY: Park Street Press.

Ross, M. (2011). *The evolution of education: Use of biofeedback in developing heart intelligence in a high school setting.* (Unpublished doctoral dissertation, University of Calgary, Alberta).

Swimme, B., & Berry, T. (1992). *The universe story.* San Francisco, CA: Harper.

Teilhard de Chardin, P. (1955). *The phenomenon of man.* New York, NY: Harper & Row.

Thomas, D., & Brown, J. S. (2009). *Learning for a world of constant change: Homo sapiens, homo faber & homo ludens revisited.* Paper presented at the Seventh Glion Colloquium, University of Southern California.

Tiri, K., Tallent-Runnels, M., & Nokelainen, P. (2005). A cross-cultural study of pre-adolescents' moral, spiritual and religious questions. *British Journal of Religious Education, 27*(3), 207–214.

Visser, F. (2003). *Thought as passion.* New York, NY: SUNY Press.

Wilber, Ken. (1999). *Integral psychology.* Boston, MA: Shambhala.

Wilber, Ken. (2000). *A theory of everything.* Boston, MA: Shambhala.

Wilber, Ken. (2006). *Integral spirituality.* Boston, MA: Integral Books/Shambhala.

Wilson, E. O. (1998). *Consilience: The unity of knowledge.* New York, NY: Random House.

Wilson, R. A. (1993). *Quantum psychology.* Phoenix, AZ: New Falcon.

Wolf, F. A. (1989). *Taking the quantum leap: The new physics for non-scientists.* New York, NY: Harper & Row.

Wolf, F. A. (1999). *The spiritual universe: One physicist's vision of spirit, soul, matter, and self.* Portsmouth, UK: Moment Point Press.

Section Three

Implications for Practice

While educators and social workers perform different and unique roles, there are convergences in their methods and values. Teaching is a key aspect of what social workers do, albeit using a different method compared to that of many teachers. At times, educators also have to attend to the mental health concerns or cultural diversities of their students in thoughtful and effective ways. Increasingly, both educators and social work practitioners are interested in working with their respective clientele/students in holistic ways for a variety of reasons, some of which are discussed in this final section of the book.

One example is the current interest in mindfulness-based practices, which are discussed in this section by Coholic and Miller. Both educators and social workers are using mindfulness as a self-care strategy for themselves, as a method and philosophy that develops therapeutic and teacher presence, and as a practice that, when taught, can assist students and clients in learning how to focus, build self-awareness, learn compassion, and much more. Educators and social workers are interested in relationships and engaging with others in meaningful ways, and mindfulness can help build these effective relationships with students and clients. Also, we are witnessing an increase in the incorporation of mindfulness strategies into schools and social work practices, because they are proving effective for a wide variety of issues and people. However, the effectiveness of learning mindfulness should not be confined to individual problems or growth. For instance, school culture can be changed when students are exposed to, and grasp, mindfulness. Programs such as MindUP report that young people become more empathic and understanding of others (http://www.thehawnfoundation.org/mindup).

Culture is another highly relevant topic for both education and social work. Within our multicultural society, we have to respectfully work with and teach people from a variety of cultural backgrounds, and some of these cultures may be inseparable from spirituality or religious beliefs. Beliefs in traditional healing practices and alternative health care are connected to culture; this topic is considered by Winchester and his colleagues. The use of alternative health practices is increasingly common, and social workers should have some knowledge regarding these. Educators and social workers teach about different cultures and explore and challenge racism; developing cultural competence has been a longstanding topic within social work. Coholic discusses how some culturally specific practice paradigms have to include people's spiritual beliefs, which encourages us to consider spirituality and how it may be implicated in life, the process of change, community development, and so forth.

Trauma and healing may be something that is more interesting for social work practitioners. That being said, Csiernik explores the matter of students having traumatic and stressful experiences during their field placements, and how spirituality can aid them in processing these events. The same can be said for some education students and their placement experiences. Cadell discusses the emerging area of post-traumatic growth, based on the theory that people can transcend traumatic and painful experiences and achieve growth beyond what has been traditionally expected. She argues that researchers have not paid enough attention to spiritual growth and change as a result of healing from trauma.

Our hope is that the material in this section will motivate educators and social workers to consider how they can, and sometimes should, broaden their perspectives to include spirituality.

Chapter 9

A Review of Spiritually Sensitive and Holistic Social Work Methods: Current Emphases and Future Directions for Research and Practice

Diana Coholic

In this chapter, I consider some of the current approaches, perspectives, and emerging trends that are prominent within the spiritually sensitive social work practice research literature. The aim of this discussion is to (a) take stock of some accomplishments to date with an eye toward future research and knowledge development, and (b) to demonstrate how social work researchers and practitioners are proving that holistic interventions are helpful and effective. Rice and McAuliffe (2009) explained that while there are differing opinions of what constitutes spiritually influenced interventions, they are practices that practitioners believe have been informed or adapted from religious or spiritual ideas, or are considered to directly engage with the spiritual aspect of a client's life. Within social work, there are three practices and methods most often discussed that fit this criteria: meaning-making, or making sense of something in one's life and how one's spiritual beliefs are often part of that process; coping, and how one copes with life events and stresses by drawing on spiritual resources and beliefs; and how some cultural practices/beliefs cannot be divorced from spirituality. I briefly consider these issues as well as holistic group work, mindfulness-based practices, and palliative hospice care. These three topics also have something highly relevant to offer the discussion and are currently emphasized in the research and practice literature about holistic helping and health practices.

In this chapter, the terms "holistic" and "spiritually sensitive" are used interchangeably. I am interested in spirituality and spiritually sensitive methods, as opposed to religion and religious practices. Nelson-Becker and Canda (2008) referred to spirituality as encompassing the human quest for a sense of meaning and purpose, and moral principles in relation to a person's beliefs and experiences about the nature of reality. In general, spirituality is one of the bio-psychosocial dimensions that comprise human beings and can involve transpersonal experiences (transcending the ordinary limits of body, ego, and linear space and time).

As both a clinical social worker and an academic researcher, I am particularly interested in understanding what makes our practices and methods effective and useful. Certainly, helping and health methods continually change and are shaped by forces that emerge not only from within helping and health professions but also from demands, needs, and interests based in a broader public domain. For example, helping and health professions are under increasing pressure to "prove" their interventions and methods work: to this end, emphasis on evidence-based practice (EBP) has become ubiquitous within social work over the past 15 years. At the same time, we have also witnessed an increasing interest in and use of holistic treatments and methods across helping and health professions, such as mindfulness-based practices and meditation, and other alternative health treatments. As P. Clark (1999) argued, the popularity and prevalence of alternative therapies can no longer be ignored by academia, the medical establishment, and government. Spiritually sensitive social work practice is one area in Western social work that has experienced substantial development in the past decade, and the impetus for this development largely emerged from practitioner and client demands and interests (Graham, Coholic, & Coates, 2006).

I conducted my doctoral study in this area in the late 1990s, a time when this field was just beginning to re-emerge (Graham et al., 2006). Specifically, I chose to conduct exploratory research in the area of feminist social work practice and spirituality because, in part, I was increasingly working with clients who brought spiritually sensitive and existential books to sessions (one example was *The Celestine Prophecy* by Redfield, 1994), and they expressed interest in talking about spiritual, holistic, and existential matters such as making sense of why a specific trauma had happened to them, or understanding the nature of life and death. My practice was changing, and I could see that other practitioners were also being challenged to work more holistically.

However, having completed my graduate social work education in 1991, I had not studied or even considered spirituality in my social work education and training. Indeed, when I began my research in this area, I encountered many practitioners and students who reported feeling anxious and uneasy about openly discussing spirituality or religion with their colleagues, peers, and teachers, and certainly this was reflected in some of the literature and debates of that time (Amato-von Hemert, 1994; J. Clark, 1994). Some practitioners feared they would be viewed as unprofessional (or worse) by their colleagues. At the same time, they expressed a strong desire for contexts within which they could feel free and encouraged to consider how spirituality was part of their work. I experienced this firsthand during the presentations I was invited to deliver on my doctoral research for community-based practitioners, which were often full to overflowing with social workers, even though I was an inexperienced public speaker and a budding academic.

Now it is more difficult, if not impossible, to keep abreast of all of the developments and research that explores spiritually sensitive methods, not only in social work but also in other disciplines and fields such as nursing, medicine, psychology, and education. In addition to the growth of research literature in this area, examples of interest include the formation of the Canadian Society for Spirituality and Social Work (CSSSW) in 2000, and earlier, the Society for Spirituality and Social Work in the United States in 1990. The fifth North American conference in spirituality and social work (a collaboration between these two societies) was held in June 2010 at the University of Calgary. Importantly, we now have access to general social work textbooks that include chapters on spirituality and existential issues (Guadalupe & Lum, 2005; Payne, 2005). These texts help to expose social work students to these topics, encouraging them to think about spirituality, and they help spiritual issues become more acceptable within social work.

Indeed, Leung, Chan, Ng, and Lee (2009) argued that contemporary trends in clinical practice are moving toward an integrative approach with interest in methods that utilize physical, cognitive, emotional, and spiritual components. Moberg (2005) also pointed out that researchers have demonstrated the importance of spirituality to human well-being and that including spirituality in helping and health practices has improved the effectiveness of clinical work and social services. Thus, practitioners today are encouraged to consider incorporating spirituality in their work (Bellamy et al., 2007).

Furthermore, Sheridan (2009) stated that there is enough of a knowledge base in spirituality and social work to draw some preliminary conclusions regarding the question of, "What are we doing, and why?" Based on an in-depth review of the literature, she found that both practitioners and students are using spiritually based interventions to a large degree. The types of interventions used most frequently included gathering in-depth assessment information; supporting aspects of clients' religion or spirituality identified as a coping resource and strength; referring clients to religious or spiritual helpers or programs; and helping clients address issues that require deep reflection, such as loss and death.

While all of this seems to reflect a greater comfort level with, and awareness of, the need for exploring spirituality within the profession, it can also be argued that we are not yet at the point where spirituality has been fully embraced by social work as a legitimate and effective practice method. Reflective of this, many (if not most) Western social work students do not receive any formal education or training in this area. Sheridan (2009) argued that, when social work programs do not include content on spirituality in social work, students are left with little guidance for professional decision-making, placing clients at risk of receiving ineffective or even harmful services. This was my experience in a research study I conducted with social work students and professors, exploring attitudes related to including spirituality in social work education. Students shared experiences related to practice with clients that they felt unprepared for and situations they were not sure how to address. One example included a client who asked the student social worker to pray with her. Another graduate student was headed for employment in an old age home where religion and spiritual beliefs were an important part of the work, but she felt that she lacked experience in this area. Moreover, she did not feel that there was space within her program to discuss these issues in class (Coholic, 2003).

The reality is that often people's religious or spiritual beliefs and practices will be an important part of our work whether we are prepared for this or not. Some examples include the client who is struggling with the decision to have an abortion, since her religious or spiritual beliefs may very well be implicated in her decision-making process; or the client who has been shunned from her family and community because she has changed her religious beliefs. Aboriginal (indigenous) clients may have strong traditional spiritual or cultural beliefs that guide their healing processes and how they make meaning out of life events. People who have suffered a trauma or a serious illness such as cancer sometimes look for meaning in the spiritual and existential realm, wondering, "Why me?"

Furthermore, this lack of education for social work students (including a dearth of professional development opportunities) indicates a need for ethical issues to be addressed, and for ethical guidelines to be developed to guide social workers who are incorporating spirituality in their work (Sheridan, 2009). For instance, Canda, Nakashima, and Furman (2004) found in a national survey of social workers that most addressed spirituality in their practice, but lacked guidelines for systematic, ethical decision-making regarding the use of spiritually oriented activities in practice. Further discussion of ethics is beyond the scope and intent of this chapter, but clearly the development of ethical guidelines is a necessary focus for social work and a part of effective social work practice.

Social workers are also beginning to study the effectiveness of specific holistic interventions and methods, which will advance the development of knowledge concerning holistic helping and health practices. Next, I consider how spiritually sensitive group methods are particularly amenable to research designs that enable investigation of practice effectiveness.

The Effectiveness of Holistic Group Work and Methods

Many studies that actually evaluated and explored the effectiveness of spiritually sensitive and holistic interventions were conducted using group methods and practices. There is likely a logical reason for this, that is, studying the usefulness and effectiveness of spiritually sensitive group methods is a highly feasible project that lends itself to deductive research designs. Once a holistic program is developed, it can be offered to many people at one time by a few facilitators trained in the group methods, and it can be compared to control and comparison groups comprised of the same client population.

A good example of this is Richards, Berrett, Hardman, and Eggett's (2006) research that evaluated the effectiveness of a spiritual group intervention for clients with eating disorders. They compared the spiritual group with a cognitive emotional support group using a randomized control group design. The spiritual group worked with a self-help workbook that included non-denominational readings about topics such as spiritual identity, forgiveness, and meditation. The researchers found that attending to a client's spiritual growth and well-being during inpatient treatment may help reduce depression and anxiety, relationship distress, social role conflict, and eating disorder symptoms.

Another example includes Antle and Lott Collins's study (2009) that evaluated the effectiveness of a breast cancer support group in promoting spiritual well-being and self-efficacy related to cancer management among a group of African-American breast cancer survivors. They found that the women who participated in a spiritually based support group reported high levels of satisfaction and significant benefits for their spiritual well-being. For some women, their illness strengthened their faith and belief that they were going to be okay. Yet another example is Layer, Roberts, Wild, and Walters's (2004) study that measured the efficacy of a spiritually based group intervention for women grieving an abortion. They found that their group program helped these women feel less shame and fewer posttraumatic stress symptoms.

In my own research, my team and I have facilitated holistic arts-based groups with children and youth in need for over five years. Spiritually sensitive social work with young people is an emerging area within the broader field of social work interventions related to spirituality that have focused mainly on adults (Cheon & Canda, 2010). In a national survey of American social workers, Kvarfordt and Sheridan (2009) found that the majority of respondents regarded religion and spirituality as relevant to working with youth, and used a wide variety of spiritually based interventions. Some of the respondents also included the spiritual/religious abuse of youth as an issue that required attention.

In the holistic arts-based groups, we use a wide variety of arts-based and experiential methods that aim to teach mindfulness-based practices (I discuss these holistic practices and philosophies later in this chapter). We also make room for holistic/existential topics and discussions, and often the children take advantage of this space by starting conversations related to the nature of life, death, and the battle between "good" and "evil" (Coholic, 2010, 2011a). The goal of the group is to assist the young people to develop their self-awareness, self-esteem, and resilience. This is a preventative program that engages youth in a meaningful and relevant strengths-based helping process. In the first three years of this project, the research was qualitative and exploratory because my team and I had to develop a group program that was feasible, suitable, and beneficial for the children and youth. Now entering the sixth year of this research project, we moved to a multiple method research design, where we continue to qualitatively analyze the group sessions and post-group individual interviews that assess each child's experience with the group, but also collect self-report scores on self-esteem and resilience. These self-report scores are collected at five different points throughout one year from the 36 children who take part in each year of the study.

The 36 children are placed into one of three streams—the first group of children participates in the holistic arts-based group first (the intervention group) and then receives no other group intervention; the second group participates in an arts and crafts group first, followed by the intervention group after a waiting period (this is the comparison group that enables us to assess factors such as group support); and the children in the third group act as the control group. After a waiting period, they participate in the intervention group. To date, we have found that some of the youth learned to understand and cope with their feelings more effectively, they learned social skills and coped better at school, and they really enjoyed the group (Coholic, 2011b; Coholic, Lougheed, & Cadell, 2009). These qualitative findings are starting to be backed up with quantitative results. Preliminary results are promising, and demonstrate that the intervention group had a statistically significant effect on helping the children to decrease their emotional reactivity, meaning that they learned to understand and cope with their feelings in more effective ways (Coholic, Eys, & Lougheed, 2011).

At this point in the discussion, it is relevant to note that the development of knowledge in spirituality and social work is occurring within a broader context that currently emphasizes the importance of evidence-based practice (EBP). The current debates about EBP may be especially relevant for us to consider, as we work within an area that some view as unscientific. EBP is part of a broader movement in the health and social service disciplines which has gained currency in social work scholarship. Essentially, EBP involves integrating clinical expertise and values with the best available evidence from systematic research while considering the client's values and expectations (McNeill, 2006). Concerns that practitioners were using harmful and/or ineffective methods with clients was a key reason for the development of EBP (Gambrill, 2006). For some social workers, it is hoped that EBP will ensure that clients receive better services, and social workers are alleged to gain increased professional confidence, improved professional status and credibility, and a greater ability to access funds (Bates, 2006; Plath, 2006; Zayas, Gonzalez, & Hanson, 2003).

However, for others, the focus on EBP is a problem precisely when it intersects with broader movements of social welfare retrenchment, cutbacks to the delivery and mandates of social service agencies, an increase in administrators' abilities to regulate and monitor front-line work, and an overall requirement to do more with less and to scrutinize and control the professional latitude of social work professionals (Clarke, 1996). Witkin and Harrison (2001) argued that EBP is incompatible with social work because the reality of practice is reflexive, interactive, and unpredictable.

One of the specific challenges with some of the arguments for EBP, particularly for our area of study and practice, is the notion that there is a hierarchy of research methods, with randomized controlled trials at the top and qualitative methods at the bottom (Plath, 2006). Broadly speaking, to date, much of the research in spirituality and social work has been exploratory in nature, and as a result it will be discounted or trivialized by some. However, we should avoid privileging any research method or hierarchy of methods, especially since these hierarchies may be limited in addressing questions about the rigour of qualitative research (Taylor, Dempster, & Donnelly, 2007). It would be prudent for us to ensure that the term "evidence-based" is widely evaluated in the field, and not conceptualized too narrowly. Also, we should understand EBP as a method from which reliable knowledge can be utilized and applied. We have a solid foundation of knowledge to build upon in the interests of advancing effective evidence-based practices and policies. As Nelson-Becker and Canda (2008) explained (with specific reference to the research in spirituality and aging), the foundation of exploratory research in this area helps to formulate future research questions and develop the next steps for research and practice. In general, we should be encouraged by research findings that indicate holistic practice methods are proving beneficial, and we need to continue to build on the solid foundation of knowledge that already exists.

Coping

How people cope with their problems, and how they can be helped to cope more effectively is a key theme in current spirituality and social work practice literature. As Farley (2007) stated, spirituality is increasingly identified as a significant component of resiliency, and can be used as a tool to enhance coping. Gockel (2009) explored spirituality and the process of healing. She found that spirituality was particularly important in helping people to reconstruct positive meanings in the face of crisis. Within the mental health field, Sullivan (2009) contended that religion or spirituality is important for client well-being and aids the recovery process. Spiritually based resources were also found, over the long term, to help women deal with their husbands' prostate cancer (Kaʻopua, Gotay, & Boehm, 2007). Kaʻopua and colleagues (2007) found that the common themes in spiritually based resources were accepting change, using adversity as an opportunity for growth, and coping proactively. Furthermore, some authors reported that meditation and mindfulness can be used as a coping intervention for clients dealing with substance abuse (Carlson & Larkin, 2009). Regarding youth, Jackson et al. (2010) examined spiritual coping mechanisms among adolescents in foster care. Based on the value the youth ascribed to spiritual coping strategies, such as praying, they made recommendations for policy and practice to include spirituality in work with this client group.

Related to coping is the matter of meaning-making, or making sense of one's life experiences and interpreting them. Helping someone to make meaning of something that has happened to them has long been a rationale for the incorporation of spirituality in social work practice, because for many people, spiritual beliefs and experiences will be integral in this process. Indeed, definitions of spirituality for social work typically include the human quest for a sense of meaning and purpose (Nelson-Becker & Canda, 2008). Along these lines, Thomas and Cohen (2006) explored older adults' meaning-making processes, and found that there were many spiritual turning points in these adults' lives that influenced their world views and interpretations of subsequent life experiences. Interestingly, they identified that much of the literature on meaning-making in adulthood actually stems from the education field, and is based on the theory of transformative learning. Thomas and Cohen (2006) found that some turning points were transformative because they enabled older adults to deepen their spirituality and transcend adversity throughout their lives, while others were incremental and added new meaning to old situations. As Nelson-Becker and Canda (2008) pointed out, older adults may increase attention to spirituality as they face the challenges of illness and mortality that can affect their sense of life meaning.

Culture and Coping

In addition to making connections between life stages and coping, researchers have also examined convergences between specific cultural practices and coping. The matter of how people cope is often connected with specific cultural practices and beliefs. Spirituality is frequently identified as an important part of how some cultural groups cope with events like natural disasters (Li-ju & Jieh-jiuh, 2009), or resettling after leaving one's country as a refugee (Sossou, Craig, Ogren, & Schnak, 2008). Lee and Chan (2009) stated that religious or spiritual coping was embedded within Chinese-American older adults' values, faith, and cultural beliefs, and that religious or spiritual beliefs were important in developing effective coping strategies. Roff, Simon, Nelson-Gardell, and Pleasants (2009) examined the importance of spiritual support for a group of African-American breast cancer survivors. Also, Banerjee and Canda (2009) discussed how a group of African-American women used their spirituality as a source of strength for coping with the challenges of poverty. Another recent example is the work by

Hodge and Roby (2010) that explored how sub-Saharan African women coped living with HIV/AIDS. They found that spirituality played some role in most of the women's ability to cope, and identified spiritual coping strategies as support from other believers, prayer, and trusting in God.

Harris-Robinson (2006) found that working-class black women used spiritual-focused coping to deal with stress, while Washington and Teague (2005) discussed how spirituality can provide protection for young African-American men by promoting healthy drug attitudes and preventing suicide. In fact, Gilbert, Harvey, and Belgrave (2009) discussed how workers in the field have been calling for an Africentric paradigm shift in social work practice with African-Americans for over a decade. They argued that Africentric interventions in social work have to be further studied so that a discourse on them as evidence-based practices can emerge. They explained that spirituality is one Africentric value that, in conjunction with other values such as collectivism, has been found to create significant change across a number of areas important in practice with African-Americans. However, they also argued that a barrier to the full integration of Africentric models in social work is the lack of cohesive documentation and replication, which limits their potential to be established as evidence-based practices.

Another current vein in the spirituality and social work literature concerns itself with culture and the delivery of culturally appropriate services, including assessments (Hodge & Limb, 2010). In fact, interest in spirituality within social work is often rationalized by pointing out the importance of attending to religious and spiritual diversity as part of the profession's overall commitment to cultural diversity (Kvarfordt & Sheridan, 2009). The reality is that in some cultures, spiritual and religious matters cannot be divorced from social work processes. Graham, Bradshaw, and Trew (2009) explained how social work practice needs to be localized in work with Muslim clients. Schiff and Pelech (2007) studied the effects of a sweat lodge ceremony, an indigenous ritual aimed at restoring the balance of spiritual, emotional, mental, and physical well-being. They concluded that this ceremony may help people to increase their sense of spirituality and connection to one another. Overall, social workers have long been concerned with developing cultural competence and delivering culturally relevant services. Research in this area is helping us understand the importance of incorporating spirituality into our work with certain cultural groups if we wish to be relevant and effective. As noted in the previous section and by Gilbert et al. (2009), future work in this area needs to build on the foundations that have been established, with the aim of developing consistent, replicable, and effective best practices.

Mindfulness

Mindfulness, a holistic philosophy and practice, deserves attention in this chapter because in the past several years mindfulness-based interventions have gained notice among researchers, helping/health practitioners, and the broader public. Kabat-Zinn (1990) explained that mindfulness meditation practice is an activity that encourages awareness to emerge by paying attention on purpose, in the present, and without passing judgment on the unfolding of experience, moment by moment. It has everything to do with examining who we are, with questioning our view of the world and our place in it, and with cultivating appreciation for the fullness of each of life's moments. According to Weiss (2004), mindfulness is meant to help people see clearly and understand themselves and others better so that they can live a more fulfilling and joyful life. Mindfulness practice is about accessing the present moment, cultivating the intention to attend to what is happening right now, and through that process, seeing things without the distortive lens of judgment, thus separating the self from feelings like acceptance or rejection, and attraction or revulsion (Bercholz & Kohn, 1993).

Mindfulness-based practices have been studied mainly within psychology and medicine, where mindfulness is usually combined with cognitive behavioural therapy (CBT) approaches and methods. Researchers working within these disciplines have demonstrated the effectiveness of mindfulness practices for a variety of people and problems (Grossman, Niemann, Schmidt, & Walach, 2004; Kabat-Zinn, 2003; Sagula & Rice, 2004; Semple, Lee, Rosa, & Miller, 2010; Smith, 2004). Social workers are also beginning to demonstrate increased interest in mindfulness. The first Canadian book written on the topic, *Mindfulness and Social Work*, was published in 2009 (Hick, 2009). Other social workers have discussed mindfulness practice as an intervention that can help social work students develop a professional identity (Birnbaum, 2005), and address feelings of discomfort in the classroom (Wong, 2004). In my research, we found that mindfulness helps improve self-awareness and coping skills such as emotional regulation (Coholic, 2006; Coholic, Eys, & Lougheed, 2011; Coholic, Lougheed, & LeBreton, 2009). Another example is spiritual self-schema therapy, which has been found to be a promising mindfulness-based individual intervention that targets addiction and HIV risk behaviours. It integrates cognitive behavioural strategies with Buddhist principles and clients' religious or spiritual beliefs (Amaro et al., 2010).

While mindfulness-based practice is rooted in a holistic philosophy, it is taught to people with diverse spiritual beliefs, or even a lack thereof (Kabat-Zinn, 1990). Facilitators of mindfulness contend that one does not have to be a Buddhist or a person with spiritual beliefs to learn, practise, and benefit from mindfulness. In fact, for many practitioners and researchers, mindfulness is not connected with any type of spirituality or holistic perspective. However, separating mindfulness from its holistic roots could lead to a diminished opportunity (perhaps even intent), to create a therapeutic space that is flexible, open, creative, and less focused on specific clinical treatment outcomes (Rosch, 2007) because a prescribed mindfulness process/program is facilitated. Within a more flexible and holistic therapeutic space, mindfulness can be facilitated using creative methods that fit clients' needs, goals, and experiences. These creative methods can include both traditional and non-traditional methods of facilitating mindfulness-based practices. Mindfulness within a cognitive behavioural framework is operationally defined, and the processes involved are broken down and measured for specific outcomes. A holistic mindfulness might be more creative, attuned to people's specific needs or goals, and open to discourse that is spiritual or holistic and existential (Gause & Coholic, 2010).

Another topic that is pertinent to this book is how practising mindfulness can help develop the therapeutic relationship to achieve "therapeutic presence" (Hick & Bien, 2008). In a paper that explored how mindfulness meditation can be used to teach new therapists how to develop therapeutic presence, McCollum and Gehart (2010) explained that therapeutic presence is understood as an availability and openness to all aspects of the client's experience; an openness to one's own experience being with the client; and the capacity to respond to the client from this experience. As they stated, some of the more difficult-to-define aspects of the therapeutic process, such as empathy, compassion, and presence, are also some of the most important.

Understanding how to be fully present with another person and to engage in effective ways to form a relationship is akin to what some conceptualize as the "art" of social work practice. Based on my experience and ten years of teaching senior social work undergraduate students, one of the most difficult things for students to learn is therapeutic presence. Instead of attending to the present moment with the client, they are often one step ahead, thinking about what to say next or worried they are going to say something "wrong" or make a mistake. While the ability to develop therapeutic presence and attend fully to the client may improve with experience, we should consider how mindfulness can help us teach this skill, particularly because we know from common factors research that 30% of client change can be attributed to the therapeutic relationship (Hubble, Duncan, & Miller, 1999). Thinking about how mindfulness can help us to be fully present with a client is convergent with Miller's discussion in Chapter 10 regarding "teacher presence." He incorporated contemplative practices and meditation in his courses to help student teachers develop teacher presence, which he described as a critical factor in effective teaching.

This summary about mindfulness is brief due to the limited scope of this chapter. However, the points relevant to my discussion include the fact that mindfulness meditation and other mindfulness-based practices are proving to be effective for a wide variety of problems and client groups, such as addressing anxiety in youth, for example. While this body of work includes mindfulness-based approaches combined with cognitive behavioural techniques, and more holistic forms of mindfulness, the latter approach is more congruent with how social workers have discussed mindfulness to date. However, embracing a more holistic version of mindfulness has not been the dominant model and method researchers have used to study its effectiveness. Given that a more holistic approach to mindfulness has not been thoroughly examined yet, there is much room for social workers and others to consider how to go about conducting studies with various client groups.

Additional Holistic Models and Theories

Social workers usually conduct assessments using a multi-systemic framework. Keeping spirituality in mind, various assessment frameworks, tools and inventories have been developed and evaluated by researchers and practitioners. Nelson-Becker and Canda (2008) provided a framework for spiritual assessment with older adults. They explained that while older adults may benefit from clinical conversations about the role of spirituality in their lives, social workers often lack understanding of how best to proceed beyond initial questions about whether spirituality is important. Gough, Wilks, and Prattini (2010) found that the intrinsic spirituality scale is a valuable tool for assessing spirituality in caregivers of Alzheimer's patients. They evaluated the psychometric properties of this scale with Alzheimer's caregivers, given this group's traditional and frequent use of spirituality as a coping resource. Hodge (2001) conducted research in the area of assessment, and provided us with a model for developing spiritual genograms with clients.

It is also common to come across practice models that are based on a combination of theory, clinical expertise, and practice wisdom. A number of holistic practice models have been proposed. For one example, Bliss (2009) used transpersonal theory as a conceptual framework to present a spiritual etiological model of alcoholism that includes the biological determinants of the disease. In part because of the religious and spiritual influence of Alcoholics Anonymous programs within the addiction treatment field, it is not at all unusual to find discussions exploring the issue of spirituality with clients who suffer from substance abuse problems (Stewart, 2008). Other examples include Jacinto, Turnage, and Cook's (2010) model, a spirituality and social support group for domestic violence survivors, and Hodge and Bonifas's (2010) model of spiritually modified cognitive behavioural therapy.

Holistic theories that encompass spirituality have also been explored and put forth as new directions for social work practice. One example is contemplative theory and practice, which is, among other things, concerned with the psycho-spiritual development of both the client and the worker, and meets the need for a spiritual component in social work practice (Sherman & Siporin, 2008). While this theory has yet to be recognized within social work, it includes a focus on mindfulness meditation as a viable method for social work that could be used with individuals, families, and groups. Transpersonal theory, which has been evident within psychology since the 1960s, has been considered by various social workers, although on the whole it has not received much attention across the profession. As outlined by Braud and Anderson (1998), transpersonal theorists are concerned with honouring human experience in its fullest and most transformative expressions. Transpersonal psychology seeks to delve deeply into profound human experiences such as personal transformation, experiences of wonder and ecstasy, and expansive states of consciousness, where people can move beyond the usual identification with their limited biological and psychological selves—beyond the limits of ego and personality. Both of these theories could offer social work a theoretical base from which to develop appropriate approaches for practice. In general, while the development and presentation of practice models can be useful and can certainly influence practice directions and emphases, at some point the effectiveness of the models and theories should be explored, particularly if we want these approaches to be more widely and positively accepted for clinical use with clients.

Finally, I note that within social work there are specialized areas of practice that are particularly amenable to the incorporation of spirituality. Palliative and hospice care is an example of a specialized area of practice within which social workers are situated. In this area, social workers incorporate spirituality—the spiritual aspects of death and dying—as an important part of their practice across different cultures (Bosma, Apland, & Kazanjian, 2010), and the lifespan (Jones & Weisenflu, 2003). In fact, it is not hard to imagine why the matter of death raises questions and existential concerns or issues regarding beliefs about life after death, the nature of life, and so forth, and so it is relevant to assess for, and support, a client's spiritual viewpoints (Furman, 2007).

However, as Yardley, Walshe, and Parr (2009) pointed out, even though spiritual care is a core component of palliative care national policies in the United Kingdom, some health care professionals express difficulties in delivering it. They examined patients' perspectives, which included the expectation that there would be opportunities to engage in spiritual care discussions. These authors reiterate the lack of training in spiritually sensitive methods and processes for social workers. Clearly there is a need for education and training in spiritually sensitive social work approaches across the profession, particularly for practitioners who will be expected to address these issues with their clients. Perhaps we are getting closer as a profession to being able to offer this to students and professionals, given the developments I have discussed in this chapter.

Conclusion

One thing is clear for current and future researchers entering this field: we have enough of a foundation for future research to expand both in detail and depth. Theories and methodologies for inquiry can also be refined (Nelson-Becker & Canda, 2008). The more we focus our energies on producing effective practice models and methods that can be replicated and taken up by others, the faster we will gain a wider acceptance for these holistic frameworks and influence the development of practice knowledge toward effective and relevant services for clients. As a field, we are well poised for this next phase of development, given that social work can demonstrate broad agreement concerning definitions for spirituality and religion, rationales for incorporating spirituality into our work, and a solid base of knowledge that is demonstrating the effectiveness and benefits of spiritual models and approaches.

References

Amaro, H., Magno-Gatmaytan, C., Melendez, M., Cortes, D., Arevalo, S., & Margolin, A. (2010). Addiction treatment intervention: An uncontrolled prospective pilot study of spiritual self-schema therapy with latina women. *Substance Abuse, 31*(2), 117–125.

Amato-von Hemert, K. (1994). Should social work education address religious issues? Yes! *Journal of Social Work Education, 30*(1), 7–11.

Antle, B., & Lott Collins, W. (2009). The impact of a spirituality-based support group on self-efficacy and well-being of African-American breast cancer survivors: A mixed methods design. *Social Work & Christianity, 36*(3), 286–300.

Banerjee, M., & Canda, E. (2009). Spirituality as a strength of African-American women affected by welfare reform. *Journal of Religion & Spirituality in Social Work: Social Thought, 28*(3), 239–262.

Bates, M. (2006). A critically reflective approach to evidence-based practice. *Canadian Social Work Review, 23*(1–2), 95–109.

Bellamy, C., Jarrett, N., Mowbray, O., MacFarlane, P., Mowbray, C., & Holter, M. (2007). Relevance of spirituality for people with mental illness attending consumer-centered services. *Psychiatric Rehabilitation Journal, 30*(4), 287–294.

Bercholz, S., & Kohn, S. (Eds.). (1993). *The Buddha and his teachings*. Boston, MA: Shambhala.

Birnbaum, L. (2005). Connecting to inner guidance: Mindfulness meditation and transformation of professional self-concept in social work students. *Critical Social Work, 6*(2). Retrieved from http://www.uwindsor.ca/criticalsocialwork/ connecting-to-inner-guidance-mindfulness-meditation-and-transformation-of -professional-self-concept-

Bliss, D. L. (2009). Beyond the disease model: Reframing the etiology of alcoholism from a spiritual perpsective. *Journal of Teaching in the Addictions, 8*(1–2), 10–26.

Bosma, H., Apland, L., & Kazanjian, A. (2010). Cultural conceptualizations of hospice palliative care: More similarities than differences. *Palliative Medicine, 24*(5), 510–522.

Braud, W., & Anderson, R. (Eds.). (1998). *Transpersonal research methods for the social sciences: Honouring human experience.* London, UK: Sage.

Canda, E., Nakashima, M., & Furman, L. (2004). Ethical consideration about spirituality in social work: Insights from a national qualitative survey. *Families in Society, 85*(1), 27–35.

Carlson, B., & Larkin, H. (2009). Meditation as a coping intervention for treatment of addiction. *Journal of Religion & Spirituality in Social Work: Social Thought, 28*(4), 379–392.

Cheon, J. W., & Canda, E. (2010). The meaning and engagement of spirituality for positive youth development in social work. *Families in Society, 91*(2), 121–126.

Clark, J. (1994). Should social work education address religious issues? No! *Journal of Social Work Education, 30*(1), 12-16.

Clark, P. (1999). To treat or not to treat: The ethical dilemma of alternative medicine therapies. *AIDS and Public Policy Journal, 14*(3), 117–131.

Clarke, N. (1996). After social work? In N. Parton (Ed.), *Social theory, social change, and social work* (pp. 36–60). New York, NY: Routledge.

Coholic, D. (2003). Student and educator viewpoints on incorporating spirituality in social work pedagogy—an overview and discussion of research findings. *Currents: New Scholarship in the Human Services, 2*(2). Retrieved from http://wcmprod2 .ucalgary.ca/currents/files/currents/v2n2_coholic.pdf

Coholic, D. (2006). Mindfulness meditation practice in spirituality influenced group work. *Arete, 30*(1), 90–100.

Coholic, D. (2010). *Arts activities for children and young people in need: Helping children to develop mindfulness, spiritual awareness and self-esteem.* London, UK: Jessica Kingsley.

Coholic, D. (2011a). Exploring how young people living in foster care discuss spiritually-sensitive themes in a holistic arts-based group program. *Journal of Religion, Spirituality and Social Work: Social Thought, 30*(3), 193–211.

Coholic, D. (2011b). Exploring the feasibility and benefits of arts-based, mindfulness-based practices with young people in need: Aiming to improve aspects of self-awareness and resilience. *Child and Youth Care Forum, 40*(4), 303–317.

Coholic, D., Eys, M., & Lougheed, S. (2011). Investigating the effectiveness of an arts-based and mindfulness-based group program for the improvement of resilience in children in need. *Journal of Child and Family Studies.* doi: 10.1007/s10826-011-9544-2

Coholic, D., Lougheed, S., & Cadell, S. (2009). Exploring the helpfulness of arts-based methods with children living in foster care. *Traumatology, 15*(3), 64–71.

Coholic, D., Lougheed, S., & LeBreton, J. (2009). The helpfulness of holistic arts-based group work with children living in foster care. *Social Work with Groups, 32*(1), 29–46.

Farley, Y. (2007). Making the connection: Spirituality, trauma and resiliency. *Journal of Religion & Spirituality in Social Work: Social Thought, 26*(1), 1–15.

Furman, L. (2007). Grief is a brutal but empowering teacher: A social worker's reflections on the importance of spiritual assessment and support during the bereavement process. *Illness, Crisis & Loss, 15*(2), 99–112.

Gambrill, E. (2006). Evidence-based practice: Choices ahead. *Research on Social Work Practice, 16*(3), 338–357.

Gause, R., & Coholic, D. (2010). Mindfulness-based practices as a holistic philosophy and method. *Currents: New Scholarship in the Human Services, 9*(2). Retrieved from http://currents.synergiesprairies.ca/currents/index.php/currents/article/view/42

Gilbert, D., Harvey, A., & Belgrave, F. (2009). Advancing the Africentric paradigm shift discourse: Building toward evidence-based Africentric interventions in social work practice with African Americans. *Social Work, 54*(3), 243–252.

Gockel, A. (2009). Spirituality and the process of healing: A narrative study. *International Journal for the Psychology of Religion, 19*, 217–230.

Gough, H., Wilks, S., & Prattini, R. (2010). Spirituality among Alzheimer's caregivers: Psychometric reevaluation of the intrinsic spirituality scale. *Journal of Social Service Research, 36*(4), 278–288.

Graham, J., Bradshaw, C., & Trew, J. (2009). Adapting social work in working with Muslim clients. *Social Work Education, 28*(5), 544–561.

Graham, J., Coholic, D., & Coates, J. (2006). Spirituality as a guiding construct in the development of Canadian social work: Past and present considerations. *Critical Social Work, 7*(1). Retrieved from http://www.uwindsor.ca/criticalsocialwork/spirituality-as-a-guiding-construct-in-the-development-of-canadian-social-work-past-and-present-cons

Grossman, P., Niemann, L., Schmidt, S., & Walach, H. (2004). Mindfulness-based stress reduction and health benefits: A meta-analysis. *Journal of Psychosomatic Research, 57*(1), 35–44.

Guadalupe, K., & Lum, D. (2005). *Multidimensional contextual practice.* Belmont, CA: Brooks/Cole.

Harris-Robinson, M. (2006). The use of spiritual-focused coping among working-class black women. *Journal of Religion & Spirituality in Social Work: Social Thought, 25*(2), 77–90.

Hick, S. (Ed.). (2009). *Mindfulness and social work.* Chicago, IL: Lyceum Books.

Hick, S., & Bien, T. (Eds.). (2008). *Mindfulness and the therapeutic relationship.* New York, NY: Guilford Press.

Hodge, D. (2001). Spiritual genograms: A generational approach to assessing spirituality. *Families in Society, 82*(1), 35.

Hodge, D., & Bonifas, R. (2010). Using spiritually modified cognitive behavioral therapy to help clients wrestling with depression: A promising intervention for some older adults. *Journal of Religion & Spirituality in Social Work: Social Thought, 29*(3), 185–206.

Hodge, D., & Limb, G. (2010). A Native American perspective on spiritual assessment: The strengths and limitations of a complementary set of assessment tools. *Health & Social Work, 35*(2), 121–131.

Hodge, D., & Roby, J. (2010). Sub-Saharan African women living with HIV/AIDS: An exploration of general and spiritual coping strategies. *Social Work, 55*(1), 27–37.

Hubble, M., Duncan, B., & Miller, S. (Eds.). (1999). *The heart & soul of change—What works in therapy.* Washington, DC: American Psychological Association.

Jacinto, G., Turnage, B., & Cook, I. (2010). Domestic violence survivors: Spirituality and social support. *Journal of Religion & Spirituality in Social Work: Social Thought, 29*(2), 109–123.

Jackson, L., Roller White, C., O'Brien, K., DiLorenzo, P., Cathcart, E., Wolf, M., et al. (2010). Exploring spirituality among youth in foster care: Findings from the Casey field office mental health study. *Child and Family Social Work, 15*, 107–117.

Jones, B., & Weisenflu, S. (2003). Pediatric palliative and end-of-life care: Developmental and spiritual issues of dying children. *Smith College Studies in Social Work 73*(3), 423–443.

Ka'opua, L., Gotay, C., & Boehm, P. (2007). Spiritually based resources in adaptation to long-term prostate cancer survival: Perspectives of elderly wives. *Health & Social Work, 32*(1), 29–39.

Kabat-Zinn, J. (1990). *Full catastrophe living: Using the wisdom of your body and mind to face stress, pain and illness.* New York, NY: Bantam-Dell.

Kabat-Zinn, J. (2003). Mindfulness-based interventions in context: Past, present, and future. *Clinical Psychology: Science and Practice, 10*(2), 144–156.

Kvarfordt, C., & Sheridan, M. (2009). Understanding the pathways of factors influencing the use of spiritually based interventions. *Journal of Social Work Education, 45*(3), 385–405.

Layer, S. D., Roberts, C., Wild, K., & Walters, J. (2004). Post-abortion grief: Evaluating the possible efficacy of a spiritual group intervention. *Research on Social Work Practice, 14*(5), 344–350.

Lee, E.-K. O., & Chan, K. (2009). Religious/spiritual and other adaptive coping strategies among Chinese American older immigrants. *Journal of Gerontological Social Work, 52*(5), 517–533.

Leung, P., Chan, C., Ng, S., & Lee, M. (2009). Towards body-mind-spirit integration: East meets West in clinical social work practice. *Clinical Social Work Journal, 37*(4), 303–311.

Li-ju, J., & Jieh-jiuh, W. (2009). Disaster resilience in a Hakka community in Taiwan. *Journal of Pacific Rim Psychology, 3*(2), 55–65.

McCollum, E., & Gehart, D. (2010). Using mindfulness meditation to teach beginning therapists therapeutic presence: A qualitative study. *Journal of Marital and Family Therapy, 36*(3), 347–360.

McNeill, T. (2006). Evidence-based practice in an age of relativism: Toward a model for practice. *Social Work, 51*(2), 147–156.

Moberg, D. (2005). Research in spirituality, religion, and aging. *Journal of Gerontological Social Work, 45*(1/2), 11–40.

Nelson-Becker, H., & Canda, E. (2008). Spirituality, religion, and aging research in social work: State of the art and future possibilities. *Journal of Religion, Spirituality & Aging, 20*(3), 177–193.

Payne, M. (2005). *Modern social work theory* (3rd Ed.). Chicago, IL: Lyceum.

Plath, D. (2006). Evidence-based practice: Current issues and future directions. *Australian Social Work, 59*(1), 56–72.

Redfield, J. (1994). *The Celestine prophecy.* New York, NY: Bantam.

Rice, S., & McAuliffe, D. (2009). Ethics of the spirit: Comparing ethical views and usages of spiritually influenced interventions. *Australian Social Work, 62*(3), 403–420.

Richards, P., Berrett, M., Hardman, R., & Eggett, D. (2006). Comparative efficacy of spirituality, cognitive, and emotional support groups for treating eating disorder inpatients. *Eating Disorders, 14*, 401–415.

Roff, L., Simon, C., Nelson-Gardell, D., & Pleasants, H. (2009). Spiritual support and African American breast cancer survivors. *Affilia: Journal of Women & Social Work, 24*(3), 285–299.

Rosch, E. (2007). More than mindfulness: When you have a tiger by the tail, let it eat you. *Psychological Inquiry, 18*(4), 258–264.

Sagula, D., & Rice, K. G. (2004). The effectiveness of mindfulness training on the grieving process and emotional well-being of chronic pain patients. *Journal of Clinical Psychology in Medical Settings, 11*(4), 333–343.

Schiff, J., & Pelech, W. (2007). The sweat lodge ceremony for spiritual healing. *Journal of Religion & Spirituality in Social Work: Social Thought, 26*(4), 71–93.

Semple, R., Lee, J., Rosa, D., & Miller, L. (2010). A randomized trial of mindfulness-based cognitive therapy for children: Promoting mindful attention to enhance social-emotional resiliency in children. *Journal of Child and Family Studies, 19*, 218–229.

Sheridan, M. (2009). Ethical issues in the use of spiritually based interventions in social work practice: What are we doing, and why? *Journal of Religion & Spirituality in Social Work: Social Thought, 28*, 99–126.

Sherman, E., & Siporin, M. (2008). Contemplative theory and practice for social work. *Journal of Religion & Spirituality in Social Work: Social Thought, 27*(3), 259–274.

Smith, A. (2004). Clinical uses of mindfulness training for older people. *Behavioral and Cognitive Psychotherapy, 32*, 423–430.

Sossou, M., Craig, C., Ogren, H., & Schnak, M. (2008). Qualitative study of resilience factors of Bosnian refugee women resettled in the Southern United States. *Journal of Ethnic & Cultural Diversity in Social Work, 17*(4), 365–385.

Stewart, C. (2008). Client spirituality and substance abuse treatment outcomes. *Journal of Religion & Spirituality in Social Work: Social Thought, 27*(4), 385–404.

Sullivan, P. (2009). Spirituality: A road to mental health or mental illness. *Journal of Religion & Spirituality in Social Work: Social Thought, 28*(1/2), 84–98.

Taylor, B. J., Dempster, M., & Donnelly, M. (2007). Grading gems: Appraising the quality of research for social work and social care. *British Journal of Social Work, 37*(2), 335–354.

Thomas, C., & Cohen, H. (2006). Understanding spiritual meaning-making with older adults. *The Journal of Theory Construction & Testing, 10*(2), 65–70.

Washington, G., & Teague, K. (2005). Young African-American male suicide prevention and spirituality. *Stress, Trauma & Crisis: An International Journal, 8*(2/3), 93–105.

Weiss, A. (2004). *Beginning mindfulness: Learning the way of awareness.* Novato, CA: New World Library.

Witkin, S., & Harrison, D. (2001). Whose evidence and for what purpose? *Social Work, 46*(4), 293–296.

Wong, Y.-L. R. (2004). Knowing through discomfort: A mindfulness-based critical social work pedagogy. *Critical Social Work, 5*(1). Retrieved from http://www.uwindsor.ca/criticalsocialwork/knowing-through-discomfort-a-mindfulness-based-critical-social-work-pedagogy

Yardley, S. J., Walshe, C. E., & Parr, A. (2009). Improving training in spiritual care: A qualitative study exploring patient perceptions of professional educational requirements. *Palliative Medicine, 23*, 601–607.

Zayas, L., Gonzalez, M., & Hanson, M. (2003). What do I do now? On teaching evidence-based interventions in social work practice. *Journal of Teaching in Social Work, 23*(3/4), 59–72.

Chapter 10

Contemplative Practices in Teacher Education: What I Have Learned

John P. Miller

In 1988, I started including a meditation component in my graduate education classes. I teach courses in holistic education and spirituality in education at the Ontario Institute for Studies in Education (OISE) at the University of Toronto. In this chapter, I reflect upon what I have learned from working with contemplative practices for over twenty years.

Rationale

I believe it is important for the reader to know a little about my own practice, and more importantly, my rationale for including contemplative practices in my classes. My own practice is *vipassana*, or insight meditation, which comes from the Buddhist tradition in Southeast Asia. It focuses on developing awareness and being present in the moment. I started this daily practice in 1974, and my first teacher was Joseph Goldstein (1975), via tape recordings. Although this is my core practice, I have also done mantra and occasionally do image work.

My reasons for introducing meditation in my classes includes several points. Most of my students are teachers who are taking graduate courses in education, so my rationale focuses on teacher development. Perhaps most important is the concept of teacher presence. Teaching, in my view, involves three basic factors. First is the theory or assumptions underlying our approach. The underlying assumptions and theories have been referred to as orientations (Eisner & Vallance, 1974; Miller, 1983). Second are the teaching strategies and practices that we employ in the classroom. Also included here are the evaluation methods used to assess student development. The third factor is the presence of the teacher. It is this last factor which is so critical. If we recall the teachers who have had an impact on us, it is not usually the material they taught that we remember, but that elusive quality of presence which somehow touched us.

The Zen Roshi Shunryu Suzuki tells a wonderful story about the presence of a teacher (Chadwick, 1999). He was head of a temple in Japan, and was looking for a kindergarten teacher for the temple school. He repeatedly tried to convince one woman to take the job, but she refused. Finally he said to her, "You don't have to do anything, just stand there." When he said that, she accepted the position. He was convinced that her presence alone would make a difference in the lives of the children. Of course she did not just stand in the classroom, but Suzuki-roshi identified this important element in teaching. Emerson (1966), in talking to teachers also emphasized the importance of presence in teaching:

> By your own act, you teach the beholder how to do the practicable. According to the depth from which you draw your life, such is the depth not only of your strenuous effort, but of your manners and presence. The beautiful nature of the world has here blended your happiness with your power. (p. 227)

Teacher presence is often ignored in teacher education, as the focus tends to be on theory and teaching strategies; yet it is critically important, particularly in holistic education.

Presence and being in the moment means that there is less chance that we will be teaching from our egos. If teaching is ego-based, it can become a frustrating series of mini-battles with students. The classroom becomes focused around the issue of control. If we teach from that place where we are present and attentive, teaching can become a more fulfilling and enriching experience. Griffin (1977) summarizes this very well,

> You do not feel set off against them [the students] or competitive with them. You see yourself in students and them in you. You move easily, are more relaxed, and seem less threatening to students. You are less compulsive, less rigid in your thoughts and actions. You are not so tense. You do not seem to be in a grim win-or-lose contest when teaching. (p. 79)

Another important reason is that contemplation is a form of self-learning. Through the process of contemplation, one learns to trust one's own deep, intuitive responses. For example, insight meditation is based on the notion that we can learn and grow by simply mindfully watching our own experience. As we notice our own thoughts and agendas, we can gain deeper insight into ourselves and the nature of experience. In contrast, the model for most learning at the university level is that the professor and the text are the sources of learning, and the student must learn from these external authorities. Contemplation provides one alternative to this model, and instead recognizes that we can learn from our own direct experience.

A final reason for engaging in contemplation is that it allows teachers to deal with the stresses in their lives. Teaching can be a very stressful profession. Research indicates that meditation is an effective tool in the relaxation process

(Murphy & Donovan, 1997; Walsh, 1999) and given the pressures that teachers face today, this aspect of contemplation should not be overlooked. The vast majority of students in my classes have seen the positive effects of contemplative practice, having fewer headaches and simply being better equipped to address stressful events that come up in their lives and in the classroom. One of my students was a secondary school vice-principal who faced many stressful events during the day. He wrote in his journal that as the pressures of his job increased, he found that he needed to engage in meditation more frequently. Teachers who meditated also found that they were less reactive in the classroom.

The Process

In two of my graduate courses and one initial teacher education course, I require students to meditate daily for six weeks. In another course, doing so is an option. In the graduate courses where it is required, I introduce the practice in the third week of classes. I first offer a definition of meditation, which is the development of compassionate attention, and I offer the rationale for doing meditation, which I described in the previous section.

I then introduce them to seven different types of meditation. We spend approximately two minutes doing each one. I suggest that they choose one to work with for the next six weeks. In brief, these include,

- *Observing the breath.* The student observes the breath, focusing on either the nostrils or the rising and falling of the belly.
- *Counting the breath.* The student counts each breath when she exhales beginning with one and going to number four. In both these breath exercises, I note that the student should not try to control the process but breathe naturally.
- *Mantra.* A sound or phrase is repeated silently.
- *Visualization.* The student visualizes a series of images, usually from an experience in nature.
- *Walking.* This practice focuses the awareness of the foot leaving and touching the ground.
- *Contemplation.* The student selects a short passage of poetry or inspirational text and repeats it silently.
- *Lovingkindness.* Thoughts of well-being are sent first to ourselves and then to others.

Students are asked to start meditating five to ten minutes a day, and over the course of the six weeks, gradually work up to twenty or thirty minutes. They keep a daily journal describing how the process is going, and are asked to report on what their bodies experience and what was prominent during the meditation (e.g., thoughts, sounds, etc.). The quotations cited in this chapter come from the journals that students submitted to me, and were used with their permission. Here is one example of a daily entry:

Aug 2nd Observing the breath
Profoundly noticeable a number of times during this session was the wave of relaxation moving through my legs from top to bottom. I could feel the tension leaving the body, flowing out through the tips of my toes. Other thoughts came and went as I attempted to return to the breathing, and the awareness of my chest moving up and down. My hands melted into my knees. I felt rejuvenated and ready for the rest of the evening.

I encourage students also to submit questions to me in their journals if any issues arise during their practice. At the end of the six weeks, they write a one- or two-page summary reflection on their practice. Here are the reflections of one woman that also includes how she brought her practice into her teaching:

Through daily meditation, I have been able to take some time for myself in order to relax, regain a sense of who I am and my physical needs. I have taken the opportunity to meditate daily for the past six weeks (and counting) in order to take into consideration the simple things that I can do for myself to help myself feel better, such as breathing properly and taking time to really enjoy little things that I experience, as opposed to moving on to the next thing without appreciating what I've just seen or felt.

I found that the energy that was generated from my meditative experience stayed with me for much of the day. I have felt great over these past couple of months and have attributed much of that to the feeling of comfort with myself and a positive outlook on things. I really have felt that meditation has had an impact on my relationships with others. My attention seemed more focused at work and in my personal life following meditation.

The relationship that I have had with my class has been a close one, yet I feel that our class meditations have brought many of us much closer. My students write journal entries about finding their "star" and going to their "garden" as they meditate on their own at home (often at bedtime as they begin their dreams!). One seven-year-old student's reflection that really stands out to me is that: "meditation makes me feel kind of in between" not happy or sad, "just calm." This, with the added energy and an overall sense of satisfaction with life, seemed to sum it up for me, too.

Some of themes that run through the journals include:

- Giving permission to be alone and enjoy their own company;
- Increased listening capacities;
- Feeling increased energy;

- Being less reactive to situations and generally experiencing greater calm and clarity. (Miller, 1994)

There are two other elements that I include in my classes. I begin each class with the lovingkindness meditation. The phrases I use are,

> May I be well, happy, and peaceful.
> May my family be well, happy, and peaceful.
> May my friends be well, happy, and peaceful.
> May my neighbours be well, happy, and peaceful.
> May my colleagues be well, happy, and peaceful.
> May all people that I meet be well, happy, and peaceful.
> May all people who may have injured me by deed, speech, or thought be well, happy, and peaceful.
> May all beings on this planet be well, happy, and peaceful.
> May all beings in this universe be well, happy, and peaceful.

Another way of doing this is to move out geographically rather than emotionally, first sending thoughts of well-being to ourselves, then to those in the room, the building, the neighbourhood, the town, the region, the continent, and the world.

The third element that I include is introducing the students to mindfulness practice in daily life. This means being attentive and present to activities during the day. I encourage them to start with one daily activity (e.g., doing the dishes, preparing a meal, brushing their teeth) and to do it without thinking about something else. Beginning with simple daily tasks can build a foundation of mindfulness that can eventually extend to the classroom, so that teachers can be more present for their students. One former student describes mindfulness experiences:

> I find these little moments kind of funny when they happen, because all of a sudden I become very aware that I'm washing the dishes or vacuuming.... And I kind of get into the moment, and it stays with me during the day.

The students in my graduate classes are mostly teachers working in public or Catholic schools. About 70 to 80% are women, and ages range from the mid-twenties to fifties.

Toronto has been identified as one of the most multicultural cities in the world, and my classes reflect that diversity. Students from Brazil, China, Indonesia, Iran, Italy, Jamaica, Lebanon, Japan, Kenya, Korea, Malta, Serbia, Tibet, and Vietnam have been in my classes. The average class size is around twenty-four students. To date, approximately two thousand students have been introduced to meditation practice in these courses. Only two students have asked not to do the assignment, as one student had been sexually abused a year before and did not feel comfortable with the practice. The other was a Christian fundamentalist. So far there has not been a student who has reported an overall negative experience with the practice during the course.

Research

A few years ago together with my graduate assistant, I conducted a follow-up with people who had done the meditation in one of the courses mentioned above (Miller & Nozawa, 2002). The study focused on four questions:

1 What is the nature of your meditation practice? (e.g., type and frequency)
2 Have you engaged in any meditation instruction since the class?
3 What have been the effects of your practice on your personal and professional life?
4 Have you experienced any difficulties or problems with the practice?

Letters were sent out to 182 former students asking if they would be interested in participating in an interview related to the questions above. Because the study involved an interview, it was limited to former students living in the Toronto area. From this group, forty letters were returned because many students had moved. In the end, 21 former students (17 women and 4 men) agreed to participate. Of the 21, 11 were teachers at the elementary or secondary level, 4 were teaching at the post-secondary level, 4 were administrators, and 2 were consultants.

The participants were interviewed by my graduate assistant, with the interviews lasting between thirty and ninety minutes. To triangulate the data, we collected the following material:

1 meditation journals from the course
2 summary reflections on the meditation submitted as part of the course
3 the interviewer's reflections on the interviews

Effects of Meditation Practice

All the participants except one commented on the positive effects meditation practice provided for their personal and professional lives.

Personal Effects. The majority of participants, thirteen (or 62%), commented on how meditation had helped them become calmer and more relaxed. One female nursing instructor commented, "I'm not as agitated … or I'm not as arousable from the point of view that things don't bother me as much.… I feel calmer, I feel more … this word 'centred' keeps coming to mind."[1]

Another main effect noted by five participants was that they felt the meditation softened them or made them more gentle. One woman who worked as a principal stated, "It made a difference in softening me in my home, in my personal life in terms of working through the process with my husband and, you know, how do you solve this?"

Finally, five participants felt that meditation helped them with personal relationships. One female administrator commented, "It affects all your relationships. They're better. They're deeper." A male consultant found that people now come to him for help: "Well, a lot of my friends, they phone me for advice. I'm sort of like their counsellor, because once you get into that whole realm of awareness and meditation and looking at things in perspective ... "

Professional Effects. Again, more than half of the participants commented on how meditation helped them to be calmer in the workplace. One principal commented that calmness is important to the whole process of change, "And to get any kind of change happening in schools, it's imperative that people are calm and are in an almost meditative state in order to make those changes that are being demanded." This principal now runs meetings that don't have an agenda: "We're just here to talk about the work that we're doing, and enjoy each other." She adds that this is "not team building, it's just kind of being together, it doesn't have a name."

A related effect the participants mentioned is that they are not as reactive, and are able to take a step back from troublesome situations. As a female teacher noted,

> You can get really frustrated with these kids, because [they] get really angry and frustrated because they can't read, and your first response is to be an authoritarian, when actuality they just need to be hugged and loved. So it [the meditation] really helps me to step back and look at what really is going on.

Another teacher simply said, "I don't remember the last time I raised my voice." She added that one of her students asked, "Miss, how come you're so calm all the time?"

A large amount of data supporting the effectiveness of meditation has been collected (Walsh, 1999). These benefits include physical ones, such as lowering blood pressure and cholesterol levels (Murphy & Donovan, 1997). Participants in mindfulness-based stress reduction programs have also shown improvements in physical and mental health measures (Lazar et al., 2003). Recent research has focused on meditation's effects on the brain; one study showed structural changes in the brain as a result of meditation associated with improvements in mental health (Holzel et al., 2011). Studies have also found that meditation can increase creativity, academic achievement, and the development of interpersonal relationships (Alexander, Rainforth, & Gelderloos, 1991; Murphy & Donovan, 1997). Our study was congruent with this general research literature. The major finding of our study was that when meditation is introduced in an academic setting, it can have positive long-term effects on both the personal and professional lives of educators. Most of the participants felt that meditation helped them become calmer and more grounded in their life and work.

What I Learned Regarding the Process of Teaching Meditation

Contemplative Practices Can Be Integrated into the Higher Education Curriculum

My experience of introducing contemplative practices to students has been a very positive one. In over twenty years I have never had a complaint from a student or administrator about asking students to engage in contemplative practice. In fact, my evening and summer classes are always full with a waiting list. The first day of class, I make it very clear that contemplative practices will be an integral part of the course. As I have already mentioned, only one student out of two thousand had concerns about meditation due to her religious background.

My Personal Practice Does Not Have to Be Compartmentalized and Kept Separate from My Professional Work

The line between personal and professional can be a fine one. I have found that I can share my own practice in a manner that supports students' development. As I have stated before, a clear rationale for doing this must be provided, particularly with reference to teacher education and teacher development. I also find that it is helpful if I share an explanation of why I have engaged in contemplative practices, so that students see the context of the practice in my own life (Miller, 2008).

Student Ownership of the Practice

I introduce several different types of practice so students can find one that will work for them. As much as possible, I try to make them feel ownership of the practice, so some students have modified their practice. For example, one student who swam every day brought mindful awareness to his swimming. Another student had been on vacation during the term, and found that sitting on the hotel room balcony and listening to the waves was contemplative. When she returned home, she imagined sitting on the balcony and listening to the waves. Students also monitor the length of time that they meditate. If they find the practice very challenging, then I suggest doing it for just five to ten minutes, while other students are more comfortable doing twenty or thirty minutes. If a student is already engaged in a sustained practice, I suggest that they just continue with that practice and not switch to one that I introduce.

Having Modest Expectations from the Practice

Some students have unreasonable expectations about meditation practice and what it will do for them. I suggest to them to adopt an approach of inquiry; in other words, try the practice and just keep an open mind about what happens. Treat each session as a unique experience. If the previous session was one where the student felt calm and relaxed, do not carry that expectation to the next session. In fact, each moment of practice should be perceived with here-and-now awareness.

Forget about Doing It "Right"

Probably the most common concern that beginning students have is: "Am I doing it right?" Because contemplative practice is so foreign to our produce-and-consume culture, students need to let go of judging their practice. The main focus is on simply settling down and developing awareness. We live in such a performance-oriented culture that students want to know how they are doing. Here is an example of how one student worried about getting it right:

> Looking back at my journal, I remember being plagued by the rush of thoughts that seemed to pour into the void in my mind when I meditated. I felt like I couldn't control or stop what was happening to me. Then panic hit: was I doing "it" right?

Eventually, this student shifted her approach.

> In the end, I thought I could take one of two paths—give up meditation or stop worrying about doing meditation the right way and just enjoy the half hour that I gave myself as a gift. At this point, I no longer felt the need to control thoughts, just to experience them and be mindful of their presence. Meditation was no longer a struggle or fight for control, but a chance to reflect and be calm.

Another student had an insight that allowed her to let go of trying to get it "right": "There were a few frustrating days at this point when I felt like giving up—I was not getting anywhere. But then I decided there was nowhere to get to, no place I had to be!"

In our daily lives, we are constantly planning something, doing it, and then evaluating what we have done. I suggest to students that in meditation we give up these activities, and as much possible, just be.

Let Go of the Story

Suzuki Roshi told his students to "welcome the thoughts, but just do not serve them tea." Story and narrative have a place in our lives, but not in meditation.

As much as possible, I encourage students to not engage the stories that come up during the practice and return to the focus (e.g., breath, mantra, and so on). This is a challenge for even the most experienced meditator, so when we do engage the story, I suggest letting go of the judgment.

Celebrate the Awareness

A session may be filled with our stories and concerns, but usually there are moments of awareness. One helpful approach is to celebrate the moment of awareness when it does arise. Instead of condemning ourselves for being lost in the thoughts, we can rejoice at the moments of awareness, no matter how brief or fleeting.

Connect to the Body

For many students, the practice allowed them to reconnect with their bodies. In our culture, and particularly in education, we tend to live in our heads. Many students began to connect more directly to the physical experience of the body. One student put it this way: "During the meditation, you have no choice but to listen to your body. It enables you to not only become in touch with our thoughts and emotions, but also to realize that everything is connected to your physical body."

What I Learned about the Relationship between Meditation and Teaching

Patience

We live in a society where we constantly witness impatience. Consider the roadways that are filled with impatient drivers, and the exasperated individuals we see waiting in lineups at the grocery store. We see impatience in our children, who are used to watching television shows and videos that are geared toward short attention spans.

As teachers, we need to cultivate patience. Children learn at different rates and in different ways. Some students can test our patience because they seem to learn slowly, while other students' behaviour in the classroom can challenge our patience. However, if we are patient and not reactive, learning and behaviour can change. Every teacher has had the experience of a student's behaviour irritating us, but if we do not react in a negative way, there can be positive change. Once I had a male student who seemed frustrated and unhappy; yet when I told his class that I would not be teaching next year because of administrative commitments, he stated that he was upset because he could not take my course in the fall. I did not react to his problematic behaviour, and found that patience rather than reactivity worked.

Meditation and mindfulness cultivate patience. Sitting quietly for twenty or thirty minutes, we learn to sit with a range of emotions and thoughts without trying to change them. People say that meditation is boring, but learning to sit with and watch the boredom cultivates patience that can be transferred into teaching.

One of my students in the Initial Teacher Education course identified patience as an outcome of the meditation practice and its place in his life and teaching.

> Patience. My fuse used to be pretty short, but now I have a lot more patience and I deal with things that come up in a different way. I'm no longer angry when a bunch of people crowd into the elevator and press every floor below mine. Now, I simply enjoy the ride. Patience has also helped me a great deal relating to the students in my classroom.

The Importance of Attention

> A student of Zen purchased a spiritual text. Bringing it to the monastery, the student asked if the teacher would write some words of inspiration in it.
>
> "Certainly," replied the teacher, who wrote for a second, then handed the book back. There the student found only a single word: "Attention!"
>
> "Will you not write more?" pleaded the disappointed student, again offering the book to the teacher.
>
> "All right," said the teacher, who this time wrote for several seconds. Inside the book the student now found three words:
>
> Attention! Attention! Attention! (cited in Walsh, p. 150)

McLeod (2002) identifies three stages for the development of attention. The first stage is formal practice, which includes meditation. Meditation practice almost always starts with focusing the attention on some object such as the breath, a sound, or an image. The next stage is extending attention into daily life, usually starting with simple activities such as walking, washing the dishes, and folding the laundry. This application of attention to tasks in daily life is also called mindfulness. The third and final stage that McLeod describes is "living in attention." Here, attention is no longer just a practice but an ongoing reality in our everyday lives. It is something that then can arise naturally in our life and work and is often the outcome of many years of meditation and mindfulness practice.

Sustained practice, then, can help teachers be more attentive to their students, and hopefully this becomes an ongoing reality in the classroom. Some of the teachers in my class have commented on how they transferred mindfulness and meditation practice to the classroom and made teaching more enjoyable.

For example, one teacher from Japan wrote,

> Being mindful in our classrooms, we are able to slow our thoughts and actions and become aware of our students' needs, see how we are meeting them, and how the students are affected and respond to our actions.... When we teach mindfully, we know what we are teaching. We are aware of the words we speak, the tone in which we speak them, we are able to deeply observe and listen to our students, and are aware of connectedness between student and teacher, and indeed all the members of the classroom community. We are able to see the presentation of the curriculum and adjust it to the situation.
>
> For teachers, there are important behaviours to be mindfully considered: body language, eye contact, and compassionate speech. As I walk down the hall from my office, where I have been handling administrative duties for my class-room, I shift my focus to my students. I try to pay attention to my walk—my posture, my speed, my gait. I relax the muscles in my face, and put on a smile. Sometimes that smile comes more naturally than at other times, but the result is always the same—my mood shifts, and I become less defensive and more recep-tive. I start each class with erect posture, looking forward and ready to meet the students. I think my body language has a strong positive impact to the start of each class.
>
> Eye contact is an extension of body language, and a very real and immediate way to focus on the students. I try to make eye contact with every student as I walk through the class. They are usually engaged in a variety of activities and conversations, but my eye contact and close physical proximity to each student allows them to refocus on the class and we connect with one another.

Presence

Attention allows the teacher to be more present for the individual student. Below is a narrative of how one elementary schoolteacher became more attentive to the needs of an individual student, and the difference she felt this made. This student, ZR, had been acting out a great deal in the classroom.

> Today ZR and I spoke briefly about his difficulty focusing. Today was particu-larly difficult for him. He did try very hard. As other students responded during our math discussion, he wiggled and wiggled in his seat. In the past, I had been frustrated with him—his distractions became the class's distractions. Today, I was mindful. I only thought of him in that moment.
>
> I felt a great deal of empathy for him. I remembered how difficult it had been (and sometimes still is) for me to sit still in class. He looked at me watching him with what seemed like a slightly guilty expression. I smiled at him and he smiled back and seemed to be trying even harder to sit still, to focus.

After the discussion was over and the students worked on their project, I went over to talk with him. (He has chosen to sit by himself, at desk right next to mine.) We had good talk. I listened, he talked. Eventually, he suggested taking breaks between his work. He promised to work hard. I said we could try it for few days and then bring the suggestion to his parents, as he also expressed concern about difficulties focusing during his homework.

Later, this teacher and ZR met with his parents.

ZR and I had a meeting with his parents after school today. We presented them with a simple "schedule" for his day—10 minutes of work, followed by a 10-minute break. I sensed by his mother's response that she was quite taken aback. This was school, and he should be able to focus. His sister did her homework without any breaks. ZR explained, as much as he could, how and why he was having difficulty, and why he felt the 10-minute breaks might help. He promised to work very hard during the 10-minute workouts. Because he had actually been experimenting, I could vouch that he had been working very hard and producing excellent work.

I think this meeting was the first that I have had in a long time where I felt that I was there. I wasn't worried about getting home. I wasn't concerned about what they would think of me as a teacher. My own experience with a "cluttered mind" made me believe that for ZR to be "here," and present, he needed breaks to immerse himself in his art. I felt comfortable. We'll monitor this strategy until the Christmas break and revisit in January.

In a world where drugs are administered to children so they can settle down, this example shows how this teacher's presence made a difference in her student's life.

Compassion

Another outcome that some teachers have identified is greater compassion for their students. This usually arises from those students who have practised the lovingkindness meditation. But even being mindful and slowing down can lead to the rise of compassion.

One teacher made the connection between being mindful and compassion:

For me, love or compassion for my students has become a central priority in my classroom. Compassion comes from the ability to focus on a student—to listen deeply to their words, empathize with their situation, and care about the outcome.... A teacher who can focus on each student is more likely to act compassionately, thus creating a true receiving of others.

An increased effort to speak more compassionately comes out of being more mindful. When I reflect on my spoken words, I am amazed by all of the things I say without deliberate consideration. I dismiss people's ideas, judge and criticize their words and actions, and fail to listen deeply to their feelings when I quickly, curtly, and sternly utter my comments. I have tried over the years to speak with more compassion. This more attentive way to speak, in turn, slows my speaking down and allows me to be more compassionate, more of an active listener who is truly responding to students' actions and words.

What I Learned about the Transformational Nature of Meditation Practice

Some students in my class reported that meditation had a transformational impact on their lives. Often this was characterized as a powerful sense of interconnectedness to others, the environment, and the universe. One teacher wrote,

> "Connectedness" is what we all crave, really! Through meditation, I have been able to re-connect with the life within me. I know that continued practice will enable me to replenish my soul, so that what once was the "drain" of teaching will become life-giving. (Also, we can find life within our students with which we can also connect!)
>
> I found meditation was a special process, but it was truly mysterious. At times I would have insights or experiences which could not be explained. "Where did that insight emerge from?" Oftentimes I felt in these situations (these rare situations) I tapped [into] something greater than me. I felt a connection to something greater. This did not feel like a religious connection ... rather a connection to the universe.
>
> I also found a certain degree of reverence for the process. It is not something you can "make it happen"—it happens to you. I couldn't help but feel many times that something else, something mysterious, was at play.

Another student wrote, "it is in these moments of complete focus that I have frequently experienced a oneness with a Higher Power. I rejoice in these moments of total oneness."

A student from China who had lived through the Cultural Revolution found the process allowed him to connect to humanity:

> In our meditation practice I have found so much in common to share with others, making me feel that human beings, be he Westerner or Oriental, are in one way or another connected in our inner worlds. Once this common point is explored, there would be opportunity for us to improve the quality of our lives.... We may gain a better understanding of what we are doing, and we see more connections with the rest of the world.

One woman who worked as a counsellor for survivors of incest, sexual abuse, and partner assault wrote of the impact of meditation in an almost poetic manner:

> Through meditation I feel that I am being gently invited to observe the nature of my own humanity. Personally I had been strongly moved and transformed through the beautiful nature of this spiritual practice. I had heard my voice and soul with amusement. I had slowly let my inner judge go away and [was] more in touch with the unspoken, the unseen, and the sacred part of myself. I had achieved a larger vision of myself and my reality, a vision that tenderly dilutes my fears, preconceptions, judgments and need for control. Because of meditation I had been able to transform my fear, anger, and resistance into joy, forgiveness, acceptance, and love.
>
> I can bring to meditation anything, that is, for the purpose of seeing it or feeling it. The reflection and contemplation offered by this practice provides a very safe and comfortable environment where my creativity, intuition, and imagination can be enlarged. I can feel, see, and reflect on my reality while I confess my own fears and personal dilemmas to the being that exists within myself. I become my own witness, my own mentor, and my own source of liberation. I can unveil the many layers that cover my real nature, so I can then be able to recognize my own needs and inclinations.
>
> Meditating has also been a road of discovery for me. I first discovered the honouring power that the soul possesses for every human being. Through meditation I discovered the unconditional acceptance that is available to the heart of every human being. It is through the practice of meditation that I had better understood the meaning and importance of accepting and honouring myself and others.

Transformation can lead to changes in how the teacher sees her students. Below are the insights of one teacher who had been doing walking meditation as her practice. She sees herself and her students as "one growing, changing organism."

> However, my thinking is expanding somewhat to stretch into a new sense of what it means to know someone, student or colleague, in a way that facilitates true and effective learning and growth. To teach from an intuitive source is to submit myself to an ocean of largeness of possibility that roars and flows with its own greatness and power, quite outside the realm of my orchestration and planning and timing. It is to let go of the illusion of my own control and expertness, recognizing instead that to limit my students to the meagre feelings of my ego is to miss the hugeness and importance of authentic, educative growth. I am reminded here of my earlier teaching days, furiously pouring over the little section on China in the Social Studies binder, pathetically planning what glorious reams of knowledge I might impart, only to realize with horror

that two-thirds of my class was *born* there. Who do I think I am? Teaching from the ego is ultimately a crash course in humiliation. It is only when I submit to the truth of my smallness as one who is learning and struggling along a humble growth road with these brothers and sisters who are my students that I come closest to teaching in truth.

.... So crucial and authentic was the experience of "teaching through living" with my students, that I have since found myself questioning the validity of some of my former practices. I am beginning to see my students and myself as ultimately one growing, changing organism, continuing to become. I am only beginning this journey; there is so much that is new and unknown to me about the scope and breadth of holistic teaching and living. I only know that it is becoming my passion and perhaps my life work to teach and to live from the fireside, to "be quiet and listen and see what we hear."

This teacher shows insight, humility, and love in this passage. For example, she realizes that many of her students probably have more knowledge of China than she does, since they were born there. She has the understanding that she cannot control the educational experiences of her students. Finally, she feels love for her students, and describes seeing "my students and myself as ultimately one growing, changing organism continuing to become." I am convinced that wisdom can come from teachers working on themselves through various mind and body practices. These practices allow teachers to move from just teaching with their heads to teaching with their whole beings. From this wholeness, wisdom can arise in our schools and classrooms.

Conclusion

I have argued in other contexts that university needs to be more holistic in its orientation (Miller, 2006, 2007). We cannot just focus on the intellect; as much as possible, we must engage whole human beings. Recently, Harry Lewis (2006), former dean of Harvard College, wrote a book on higher education entitled *Excellence without a soul*. Although he does not make an argument for incorporating contemplative practices, he suggests that the universities' image of the student is a "brain on a stick," and argues that we need to find a more soulful approach to learning. I believe that my experience is one example of how to bring a more holistic approach to higher education. I have made the argument in terms of teacher education, but believe that contemplative practices can be explored in other parts of the curriculum. The Center for Contemplative Mind in Society has offered programs and scholarships for professors interested in integrating contemplation into the university curriculum. Indeed, the biggest development in the last ten years has been in the area of mindfulness practice in education. This is evident in the number of books that explain how mindfulness practices can be used in public school settings. Two recent books were written by Schoeberlein (2009) and Willard (2010). There also has been extensive media coverage. A recent example can be found in an article published in the *Shambhala Sun* (Joyce, 2011), which describes the introduction of mindfulness practice to students in Newark, New Jersey and Oakland, California. These are students living in inner cities who are facing major life challenges. In Vancouver, there is the MindUP program that is being used in public schools. The Mindfulness in Education Network (MIEN) has also been instrumental in connecting teachers and researchers working with mindfulness practices.

I believe the reasons for the rising popularity of mindfulness practice are twofold. First, there is the research which began in the health field initially under the direction of Kabat-Zinn (2005). The evidence found has been persuasive enough that it has encouraged educators to introduce mindfulness into classrooms. Second, the term mindfulness has less religious overtones than the word "meditation." The concept of being mindful is accessible, and in our era of multitasking, provides an appealing alternative. With its popularity, there is a danger that mindfulness practice will be packaged and sold as a commodity. Still, this work done on mindfulness in education is an encouraging development.

In conclusion, this is not new terrain. We have examples of holistic higher education from the past. The ancient university of Nalanda in India had rooms for meditation, along with lecture halls and the library. These rooms are visible in the ruins. Plato's Academy included contemplative practices (Hadot, 2002). Today, Naropa University in Boulder, Colorado, incorporates contemplative practices throughout its curriculum. Considering these examples, we need to continue exploring alternative approaches to higher education so that the whole student is engaged, not just the intellect.

Note

1 This quote and all those that follow in this section are taken from the interviews conducted by A. Nozawa for the qualitative study we conducted on meditation at OISE in 2002.

References

Alexander, C. Rainforth, M., & Gelderloos, P. (1991). Transcendental meditation, self-actualization, and psychological health: A conceptual overview and statistical meta-analysis. *Journal of Social Behavior and Personality* 6, 189–247.

Chadwick, D. (1999). *Crooked cucumber: The life and zen teachings of Shrunryu Suzuki.* New York, NY: Broadway Books.

Eisner, E., & Vallance, E. (Eds.). (1974). *Conflicting conceptions of curriculum.* Berkeley, CA: McCutchan.

Emerson, R. W. (1966). *Emerson on education* (E. M. Jones, Ed.). New York, NY: Teachers College Press.

Griffin, R. (1977, February). Discipline: What's it taking out of you? *Learning*, 77–80.

Hadot, P. (2002). *What is ancient philosophy?* Cambridge, MA: Harvard University Press.

Hölzel, B. K., Carmody, J., Vangel, M., Congleton, C., Yerramsetti, S. M., Gard, T., Lazar, S. W. (2011). Mindfulness practice leads to increases in regional brain gray matter density. *Psychiatry Research: Neuroimaging, 191*(1), 36–43.

Joyce, B. (2011, May). Making peace in America's cities. *Shambhala Sun*, 32–41.

Kabat-Zinn, J. (2005). *Coming to our senses: Healing ourselves and the world through mindfulness.* New York, NY: Hyperion.

Lazar, S. W., Bush, G., Gollub, R. L., Fricchione, G. L., Khalsa, G., & Benson, H. (2003). Functional brain mapping of the relaxation response and meditation. *NeuroReport, 11*(7), 1581–1585.

Lewis, H. R. (2006). *Excellence without a soul: Does liberal education have a future?* New York, NY: Public Affairs.

McLeod, K. (2002). *Wake up to your life: Discovering the Buddhist path of attention.* San Francisco, CA: Harper.

Miller, J. (1983). *The educational spectrum: Orientations to curriculum.* New York, NY: Longman.

Miller, J. (1994). *The contemplative practitioner.* Westport, CT: Bergin and Garvey.

Miller, J. (2006). *Educating for wisdom and compassion: Creating conditions for timeless learning.* Thousand Oaks, CA: Corwin.

Miller, J. (2007). *The holistic curriculum.* Toronto: University of Toronto Press.

Miller, J. (2008). A journey of transformation of a Vietnam war resistor. In M. Gardner & U. Kelly (Eds.), *Narrating transformative learning in education* (pp. 223–233). New York, NY: Palgrave Macmillan.

Miller, J., & Nozawa, A. (2002). Meditating teachers: A qualitative study. *Journal of In-Service Education, 28*, 179–192.

Murphy, M., & Donovan, S. (1997). *The physical and psychological effects of meditation.* Sausalito, CA: Institute of Noetic Sciences.

Schoeberlein, D. (2009). *Mindful teaching and teaching mindfulness.* Boston, MA: Wisdom.

Walsh, R. (1999). Asian contemplative disciplines: Common practices, clinical applications and research findings. *Journal of Transpersonal Psychology, 31*, 83–108.

Willard, C. (2010). *Child's mind: Mindfulness practices to help our children be more focused, calm and relaxed.* Berkeley, CA: Parallax Press.

Chapter 11

Toward Better Holistic Medical Education: What Can We Learn from Spiritual Healers?

Ian Winchester, Russell Sawa, Nancy Doetzel, Hugo Maynell,
Debbie Zembal, and Robbi Motta

Introduction

My colleagues and I are interested in improving medical education by considering holistic healing that involves what one might term a spiritual component. The basic approach to date in Canadian medical schools has largely been to give lip service to the notion of holistic healing, though where actually mentioned in the medical curriculum, it encompasses placing patients in their family or social setting, listening to patients' descriptions of their symptoms, carrying out obvious physiological tests and blood, urine, or other fluid studies, and sometimes discussing patients' concerns with family members present or involving them in such discussions. This, of course, is a great improvement over merely getting a quick history from the patient and doing some blood or urine tests and prescribing a pill or an operation, however effective these may prove to be, but certainly does not encompass a holistic approach.

Our interest has been anticipated by a number of authors, such as Dr. Aldridge (1991) of the Faculty of Medicine at Witten Herdecke University, Germany, who wrote the article Spirituality, healing and medicine, published in the *British Journal of General Practice*. Al-Krenawi, Graham, and Maoz (1996) have also explored the healing practices among the Bedouin that involve a spiritual component, from the vantage point of social work. Findings from both of these studies are very supportive of our present research activities.

Aldridge puts our common interest succinctly:

> The natural science base of modern medicine influences the way in which medicine is delivered and may ignore spiritual factors associated with illness. The history of spirituality in healing … reflects the growth of scientific knowledge, [relates to] demands for religious renewal, and [responds to] the shift in the understanding of the concept of health within a broader cultural context. General practitioners have been willing to entertain the idea of spiritual healing and

> include it in their daily practice or referral network. Recognizing patients' beliefs
> in the face of suffering is an important factor in health care practice. (Aldridge,
> 1991, p. 224)

In fact, there has been considerable impetus in recent years in England, Scotland, and Australia's medical communities encouraging physicians to follow the lead of the World Health Organization which roughly a decade ago began to consider the possibility of adding "spirituality" to its definition of "health." (See, for example, Cheungsatiansup's 2003 article that proposes the inclusion of spirituality in assessing health.)

In Scotland, the Scottish Executive Health Department (SEHD) requires all physicians to consider the spiritual state of their patients part of their responsibility, and in guidelines circulated to the Health Boards in 2002, the SEHD required NHS organizations "to develop and implement spiritual care policies that are tailored to the needs of the local population." Indeed, the Health Minister for Scotland had earlier expressed his determination to make spiritual care a central element of the way the National Health Service cares for people, and that such care should be undertaken by the whole health care community (Chisholm, 2002).

In Australia, Peach has written a number of articles on the necessity of taking the relationship between spirituality and health seriously, as well as the need for more research into linkages between the two. In her 2003 article in the *Medical Journal of Australia*, she argues that a survey of the more rigorous studies looking at religiosity and the onset of or recovery from a broad range of medical conditions suggest a positive association between greater religiosity and better health outcomes. The evidence, she argues, could indicate a causal association, but it is not conclusive.

In another article published in the *Medical Journal of Australia*, Williams and Sternthal (2007) argue that "there is mounting scientific evidence of a positive association between religious involvement and multiple indicators of health" (p. 248). Their main source for this claim is the reference in Koenig, McCullough, and Larson's *Handbook of Religion and Health* (2001) which identifies 1,200 studies that examined the relationship between some aspects of religious belief or activity and some indicators of health, and concluded there was a positive association between religion and physical and mental health. They conclude, as do we, that it is not helpful at this stage to try to distinguish "spirituality" clearly from "religion." Spirituality appears to mean different things to different people, and often refers to an individual's attempts to find meaning in life, which can sometimes include a sense of involvement in the transcendent, outside institutional boundaries. Religion tends to refer to aspects of human belief and action, including spirituality that are related to the sacred or supernatural, and grounded in a religious community or tradition. Like Koenig et al., we think that most of the research in this area tends to have been based on measures of religiosity rather than spirituality.

We conclude that there is considerable support in the medical research community for further work exploring the relationship between spirituality, religion, and health, and in this chapter we wish to report, in a general way, what our research group has been doing to add to the work done so far. So far as we can see, except for the work of Al-Krenawi, Graham, and Maoz, along with a few others looking at spiritual practices in diverse cultures, there is very little research about the wide range of spiritual healers who ply their trade in the North American context. To fill this gap, we have engaged in the work we relate here.

What Is Our Research About?

For the last five years, we have been interviewing a wide range of "holistic" healers drawn from a number of healing traditions that may be loosely described as "spiritual" healing practices. Most of these healers have been in Canada or the United States, though their origins are often wider than this. Sawa, our leader and a physician himself teaching at the University of Calgary Medical School, conducted interviews with thirty healers who may be so loosely described. The interviewees were a purposeful sample drawn from a wide spectrum of healing practices. They were identified through word of mouth, often by healers who were interviewed earlier. These healers included Aboriginal, shaman, Christian (both Protestant and Roman Catholic), Hindu, Buddhist, Chinese, Wiccan, and "energy" healers, including Reiki practitioners. Our object was to discover something of their claims to healing or even to curing, and also to gain some understanding of their approaches to healing that might prove useful to mainstream medical practice in North America.

We asked each of the thirty healers studied to offer narratives of their healing experiences. There was no definite set of questions chosen in advance, and they proceeded to tell their stories to the interviewer in whatever manner they chose. New interviews were added as themes arose and required more data for explanation. Whenever new questions arose, they were asked in subsequent interviews. Audiotapes were made of each interview and transcribed in totality. Our approach was reviewed and approved by the Ethics Committee of the Faculty of Medicine at the University of Calgary. Whenever a transcribed interview was available, our team met to discuss the interview in detail and to summarize it in a collection of definite propositions representing the content of the interview for further discussion and comparison. Our approach was based centrally in the qualitative research tradition and followed, in large measure, the approach suggested by Lonergan in his book *Insight*. But it is probably also true to say that we were guided in large measure by everyday common sense in our attempt to understand what study participants told us.

Who Are We?

Our team of researchers consisted of Russell Sawa, a physician and associate professor in the medical school at the University of Calgary, Nancy Doetzel, an educator and sociologist who teaches at both Mount Royal University and the University of Calgary, Hugo Maynell, a retired professor of philosophy of religion, Debbie Zembal, a practising nurse and energy healer in the Reiki tradition, Robbi Motta, an intuitive healer and Reiki practitioner who works both with people and animals, and myself, Ian Winchester, a physicist, former student of medicine, philosopher of science and sometime Dean of Education at the University of Calgary. As this chapter depends on the work of us all, every team member is included as an author, but since the writing and viewpoint is entirely my own (Ian Winchester's), I do not wish to claim that everyone in the research group agrees with everything that I have written.

What we discovered early on was that there were some striking similarities in the practices and claims of all of the healers we interviewed. But equally important, there were also striking differences among them. We will not go into much detail concerning these findings healer by healer, but instead try to summarize the most important similarities and differences. While each healer brought interesting cases to the interview, and while all such cases were plausibly characterized by what struck us as very honest and believable interviewees, we were disappointed on one point with all of the alternative healers interviewed. Not one of them kept good records about the physical or mental state of the patient before or after the healer's intervention. As future research will proceed with us actually observing such healers in the context of their practice, we are determined to make sure that such records are always kept in a way that is clear and unquestionable.

Interventions in all cases involved the healers listening carefully to the patients coming to them with a complaint, and subsequently making suggestions as to what the patient might do next or what treatment to follow. Often the narrative involved the patient coming to the healer with a prior diagnosis made in the course of ordinary Western medical practice. These diagnoses might involve such things as broken bones, tumours or cancers, infections that would not heal or go away or, in one interesting case, a patient who was unable to enter the kitchen in his apartment due to a headless man blocking the way. In practically every case relayed to us, the healer claimed to have provided a form of healing for the disorder.

Healing versus Curing

In the course of the interviews, we initially assumed that when healers talked about successful treatment results they meant a "cure" in the standard Western definition of the term. But in fact, in most cases, the physical disorder was often described as still present, although it no longer blocked the patient from getting on with his or her life in a normal or practically normal fashion. In some cases, not only did healers claim to have "healed "the patient in this sense but also they stated they were involved in the complete elimination of the patient's physical or mental disorder; that is, they provided a "cure" in the standard Western medical sense. However, we were not offered the kind of supplementary evidence we like to see for any of the cases, such as a prior medical diagnosis of the physical disorder with appropriate pathological study, or post-treatment study indicating the disappearance of the disorder.

Because we were forced to make this distinction frequently in our earliest study of these interviews, we began to define "healing" and "curing" in different ways. This is a distinction that, in one sense, is clear from our own everyday experience: when small children who have bumped or bruised a limb come to us to "kiss it better," adults effect a "healing" of their distress, enabling them to endure the residual pain while the bruise or bump remains, which will eventually be "cured" or disappear. Something like "kissing it better" appeared to be systematically going on in the actions and results of practically all of the alternative healers who used what they frequently considered a spiritual means of intervention.

Ordinary versus Paranormal Intervention

Another distinction we were forced to make early on in our study of the interviews was between what we call claims of ordinary spiritual intervention and claims of paranormal intervention.

Ordinary Spiritual Intervention

Ordinary spiritual intervention was invariably connected with the concern of the healer to listen to and understand the cultural, religious, or philosophical presuppositions of their patients and how these people understood the disorder, ailment, or trouble that had brought them to the healer in the first place. One might say that the healers treated patients' "spiritual understanding" according to the German notion of *geisteswissenshaft*, which defines "spirit" as intrinsically related to how a person is embedded in their particular culture or understanding of that culture. There is no equivalent for this word in the English language, and that makes it rather difficult to easily discuss the relationship of "spirit" to "culture." We could refer to the social sciences in this context, but that papers over the possibility that most of the human spirit resides in the context of human culture, a culture that is entirely man-made but just as real for us as bumping into a rock or a tree, or being pulled down to earth by the force of gravity, according to the laws of physics. In all "ordinary spiritual interventions," while there is understanding of the patient's world view from the vantage point of the spiritual, holistic, or non-traditional healer, the healer's primary goal is a compassionate regard for the patient and wise suggestions for better conduct of one's daily life. This intention to help and the invocation of manifest love in the sense of *caritas* in Latin or *agape* in Greek was claimed by practically all of the healers we interviewed.

To take a typical example, one patient came to a healer with an apparently incurable cancer. The patient was terrified of dying of cancer, and this fear caused the individual to stop functioning in everyday life. The healer was able to convince the patient that the best chance for a cure was to come to grips with that everyday life, and carry on much as before. The patient understood this, and with the aid of the healer, began functioning again. The physical symptoms of the cancer subsided, and the patient went back to a productive and useful life for a number of years before ultimately succumbing to the disease. This patient, in our terminology, was healed but not cured.

The reverse possibility also exists. For example, suppose someone comes to a healer after having a breast removed to treat breast cancer, but the patient cannot get through a day for the rest of her life without worrying about the recurrence of the cancer either in the remaining breast or somewhere else in her body. Even though this patient might live into her nineties and suffer no recurrence of the cancer, she has been medically cured, but certainly not healed. What our non-traditional healers often do is help such people toward healing, given a prior medical intervention of the curative kind, so that they can get on with their lives in a normal fashion.

Paranormal Claims

Conversely, while a number of our healers engaged in what we might term an "intervention" by establishing an immediate cultural understanding of the patient in ways that are like "kissing it better" with a child, others claimed they invoked special and uncommon powers or interventions by themselves, by some guide in a world outside our everyday one, or by the invocation of a higher power similar to that in, say, Alcoholics Anonymous. Such claims were common among Roman Catholic, Hindu, shamanistic, Reiki, and other energy healers. They were not part of the claims of Wiccan or Buddhist healers.

Here are a couple of examples.

The case of Headless Max. We refer to one of our interviews as the case of Headless Max. It involved a patient coming to a spiritual healer who could not enter the kitchen in his flat because he invariably encountered an apparition with no head behind the counter that he called Headless Max. This headless being was so frightening, he blocked the way into the kitchen for the patient in question. The patient worked in northern Alberta with an oil exploration firm. His daily work involved flying into remote lake and forest regions of that province in search of geological information, usually with a colleague. In order to fly in and out of the remote locations, the patient and his colleague both arrived and departed by helicopter. Sometimes the terrain was too rough for the helicopter to land, so the two had to be picked up by climbing onto a rope hanging from the helicopter. On one fateful occasion the patient climbed up first, and the colleague second. At some point while flying to a more secure landing point to allow the men to get into the helicopter, the patient's colleague simply fell off the rope and disappeared, his body never to be found. On returning to his flat after this mishap, the patient always saw Headless Max in his kitchen. The healer was a Roman Catholic priest, who told the patient that he was suffering from possession by a demon, something that the patient, himself a Roman Catholic, believed possible. The healer told the patient he would exorcize the demon, which he did, following standard church procedures. Headless Max disappeared, never to return. In this case a higher power was invoked, namely God, acting through the Holy Spirit referred to in the Apostles' Creed as a member of the Holy Trinity.

Perhaps of all our cases, this one, which came early in our experience, has been most important, for it permitted us to see a situation in which the separation between healing and curing, which was generally an important distinction for us, dissolved or appeared to dissolve. At the same time, it posed a number of puzzles for us in its own right. Was this a case of psychological illness that could only be cured by "spiritual" means? Was it important to this patient, for example, to believe that "demons" objectively exist who could possess an individual in such a way that made it impossible to get on with everyday life, not even allowing the man to go into his own kitchen?

Some in our research group believed in the existence of demons, others in the possibility of their existence, and some thought that such beliefs could not generally be part of the common experience of mankind, though they were "real" for some individuals. Was it sufficient that both healer and patient (or sufferer, perhaps) believed in the existence of demons on the one hand and the possibility of exorcizing them through religious means on the other? Or was it even possible that while a patient had to believe in the demons that "possessed" him or her, the healer need only enter into the "personal world" of the patient and offer the exorcism as a treatment that the patient believed could affect a cure without actually sharing the reality of the patient's world view? Could the healer be effective even if he or she did not share the personal world view of the patient? We have not resolved these questions to our satisfaction as a research group, but we continue to explore cases in which the healer appears to be good at entering the personal world of the ill person in such a way that healing, if not curing, is possible through intervention.

The case of an Aboriginal patient and healer: Common reality and extraordinary reality. In another case, an Aboriginal patient was suffering from personal difficulties related in part to family relations and in part to physical symptoms. The healer, also an Aboriginal, suggested to the patient that he would dream one night, and that he, the healer, would join him in his dream. Together they would visit some of the patient's wise ancestors to find out what to do. The patient believed in this course of action, engaged in the dream exercise with his healer, and listened to his ancestors in the dream by following the guidance of the spirit that the healer had invoked for the journey to the dream land. Afterward, the patient engaged in the suggested course of action, and was no longer bothered by his personal difficulties or physical symptoms.

This again raises questions for us relating to the "worlds" inhabited by the healer and the patient seeking intervention. It suggests, perhaps, that we have to distinguish between the common world of everyday waking life for most of us, the world of common sense and natural science, and the personal worlds that are so real for the patients who approach alternative healers. Again, some in our research team think that if something is part of the personal world of an individual seeking healing intervention, then that personal world is, in fact, part of the "real" world, though perhaps an unusual extension of it. For others on our team, a distinction has to be maintained between the world of common sense and natural science, a world that all of us experience, where we can engage in common and repetitive activities on the one hand, and the private (or in any event) unique world of individuals in which they experience extraordinary things on the other. For those of us with this latter view, the experiences of the world of common sense and natural science are real experiences for us all, but the extraordinary experiences that are part of the world of some patients and healers is real only for them, not for the rest of us.

Other cases. Generally, for most cases related to us, the healer not only found out how the patient's suffering, disorder, disease, or distress was related to their personal beliefs but also they invoked a hypnotic state, meditation, or prayer with the patient. Sometimes this involved the healer describing to the patient how he had entered the patient's mind and met a spirit guide to the patient's mental and physical states, perhaps by moving to the "Buddha plane" and directly experiencing the patient's troubles, and once he knew what the difficulty was, he returned to the everyday world to suggest a course of action. One healer, a Western-trained physician of Chinese origin, accepted Western diagnoses of the patient's disorder, claimed he simply suggested that he and the patient pray together, and often the disorder was ameliorated or disappeared. Or if this did not happen, the patient was nonetheless able to continue with their everyday life. Thus for this healer, sometimes a cure and sometimes healing was invoked through paranormal means, namely, in apparent answer to a joint prayer.

While a number of our healers were drawn from shamanistic, Aboriginal, Wiccan, Buddhist, Hindu, or energy healing traditions, many others were drawn from the Roman Catholic faith—priests, bishops, or lapsed priests now actively engaged in healing full time. It was perhaps not surprising that the healers from the Roman Catholic faith believed that such healing as they could bring about was due to the power of God's spirit, a spirit the healers felt they were, at best, a conduit for. But the healers from most of the other traditions, shamanistic, Aboriginal, energy, and Hindu for example, also saw themselves as the conduit of a healing power, energy, or spirit that was not their own. Indeed, only the Wiccan healer claimed to have healing power herself and to possess special abilities not related to a higher power as such.

Conversely, healers from non-Christian traditions did not speak of the intervention of the "Holy Spirit" or God directly, but often referred more generally to the intervention of a "higher power."

Energy healers often invoked a notion of "energy" which they sometimes claimed was identical to the ordinary notion of energy referred to in contemporary physics. This energy might be involved both in the process of diagnosis and in treatment, the patient's energy conveying to the healer what was wrong and the healer's energy passing to the patient and effecting healing or perhaps even a cure of the disorder.

We retain an open mind to these very diverse claims of special powers, related either to long years of training or to the healer being in possession of special and unusual paranormal powers. Indeed, only the Wiccan healer claimed to have healing power herself and to possess special abilities not related to a higher power as such. While the Buddhist healer did not invoke a higher power, neither did he claim to be the source of healing himself, but rather that he was leading the patient to a better path.

Discussion

Perhaps our most important findings were the distinctions we found ourselves having to make, given the material at hand in the interview narratives. First we had to distinguish between healers telling us of those patients who were able to go on with their everyday lives after the healers' interventions, and those who we referred to as healed.

Second, we had to acknowledge claims made by the healers about patients who appeared to them to be free completely of their presenting symptoms, and who they pronounced as cured. Some of these patients seemed destined to spend the rest of their days distressed by their presenting ailment or complaint, such as a now "cured" or completely removed cancer. However, the reverse was more often true; namely, while the patient was rarely cured in a medical sense, in that their presenting disease or disorder completely disappeared, never to return, commonly they were able to go on with their lives as if the ailment was largely unimportant and no longer an impediment to living fully.

Third, it became clear to us that all of our healers worked with patients who came to them hoping to be healed, perhaps cured, and that all of the healers had definite compassionate intentions to heal and perhaps cure. Thus we believe that the intentions of both the patient to be healed, and the compassionate, loving intentions of the healer to heal in the sense of *caritas* or *agape* are both crucial for the success of non-Western healing traditions. And a major part of this compassion was the ability to listen to and enter into the patient's cultural world, the world of deeply held beliefs. The distinction between the healer who works by listening to and entering into the world of the patient before offering advice or treatment, and the healer who invokes special or unusual powers to heal, appears to us to be central.

There was a meditative component in many of the interventions of our healers which paralleled, in some respects, the approach of the Aboriginal healers who had their patients enter into a dream world with them. The invocation of prayer, meditation, breathing exercises, relaxation, and perhaps hypnosis seemed to be of this nature to us in the claims of many of our healers.

We intend to study these claimed unusual, perhaps paranormal powers more fully in future studies that will involve healers similar to those whose narratives we have just examined, and we are planning joint work with scholars in India and Israel as well as in Canada. In these studies, however, we will not simply ask the healers to tell their stories; we will work with both healers and patients to follow their course of diagnosis and treatment, making sure that adequate prior diagnostic tests and medical follow-up is not ignored.

Implications for Medical Education

Although our intentions are ultimately to develop important suggestions for holistic healing ambitions and a better understanding of traditional healing practices by students and staff of Canadian medical schools, our sense of the implications for medical education at the moment are very limited. As mentioned in the introduction, the Scottish Health Department has a number of suggestions in the form of practical steps that physicians might take to involve a spiritual or religious dimension in the lives of their patients that may aid in healing. Some of the steps suggested include

[the] ready availability of Bibles and other useful spiritual books; chaplains and their assistants be recognized as specialists in spiritual care and that the two

should meet on terms of equality; spiritual provision for those who do not belong to the Christian faith be made without downgrading the historic provisions for Christians; medical students should be taught to include the spiritual/religious dimension in history-taking and Chaplains should be more directly involved in student teaching (for example, in ethics seminars and in planning "spirituality" teaching modules; doctors should engage more meaningfully with their nursing and therapy colleagues to discuss ways in which spiritual needs may be met; doctors who themselves have little or no interest in spiritual or religious elements in their patients' care could, nevertheless be encouraged to countenance increased provision for these needs in their wards and units; and finally, further research should be undertaken to determine precisely which elements of spiritual care are effective. (Chisholm, 2002, p. 25)

How does our study of these thirty spiritual healers support or detract from these suggestions? Our discovery that each of our healers was entering into the cultural world of their patients with great care and compassion before offering any advice seems to support all of these recommendations. Certainly from the point of view of medical education, it suggests the importance of teaching medical students how to include the cultural and spiritual dimensions of a patient as part of the medical history, dimensions which to us appear to be very much one and the same.

The distinction between healing and curing that we were forced to make also relates centrally to the World Health Organization's definition of health; namely, that health is a state of complete physical, mental, and social well-being, not merely the absence of disease or infirmity. For if (as appears to be the case with those patients who work with the diversity of holistic healers we interviewed) patients whose sense of well-being, physically, mentally, and socially is improved by the intervention of spiritual healers, then they are making a very important contribution to their health by listening to their patients, by taking their "cultural" or spiritual concerns seriously, and by intervening from the vantage point of their cultural or spiritual beliefs, not just their physical or mental complaints.

Perhaps the most important result of our study is that all of our holistic healers, from every tradition, listened carefully to their patients, attempted to understand and enter into their cultural heritage and world view, and offered suggestions and treatments with love and compassion that arose from that understanding. If this approach was encouraged in all of the next generation of physicians, surgeons, and family practitioners coming out of Canadian medical schools, it would most likely improve patient health.

Finally, the suggestion of the Scottish Health Department (Chisholm, 2002) that further research should be undertaken to determine precisely which elements of spiritual care are effective will be at the centre of our future research undertakings.

References

Aldridge, D. (1991). Spirituality, healing and medicine. *British Journal of General Practice*, *41*(351), 224–227.

Al-Krenawi, A., Graham, J. R., & Maoz, B. (1996). The healing significance of Negev's Bedouin dervish. *Social Science and Medicine*, *43*(1), 13–21.

Cheungsatiansup, K. (2003). Spirituality and health: An initial proposal to incorporate spiritual health impact assessment in the World Health Organization, Examples of health impact assessments. *Environmental Impact Assessment Review*, *23*(1), 3–15.

Chisholm, M. (2002). Speech delivered at the Spiritual Care in the NHS Conference on 16 November, 2001. *Scottish Journal of Healthcare Chaplaincy*, *5*, 24–26.

Koenig, H. (2001). Religion, spirituality and medicine: How are they related and what does it mean? *Mayo Clinic Proceedings*, *76*, 1225–1235.

Peach, H. G. (2003). Religion, spirituality and health: How should Australia's medical profession respond? *Medical Journal of Australia*, *178*(8), 415.

Williams, D. R., & Sternthal, M. J. (2007). Spirituality, religion and health: Evidence and research directions. *Medical Journal of Australia*, *186*, 247–250.

Chapter 12

Stress, Coping, Growth, and Spirituality in Grief

Susan Cadell

Introduction

> I've learned a huge amount about how I should live life.... About my capacity for
> pain and joy and ... sadness and grief and tenderness and love. Learning that I
> have tremendous depths and also learning how to live with sadness and joy and
> loss and all those things. So it makes.... Either I transformed or I would burn
> out. And so I chose to transform.

These are the words of a woman whose brother died of AIDS-related illness.
In addition to her personal loss, she experienced dozens of other deaths in her
work at an AIDS organization. She was thoughtful and spiritual about the
changes, both positive and negative, that had occurred in her life as a result of
her grief experiences.

This chapter addresses a number of the concepts that can be involved in
grief, such as stress and coping, growth and spirituality. First I will address
the concepts that are used in the chapter and then, using quotes from research
projects with bereaved individuals, I will explore stress and growth in grief and
examine the role of spirituality in that framework. I hope to demonstrate that
spirituality is foundational in growth, and review the work of others who are
posing similar questions. I will end the chapter by exploring some of the implications this knowledge has for social work.

Concepts

All of the concepts addressed throughout this chapter have undergone years of
research scrutiny and even more of human experience. In the last few decades,
there has been a significant shift in thinking about adverse circumstances, a
movement in many disciplines to include more positive aspects of various
negative experiences. In social work, Saleebey (1992) pioneered this paradigm

shift with the strengths perspective. The phenomenon is not new; in fact, stories of triumph over adversity are ancient (Tedeschi & Calhoun, 1995).

The need to treat illness, including mental health issues, requires a thorough understanding of (psycho)pathology, but somehow the focus remained exclusively there instead of moving back to a holistic or salutogenic lens (Antonovsky, 1979) once the pathology was understood. Research has typically followed this exclusive direction and trauma is an excellent example of this focus. A great deal is studied about posttraumatic stress disorder (PTSD), despite the fact that the majority of people exposed to a traumatic incident do not go on to develop it. In contrast to the vast knowledge we have about PTSD, very little is known about people who are exposed to adverse circumstances who do not become traumatized. The study of posttraumatic growth grew specifically from the experience of two psychologists, Richard Tedeschi and Lawrence Calhoun, who recognized that some people actually experienced benefits in the face of difficulties (Tedeschi & Calhoun, 1995).

Researchers in many disciplines have been making an effort to move away from a solely pathological lens of understanding the human experience to a broader and more positive one. In social work, the strengths perspective (Saleebey, 2006) has been at the forefront of this movement. Positive psychology (Joseph & Linley, 2008) and family-centred medicine have also contributed to the changing discourse, as well other disciplines. I will address the shifts in thinking concerning grief, stress and coping, growth, and spirituality specifically in the following sections.

Grief

Grief is the emotional reaction to a loss (Attig, 1996). Loss can occur in many circumstances, and can cause grief. This chapter examines reactions to the death of a person and the grief that is experienced in that circumstance. Bereavement is also a term used in relation to the experience of someone dying. Grief and bereavement can be considered different concepts; here they are used interchangeably, as two sides of the coin of experiencing a death. This man, whose partner died four years earlier, captured both the interconnection and complexity of grief and bereavement well:

> When he died there was a huge, huge, huge void in my life ... I once said to him, *Tu es ma raison d'être.* You're my reason for being. And he got very upset and said, nobody should ever say that about anyone else. And he's right, because in terms of how things have changed since he died, I, er ... still miss him a lot, and in some ways it's difficult to talk about because it's embarrassing to still be choked up four years later.

While the experience of death is universal, theoretical understanding of grief in the Western world has shifted from a detachment model to an understanding of the continuing bonds that are formed with the person who has died. These bonds entail new ways of relating to the deceased. While the relationship has changed, it has not ended. As one man whose partner died said, "We were one body.... It's as if I am missing my arm.... You have the impression that is your arm because the other was so important."

Stress and Coping

Stress arises when individuals perceive that they cannot adequately cope with the demands being made on them or with threats to their well-being (Lazarus & Folkman, 1984; Folkman, 1997). Stress results from an imbalance between perceived demands and resources. It is very much determined by a person's appraisal of the situation as challenging or threatening. If an event is not perceived as being harmful it does not cause stress, and coping is not required. One man whose partner died of AIDS-related illness expressed his personal challenge coping with grief: "I don't feel complete. If I were a ship, I would be rudderless. Yes, I guess that is what I have in my mind, I am adrift."

The paradigm shift in stress and coping is exemplified in Folkman's (1997) reworked model. In its original conceptualization, positive emotions were only possible in the coping model when the outcome of an event was favourable. However, in Folkman's longitudinal study of HIV caregivers, there were no favourable resolutions to the reality of a loved one having a life-threatening disease. A bereaved parent expressed a similar sentiment: "I will never, ever be in the same world that I was in before—ever." Despite there being no favourable resolutions, the HIV caregivers were reporting positive aspects in their experiences (Folkman, Moskowitz, Ozer, & Park, 1997). Folkman (1997) revised the model to include the possibility of positive emotion when there is an unfavourable outcome or no resolution to the coping process. This involves meaning-based coping of which spiritual beliefs are a component.

Growth

Growth refers to positive aspects or outcomes of an adverse experience, a traumatic event, or life crisis (Calhoun & Tedeschi, 2006). Specific terms used to describe this concept are posttraumatic growth (Tedeschi & Calhoun, 1995), stress-related growth (Park, Cohen, & Murch, 1996), adversarial growth (Linley & Joseph, 2004), thriving (Ickovics & Park, 1998), benefit-finding (McMillen, 1999), and perceived growth (Tomich, Helgeson, & Nowak Vache, 2005). Although the term posttraumatic growth (probably the one most commonly used) contains the word trauma, growth is not limited to traumatic incidents. Rather, posttraumatic growth is considered to be possible, although not always present, in the struggle with significant life challenges (Calhoun, Tedeschi, Cann, & Hanks, 2010). Grief is often not traumatic, but is certainly one of the areas in which growth has the potential to occur. One bereaved mother commented,

> I think, you know, I have had an amazing life, and all of that. People don't like to talk about sad things, but, even the bad ... I didn't wish for her to die, but good things have happened because of it.

The term posttraumatic growth was coined in the 1990s by Tedeschi and Calhoun (1995), two psychologists who recognized, in working primarily with widows, that the experiences their clients discussed were not exclusively negative. The process of growth is presented as co-occurring along side the distress and negative aspects that are traditionally given prominence when considering the outcome of trauma, stress, or grief (Tedeschi, Park, & Calhoun, 1998). A woman who had experienced numerous AIDS-related losses encapsulated this point well:

> wouldn't it be a sad commentary on the years and years of pain and grief if we couldn't celebrate people's lives and how much they've contributed to the world, mixed and mingled with the overwhelming sense of loss that their lives were cut too short. So it is the combination of ... pride and celebration and joy and sadness and despair and apathy. And it is a mingling. It is not separate from.

The body of work on positive aspects of negative events is growing tremendously. Tedeschi and Calhoun (1995; Tedeschi, Park, & Calhoun, 1998; Calhoun & Tedeschi, 2006; Kilmer, Gil-Rivas, Tedeschi, & Calhoun, 2009) themselves have written widely and expanded their clinical view (Calhoun & Tedeschi, 1999) to working with bereaved parents (Tedeschi & Calhoun, 2004). Many others have built upon their work as well, including Weiss and Berger's new book on global perspectives on growth (2010).

Spirituality

> I guess it all depends on what you define spirituality as ... you should give back things that you take and I believe that you should take care of the people around you. I mean, I'm sure that a lot of what I believe comes from this religion and that religion.

The words of this bereaved HIV carer reflect a reality: there are many definitions of spirituality. The one that I prefer is Hardy's (1982); he describes it as "that attitude, that frame of mind which breaks the human person out of the isolating self. As it does that, it directs him or her to another in relationship to whom one's growth takes root and sustenance" (p. 154). Hardy encapsulates both religious and non-religious spirituality, as his definition is inclusive of religion, but not exclusively limited to it. The connection to another may be divine or may be human, and transcendence is the act of going beyond oneself. A bereaved mother commented,

> And the times when I felt like I was falling down that black hole and you don't know how deep it's gonna be and you can't see the bottom, there was also a sense that there was a safety net there. That, that God was holding a safety net there and that I wouldn't hit the bottom.

Hardy's definition of spirituality (1982) involves three essential aspects that will be further demonstrated in the themes below. The first is that spirituality is an attitude or frame of mind. The second is that it involves connection to "an other" who may be a divine other or a human other. Transcendence, or the experience of going beyond oneself, is the third vital aspect of this definition. Some or all of these components of spirituality will be demonstrated by each of the quotes to illustrate how growth is experienced in the context of grief and bereavement.

Posttraumatic Growth in Grief

The quotes I have used throughout this chapter are from two research studies with bereaved individuals. The first study examined the experiences of people who cared for someone who had died of AIDS-related causes (Cadell, 2007; Cadell, Regehr, & Hemsworth, 2003). The second explored positive aspects of the experience of parental bereavement (Cadell, Janzen, & Fletcher, 2004). The methods are fully explained elsewhere, but I will address them briefly. Both studies involved open-ended interviews, and data was analyzed using the constant comparative method (Lincoln & Guba, 1985). The bereaved HIV carers were chosen based on scores of growth collected in the first quantitative phase of the research involving people throughout Canada. Half of the individuals interviewed during the second qualitative phase had high growth scores and half had low scores. Despite the differences in scores, all recounted positive aspects of their experiences (Cadell & Sullivan, 2006). The bereaved parents who participated in the second study were recruited through a hospice bereavement group in British Columbia and a peer support bereavement organization in Ontario. Each parent filled in a short questionnaire at the time of interview including a measure of growth, but only qualitative data is reported on here.

The posttraumatic growth inventory (PTGI; Tedeschi & Calhoun, 1996) is a tool widely used to measure growth after a stressful incident. It was designed with five subscales: new possibilities, relating to others, personal strength, appreciation of life, and spiritual change. Of the 21 questions in the PTGI, only two address the final subscale of spiritual change. These two questions are numbers (5) I have a better understanding of spiritual matters, and (18) I have a stronger religious faith. The questions do not even begin to fully capture the depth of spirituality inherent in a grief experience. It is my opinion that Tedeschi and Calhoun have underestimated the importance of spirituality in the experience of growth. In order to illustrate the significance of spirituality, I use quotes from both bereavement studies: the parents, and the HIV carers to illustrate each subscale in an effort to demonstrate the spirituality inherent in each. These exemplars of the five posttraumatic growth inventory categories were generated through content analysis of the primary qualitative data (Creswell, 2007).

New Possibilities

The first of the domains of the posttraumatic growth inventory is new possibilities. This category captures the notion that opportunities and prospects may arise during or in the aftermath of an adverse event. All of those interviewed identified at least one new possibility that they had found in life after the death of their child or the person they cared for. One mother identified how big the task was:

> I think the best thing that parents can do for themselves is just to stop trying to change everyone and change themselves, in the sense of learning to accept the impossible, learning to accept [that you] will never accept it, that you can never change it, that this is it, this is the way it is and start a new life, you have to start a new life.

Many of those interviewed formed new connections and learned from others who had been through similar experiences. One mother whose child had died commented,

> [the other parents in the peer support group] innately know what … you're going through 'cause they've been there. And that's why it's such a safe, comforting environment; for me it was very, very comforting.… I picked up really quite a lot of information and things that I could apply to my way of dealing with issues.

For many of those interviewed, new possibilities took the form of giving or service to others. All of the bereaved parents who were interviewed were part of a support network, either led by peers or professionals. As they moved through their grief experience, the parents in both models of support talked about becoming role models for other bereaved parents who were newer to grief and loss. Some of the bereaved individuals, both parents and HIV carers, also performed their paid work in new and more meaningful ways. Volunteerism became prominent for some. One HIV carer stated,

I decided to do prevention work in schools. It has been five years since I have been doing that with young people. I know that I am doing good because I save, maybe in a class, two lives and that gives me the strength to continue. I could say that it's my breath of life.

The new opportunities in life after the death of someone important demonstrates the three aspects of spirituality that Hardy (1982) touches on—one's attitude or frame of mind, a connection with an other, and going beyond oneself. All of the above examples include an attitude toward the loss that allows for finding meaning in one's situation. A connection to others is demonstrated in reciprocal support and learning. The altruism displayed through these experiences has, in turn, taken these bereaved individuals beyond themselves.

Relating to Others

The second domain is that of relating to others. The bereaved individuals who were interviewed experienced positive outcomes in how they related to others. The relationships for bereaved individuals are so complex and varied that I have divided this domain into three types of relationships: family, friends, and the person who died.

Relating to Others: Family. Positive changes in family relationships included parents, siblings, and extended family. One bereaved HIV carer commented about her relationship with her mother:

> Well, you know, she's kind of the only person that's been there through no matter what crap I've put her through…. My mom, who I can still call at three o'clock in the morning even though she needs her sleep, and I can phone her crying my eyes out and she would still be there for me …

For the bereaved parents who had other surviving children, they appreciated the relationships that they had with these children in a new way. One mother reflected,

> [My surviving son] certainly is not replacing [my son who died] because it is a different feeling, that mother feeling, but I am just so much more aware of [my surviving son]. I consider that the best gift. I may have lost a son, but I gained one too. I know that sounds kind of funny.

Some of the bereaved mothers learned to accept that their spouses mourn differently than them and this improved their relationships. "My husband and I have found a new sort of level to our relationship … there's a new openness and honesty and closeness … we're more romantic and we're more loving." They also learned new ways of relating to one another that helped:

And I think for [my husband and I] relationship wise, it's done us a world of good because instead of, um, not that we ever swept things under the carpet 'cause I'm just not that way, but maybe letting things slide a little in our day-to-day lives. We don't do that anymore.

Relating to Others: Friends. The second subcategory in relating to others is friends. Participants forged or discovered positive aspects of friendships. For some, this meant finding friendships with new people, for others it meant stronger bonds in their existing friendships. A bereaved mother related,

[my one close friend and I] have had our ups and downs, again because she's never been through it, she doesn't get it, she doesn't understand, and we have had a few little set-tos ... it was on the anniversary of [my son]'s passing and she didn't call, which really set me off and I told her exactly, exactly how I felt, and I find most times people are more than willing to take it because it actually helps them understand where I live and where I come from. So they're better able to talk or say things thereafter.

For some, changes in friendships meant divesting themselves of relationships that were no longer fulfilling. Another bereaved mother commented,

I'm tired of excuses; there is nothing wrong with picking up the phone, you know, a couple of weeks after the funeral and saying, "how you doing, do you want to go for a drink?" Sorry, nothing wrong. I'm tired, and I'm tired of excuses, as a bereaved mother who for all intents and purposes has made it through and I'm on the other side. I am tired of excuses from people.

All participants expressed the need to have someone in their life they can be completely honest with talking about their bereavement and the deceased person. These relationships allow them to talk in-depth about the bereavement experience without the worry of burdening the other person. One bereaved parent described these as being reciprocal relationships: "People that listen. You know, people that are there for you, you are there for them."

Relating to Others: The Person Who Died. The third area of relating to others is the relationship to the person who died. In contrast to earlier ideas about grief, that its purpose was to entail detachment from the deceased, we have come to the realization that bonds are not broken, but take on new aspects. One HIV carer whose partner died said, "your love doesn't die. One would say that it connects us still."

All bereaved parents reported a close and strong relationship with their deceased child. The bereaved HIV carers also expressed ways that they maintain connections with the deceased. This can mean having conversations with the person, feeling the person's presence, or discussing the person. A bereaved HIV carer shared how she stayed connected to those who had died:

> I travel all around the world to places that my friends would want to go. The ones that I've cared for. And I bring a picture of them and I let it float in the water: I let it go, you're here now ...

For bereaved parents, maintaining a connection could also be discussing the deceased child with their other children. One mother illustrated how her deceased son remains connected to all members of the family:

> [My son] sits on my shoulder every day, and has since the day he died. I view him as my guardian angel, my mentor, someone who is looking out for me and hopefully his dad and his brother, and I am sure he is ...

One bereaved HIV carer wanted to be clear that this connection did not make memories of the person perfect:

> My angels are different than other people's angels. My angels are all the people that have died of AIDS that I've loved. They're my angels. But they're not perfect by any stretch of the imagination, but ... I mean they're dead, but they're human beings. The essence of everything they were when they were alive.

In all three categories of relating to others, spirituality is clearly demonstrated via the connections to others—those living and dead. These relationships all reflect a frame of mind toward the loss and the experience of transcendence is evident.

Personal Strength

The third domain of the posttraumatic growth connected to spirituality is that of personal strength. The bereaved individuals interviewed reported that they had more strength after the experience of death than they ever expected to. Themes of personal strength derived from facing the adversity of loss were well developed. One bereaved mother related,

> But I just knew that ... I was gonna get through; like I—I had survived to here, that was a miracle because, you know, leaving the hospital, looking at my watch and thinking oh my god, [I'm] too young to do this ... I am getting through this. I'm putting one foot in front of the other. I'm learning how to live a life again without that child.

Many parents of children who died of illness and HIV carers found that they had more of a capacity to deal with hardships than they thought they did. The acts of caregiving for someone ill and dealing with the health care system can be extremely taxing, and this was a frequent theme that generated strength as well. One HIV carer commented, "I kept saying in my mind, 'you know, you're a strong person and a hard worker.' I didn't believe it; but I found out that I am a strong person." All of them confronted mortality and a situation that they never expected. "Now I have no fear of death myself because I've seen so much of it. It's made me a stronger person."

The attitude or frame of mind of the bereaved individuals allowed them to find strength within themselves at a time when many did not think they would be able to go on. In a sense, they found a new connection as they transcended their former selves and moved beyond who they once were, or thought themselves to be. The realization of personal strength through grief demonstrates spirituality.

Appreciation of Life

The fourth category of growth is appreciation of life. Over time, the participants came to appreciate life in new ways, or experienced a change in their overall philosophy on life. For some this meant a renewed appreciation of the work that they did as paid employees or volunteers. One woman who worked with people living with HIV said,

> I think the work we do is very spiritual. It is, yeah.... It's work of the soul. There is all kinds of administration and paperwork.... But what we're really doing is walking beside somebody on a journey that is, umm ... the last journey of their lives.

The bereaved individuals also often discovered a new way of relating to their own mortality. A bereaved mother shared her view:

> I used to be afraid to die, of course, because my greatest fear would be saying goodbye to my children, and I had to do that, didn't I? So I guess I was forced to, to face that fear. The way I look at it now is, when I die, I will be going to [my son who died]. I will be sad to be leaving [my remaining child], but I will be going to [my son who died], so it is a fifty-fifty split. So I am not afraid anymore.

A number of the bereaved HIV carers were HIV-positive themselves. One found that he had so much renewed appreciation for life that it came to include his identification as an HIV-positive person:

> It's going to sound crazy I guess, but I think [being HIV-positive and having friends die has] enriched my life. I think I've lived with the disease for so long now that if they came tomorrow and said I didn't have this disease, I was cured, that you know, I think I'd be more devastated than when I got it.

Once again, Hardy's (1982) three aspects of spirituality—attitude or frame of mind, connection with "an other," and transcendence, are all present in the examples.

Spiritual Change

The final domain is spiritual change. This domain is conceptualized as involving a strengthening or dissolution of a religious or spiritual connection. The bereaved individuals talked about what they experienced in terms of spirituality and, for some, religion. Many of those bereaved talked about how their spirituality or religion sustained them throughout the process of loss. For one HIV carer, her sense of Aboriginal spirituality was strengthened:

> with all the work ... that I'm doing and all the caregiving and stuff, just knowing that I can feel better about myself and I can talk about it, like when we go in sweat lodges and you know, we have native ceremonies, we burn sweetgrass.... Yeah, so it's brought me closer to my culture.

For another bereaved carer, spirituality involved seeking meaning: "There's a purpose behind everything, and I feel, well, there's a purpose behind this so now I'm searching into that. And I'm exploring that whole avenue ..."

Searching for meaning is viewed as a chance by the bereaved to learn more about themselves, their views of life and death, and their relationship with religion or spirituality.

Discussion

The notion of posttraumatic growth as conceptualized by Tedeschi and Calhoun (1996) encompasses spirituality. However, the conceptualization of spirituality in growth is limited to a change in spiritual or religious beliefs. Rather than viewing growth and spirituality as two interconnected entities, they are typically discussed in the literature as separate concepts. While spirituality is described as one area where growth may occur, the significance of spirituality in relation to all areas of growth has been grossly overlooked in much of the discourse on positive change following adversity. With the quotations in this chapter pulled from two different populations of bereaved individuals, I have tried to demonstrate that spirituality is more pervasive than many growth theorists have acknowledged. For example, it is a larger component of growth than just the domain of spiritual change as conceptualized in the PTGI (Tedeschi & Calhoun, 1996). Using Hardy's (1982) definition of spirituality, I have attempted to illustrate the presence of spirituality in all the areas of growth outlined by Tedeschi and Calhoun: new possibilities, relating to others, personal strength, appreciation of life, and spiritual change.

Hardy (1982) posits that spirituality is an "attitude or frame of mind which breaks the human person out of the isolating self" (p. 154). The quotes illustrate well how the bereaved individuals have a perception of their situation that allows them to connect to others. People often feel alone in their grief, and these individuals continue to feel that way at times. In addition, they shared how they connected to others in their grieving experiences, and how they have come to see themselves as changing, even transcending in the process, by realizing their own strength, moving from the supported to the supporter, the learner to the role model. This then is what "breaks" them out of "the isolating self" and further "directs him or her to another in relationship." The increased appreciation bereaved individuals had for certain relationships, along with the greater closeness to others, as evidenced by the quotes, illustrates this well. The quotes also illustrate how bereaved individuals often feel directed to more meaningful work or volunteer experiences that serve to form new connections and relationships.

And in those relationships, according to Hardy, (1982) "one's growth takes root and sustenance" (p. 154). All of the bereaved individuals interviewed, parents and HIV carers alike, reported some positive aspect of the experience of loss. Some of these individuals were chosen according to their low scores on the PTGI, and yet they still had positive aspects to recount. Some of the bereaved individuals had fewer relationships. This was purposeful on their part, as they grew to realize what was really important for them and eliminated the relationships that did not provide what they needed. They required sustenance in their relationships, and they strengthened the relationships where they got what they required and divested themselves of those where they did not.

The concept of posttraumatic growth has generated much interest since it was introduced in the 1980s, and our understanding of it is still evolving as more evidence is gathered. Tedeschi and Calhoun have recently begun to consider that more spiritual issues are involved, although they have labelled these as existential. In an article discussing growth after bereavement, they address how a person's world views can be challenged by loss (Calhoun et al., 2010). Existential suffering and/or growth can be one result of the struggle to make meaning of a death. They have also discussed the role of spirituality in various ways, most notably in relation to different populations with varying emphases on organized religion (Calhoun, Cann, & Tedeschi, 2010). Their sense that the United States has a greater emphasis on organized religion than European or other countries is questionable, and may be underestimating the spiritual or non-religious aspects of the growth people experienced.

Although growth theorists may neglect to consider or else minimize the relationship between growth and spirituality, many of the personal narratives written by bereaved individuals do acknowledge the relationship. Abigail Carter's husband died in the attacks on the World Trade Center in New York on September 11, 2001 (2008). She has written a moving account of her transformation after his death and about what she terms the silver lining of grief. There is indeed a silver lining possible in grief, or in any other negative circumstance. Carter's account is a powerful one of her own struggle with young widowhood with two small children. She continues her story in a blog (www.abigailcarter .com), and maintains that this process is deeply personal and individual. Carter started out not at all spiritual or religious, and sees herself as having become very spiritual. She organizes her book and story according to the ancient three-part process of alchemy: the blackening, the whitening, and finally the reddening of lead as it turns to gold. She was given a book about spiritual alchemy that led her to this knowledge. Her story is one among many examples of growth through grief in the popular media, but hers has particular resonance with spirituality as I define it here.

Implications for Social Work Practice and Other Thoughts

Stress occurs when an adverse circumstance taxes an individual's capacity to cope with a situation. The death of someone and the resulting grief is one such situation that can cause such stress. While death has been experienced throughout human history, in Western society today it has come to be understood as an adverse experience, rather than a natural one. Our theoretical understandings of the grief experience have been rooted in such attitudes. And yet, our attentions have recently turned to include positive aspects of negative experiences such as loss. Growth, being one positive outcome, is possible in the face of difficult life experiences. The paradigm has shifted to include positive aspects in such fields as stress, coping, and grief.

Grief is a universal human experience, one that is seldom discussed in our death-denying society (Granek, 2010). For some, this means that their grief becomes disenfranchised and silenced. This experience serves to further isolate the bereaved. People who are grieving often talk about the need to hear the name of the person who died. At the same time, people around those who are grieving often express fear that they will say the wrong thing, and so say nothing at all. This silence of those around them often hurts and bewilders the bereaved, who experience this as not wanting to hear about the grief. Social workers and other professionals working in a clinical role often receive little or no training about grief and loss. This can lead to professionals feeling uncomfortable discussing such issues. All professions can benefit from an increased ability to interact effectively with people who have experienced a loss. And given that all professionals are humans who may have already or will experience death themselves at some time in their lives, education in grief and loss can only be of benefit, both professionally and personally. Calhoun et al. (2010) offer an excellent framework of intervention for working with grieving people as expert companions that acknowledges the humanity of both the professional and the person who is being helped.

Parental grief is often construed as the worst kind of grief. While I believe that this attitude is intended to reflect respect for the untimely nature of a child's death before parents, it can also serve as stigmatization. Social work often tends to dichotomize, which in turn alienates the individuals we are striving to support (Grant & Cadell, 2009). The construal of parental grief as worse than any other carries the risk of having this effect and further isolating parents who already feel very alone when a child dies.

Social workers and other professionals should be able to open conversations with people about their faith, beliefs, and practices. We need to be able to ask the questions in a way that is inclusive of any possible connection, not just established practices that we are familiar with. We need to be cautious about making assumptions about one's faith that may be based on gender, age, or culture. We need to be educated and educating about these conversations, and we need to be using and modelling them in practice. Many social workers work in inter-professional or multidisciplinary settings. We need to have these dialogues with the people we serve and the professionals we work with. I believe that this is a matter of ongoing dialogue with our own beliefs and values in order to situate ourselves. Before we can be effective in talking to others about their faith, we need to have an understanding of our own beliefs. But it does not end there, because we need to know and discover on an ongoing basis about others.

In this chapter, I have attempted to demonstrate that spirituality is more central to the process and outcomes of growth, be it in the context of grief or any other adverse circumstance, than it has been given credit for. I would go so far as to say that spirituality is foundational to growth. It is through spiritual connections that meaning is generated, benefits are understood, and growth is realized. The underestimation of spirituality in the conceptualization of posttraumatic growth and the more recent move to reflect on its greater importance parallels the rediscovery of spirituality and religion in many disciplines, including social work. Spirituality is coming back into many aspects of practice, teaching, and research.

In closing, I return to the words of the wise woman who had lived through numerous losses about her struggle to make sense of the experience:

> I've learned a huge amount about how I should live life.... About my capacity for pain and joy and ... sadness and grief and tenderness and love. Learning

that I have tremendous depths and also learning how to live with sadness and joy and loss and all those things.... Either I transformed or I would burn out. And so I chose to transform.

References

Antonovsky, A. (1979). *Health, stress and coping: New perspectives on mental and physical well-being.* San Francisco, CA: Jossey-Bass.

Attig, T. (1996). *How we grieve: Relearning the world.* New York, NY: Oxford University Press.

Cadell, S. (2007). The sun always comes out after it rains: Understanding posttraumatic growth in HIV carers. *Health & Social Work, 32*(3), 169–176.

Cadell, S., Janzen, L., & Fletcher, M. (2004, November). *Parents finding meaning: Examining post traumatic growth and the role of support with two bereavement programs.* Research paper presented at the National Hospice Palliative Care Organization's First Pediatric Palliative Care Conference, Dearborn, MI.

Cadell, S., Regehr, C., & Hemsworth, D. (2003). Factors contributing to posttraumatic growth: A proposed structural equation model. *American Journal of Orthopsychiatry, 73*(3), 279–287.

Cadell, S., & Sullivan, R. (2006). Posttraumatic growth in bereaved HIV caregivers: Where does it start and when does it end? *Traumatology, 3*(12), 45–59.

Calhoun L. G., Cann, A., & Tedeschi, R. G. (2010). The posttraumatic growth model: Sociocultural considerations. In T. Weiss & R. Berger (Eds.), *Posttraumatic growth and culturally competent practice: Lessons learned from around the globe* (pp. 1–14). Hoboken, NJ: John Wiley & Sons.

Calhoun, L. G., & Tedeschi, R. G. (1999). *Facilitating posttraumatic growth—A clinician's guide.* Mahwah, NJ: Lawrence Erlbaum Associates.

Calhoun, L. G., & Tedeschi, R. G. (2006). *The handbook of posttraumatic growth: Research and practice.* Mahwah, NJ: Lawrence Erlbaum Associates.

Calhoun L. G., & Tedeschi, R. G., Cann, A., & Hanks, E. A. (2010). Positive outcomes following bereavement: Paths to posttraumatic growth. *Psychologica Belgica, 50*(1&2), 125–143.

Carter, A. (2008). *The alchemy of loss: A young widow's transformation.* Deerfield Beach, FL: Health Communications.

Creswell, J. W. (2007). *Qualitative inquiry and research design: Choosing among five approaches.* Thousand Oaks, CA: Sage.

Folkman, S. (1997). Positive psychological states and coping with severe stress. *Social Science and Medicine, 45,* 1207–1221.

Folkman, S., Moskowitz, J. T., Ozer, E. M., & Park, C. L. (1997). Positive meaningful events and coping in the context of HIV/AIDS. In B. H. Gottlieb (Ed.), *Coping with chronic stress* (pp. 293–314). New York, NY: Plenum Press.

Granek, L. (2010). Grief as pathology: The evolution of grief theory in psychology from Freud to the present. *History of Psychology, 13*(1), 46–73.

Grant, J., & Cadell, S. (2009). Power, pathological worldviews and the strengths perspective in social work. *Families in Society, 90*(4), 425–430.

Hardy, R. P. (1982). Christian spirituality today: Notes on its meaning. *Spiritual Life, 28*, 151–159.

Ickovics, J. R., & Park, C. L. (1998). Thriving: Broadening the paradigm beyond illness to health. *Journal of Social Issues, 54*(2), 237–244.

Joseph, S., & Linley, P. A. (2008). *Trauma, recovery, and growth: Positive psychological perspectives on posttraumatic stress.* Hoboken, NJ: John Wiley & Sons.

Kilmer, R. P., Gil-Rivas, V., Tedeschi, R. G., & Calhoun, L. G. (2009) *Meeting the needs of children, families, and communities post-disaster: Lessons learned from Hurricane Katrina and its aftermath.* Washington, DC: American Psychological Association.

Lazarus, R. S., & Folkman, S. (1984). *Stress, appraisal, and coping.* New York, NY: Springer.

Lincoln, Y. S., & Guba, E. G. (1985). *Naturalistic inquiry.* Beverly Hills, CA: Sage.

Linley, P. A., & Joseph, S. (2004a). Positive change following trauma and adversity: A review. *Journal of Traumatic Stress, 17*, 11–21.

McMillen, J. C. (1999). Better for it: How people benefit from adversity. *Social Work, 45*(5), 455–469.

Park, C. L., Cohen, L. H., & Murch, R. L. (1996). Assessment and prediction of stress-related growth. *Journal of Personality.* 64(1), 71–105.

Saleebey, D. (1992). *The strengths perspective in social work practice.* New York, NY: Longman.

Saleebey, D. (2006). *The strengths perspective in social work practice.* (4th ed.) Boston, MA: Pearson.

Tedeschi, R. G., & Calhoun, L. G. (1995). *Trauma and transformation—Growing in the aftermath of suffering.* Thousand Oaks, CA: Sage.

Tedeschi, R. G., & Calhoun, L. G. (1996). The Posttraumatic Growth Inventory: Measuring the positive legacy of trauma. *Journal of Traumatic Stress, 9*, 455–471.

Tedeschi, R. G., & Calhoun, L. G. (2004). *Helping bereaved parents: A clinician's guide.* New York, NY: Brunner Routledge.

Tedeschi, R. G., Park, C. L., & Calhoun, L. G. (1998). *Posttraumatic growth: Positive changes in the aftermath of crisis.* Mahwah, NJ: Lawrence Erlbaum Associates.

Tomich, P. L., Helgeson, V. S., & Nowak Vache, E. J. (2005). Perceived growth and decline following breast cancer: A comparison to age-matched controls 5 years later. *Psycho-Oncology, 14*(12), 1018–1029.

Weiss, T., & Berger, R. (2010). *Posttraumatic growth and culturally competent practice: Lessons learned from around the globe.* Hoboken, NJ: John Wiley & Sons.

Chapter 13

The Role of Spirituality in Mediating the Trauma of Social Work Internships

Rick Csiernik

Introduction

While the social work profession in North America was in many ways founded upon Judeo-Christian principles, spirituality has historically not been associated with social work education. This is partially because social work as a client-centred profession philosophically and theoretically supports each client's right and entitlement to self-determination, which at times directly conflicts with religious teachings (Adams, 1982; Csikai, 2004; Gitterman & Germain, 2008; Tower, 1994). However, researchers have been increasingly focused on the importance of the broader concept of spirituality among Canadian social workers over the past decade (Cadell, 2007; Coates, Graham, & Schwartzentruber, 2007; Coholic, 2006; Ebears, Csiernik, & Bechard, 2006, 2008a, 2008b; Graham, 2008; Graham, Coholic, & Coates, 2006), building on the earlier work of prominent social workers such as Edward John Urwick (Moffatt, 1994; Graham & Al-Krenawi, 2000), Towle's (1957) *Common Human Needs* and Spencer's (1956) *Religious and Spiritual Values in Social Casework Practice.*

Canda (1989) wrote that religion significantly affects clients, and that individuals possess spiritual needs that assist in providing an understanding of and purpose for life. He stated that the poorly prepared social work student could be a danger to a client if his or her spiritual growth crisis or mystical experience were to be mistaken for psychopathology. He further advocated for a comparative approach to teaching spiritual and religious content in schools of social work that would

1 examine religion and spirituality as general aspects of human culture and experience;
2 compare and contrast diverse religious behaviours and beliefs;
3 avoid sectarian and anti-religious bias;
4 encourage dialogue that is explicit about value issues and respect value differences;

5· examine both the potential benefit and the potential harm of religious beliefs and practices; and,

6 emphasize the relevance of the social work student's understanding of religion to provide effective service to clients.

Many have cautioned that one should not confuse spirituality with religion, and this is a wise recommendation. However, for social work students these distinct concepts are often not clearly differentiated when they are in university. In a study of undergraduate social work students, Csiernik and Adams (2003) found that while there was a broad range of thoughts on what spirituality meant, the most common were centred around God the creator, or another supreme being. Themes pertaining to inner piece, religious traditions, and eternal life dominated responses. Likewise, social work undergraduate respondents indicated that the most common means used to meet their spiritual needs were prayer, reflection and mediation, and attending religious services.

While spirituality is not typically part of social work education, what is taught are practice skills at three distinct levels of intervention: micro, mezzo, and macro. Education about values within this framework characteristically includes an examination of the professional code of ethics along with a reflection upon personal beliefs and how they have been influenced and shaped by family, peers, mentors, and societal institutions prior to entering a school of social work (Kirst-Ashman & Hull, 2008; Turner, 2002). However, despite the support of some academics (Canda, 1998; Canda & Furman, 1999; Coates & Ouellette 1997, 1998; Dudley & Helfgott, 1990; Sheridan & Amato-von Hemert, 1999), the topic of spirituality has typically been omitted from mainstream curricula in schools of social work. This has been done despite concerns about the ability of new practitioners to separate their personal beliefs from those of their clients, and the potential clash between fundamental beliefs and the ethical principle of client self-determination and support for diversity (Sheridan, Wilmer, & Atcheson, 1994).

Derezotes (1995) explored the relationship of spirituality and religiosity to the practice and lives of social work students, faculty, and practitioners. The majority of respondents in his study indicated that they believed there was a direct association between spirituality and psychosocial problems, and that training in spirituality should be a component of social work education. Kaplan and Dziegielewski's (1999) research, focusing exclusively upon the attitudes of graduate social work students, found that the majority valued the role of spirituality and religion in both their personal and professional lives. However, the 84 respondents indicated that they were generally not able to successfully integrate spiritual and religious concepts into their social work practice with clients, nor were they typically comfortable in doing so. The graduate students stated that they lacked adequate training and preparation to fully deal with this complex concept appropriately. Kaplan and Dziegielewski concluded that the low number of students willing to incorporate spirituality into their early practice was indicative of the confusion the new practitioners felt concerning their roles and responsibilities around this issue. Interestingly, there was also no discussion on how the social work students used spirituality for their own well-being.

In an examination of undergraduate students from an Atlantic school of social work, Coates and Ouellette (1997, 1998) reported that participating in a course on spirituality had a positive impact upon the participants' spirituality. They found that attention to spirituality "fosters openness and acceptance of diversity, encourages creativity and problem-solving in a context of collectivity, community and support rather than one of individualism and self-interest" (1997, p. 1). They stated that spirituality also assisted social work students in dealing with stress, particularly during this time of societal transition. Similarly, Kamya (2000) in her study of 105 social work students found a relationship between hardiness, spiritual well-being, and self-esteem, with spiritual well-being and hardiness being strong predictors of self-esteem. Staral (1999) stated that while assisting her students to develop competency, she stressed "respect for religious thought, importance of critical thinking, valuing client self-determination and drawing relevant boundaries for the discussion of religion and spirituality" (pp. 109–110).

A study of undergraduate social work students at King's University College, a Canadian Catholic university, found that spirituality was very important to this group; indeed, more important than it was to a random sample of their undergraduate peers. Social work students in the study were found to have quite traditional views of what spirituality entailed: the majority believed in a supreme being and in the importance of following traditional religious teachings. Parents and the church were the primary spiritual influences for both groups, and when spiritual needs were not met because of competing academic demands, the consequences were viewed as profoundly negative. A key finding of this study was the nearly unanimous response from social work students that their spirituality, education, and career goals were all linked, and to a more significant degree than those attending other liberal arts programs within this Catholic post-secondary institution. In a series of closed-ended questions, social work students consistently had a greater mean score when indicating the importance of spirituality in various facets of both their lives and education. They also expressed a greater comfort in discussing spirituality than did members of the comparison group, and showed a significantly greater mean score on the standardized JAREL spirituality well-being scale (Csiernik & Adams, 2003).

A follow-up study of the same group just prior to graduation reported that their undergraduate social work education had positively impacted their spirituality, despite the lack of any formal course or program objectives concerning this theme. A shift in how they perceived spirituality was observed over their two years of study. When the social work students had begun their studies there was a significant association between spirituality and the importance of a supreme being in their lives, while at graduation there was a greater focus upon spirituality as being a way of life that included becoming more connected with others. Family also became much more closely associated with spirituality for these students during the course of their education. Spirituality was more associated with the choice of post-secondary studies for social work students than it was for the comparison group, though a minority of social work students reported that their spiritual development did not truly start until they began their social work studies. While social work students reported that spirituality was of great importance in their personal lives in both studies, the importance of post-secondary education in strengthening their spirituality grew during their time within the social work program, while no change in this area was reported by the comparison group of liberal arts students (Adams & Csiernik, 2002).

The Social Work Internship and Trauma

A vital aspect of all social work education is the internship, or practicum. The practicum is typically the first opportunity for a student to experience a professional practice role and allows him or her to begin to integrate learned knowledge and theory in an actual social work environment. The importance of understanding the complex needs and dilemmas of social work students in their placements, including the role of various forms of trauma and exposure to trauma, has been discussed by several authors (Furman, Benson, Grimwood, & Canda, 2004; Miller, 2001; Rey, 1996). Secondary trauma is the emotional duress people experience after having close contact with a trauma survivor (Figley & Kleber, 1995; Geller, Madson, & Ohrenstein, 2004; Hesse, 2002). Vicarious trauma is defined as the permanent transformation of the counsellor's inner experience as a result of empathic engagement with clients' trauma experiences and responses. Signs include disturbances in one's cognitive frame of reference, identity, world view, and spirituality (Hyman, 2004; Pearlman & Saakvitne, 1995). The main differences between the two are a focus on symptomatology versus theory, the nature of the symptoms, observable reactions versus more covert changes in thinking, relevant populations, and a critical amount of exposure to trauma survivors (Figley, 1995). Whereas secondary trauma may be experienced by having contact with a client, vicarious trauma results from cumulative exposure to a number of traumatized clients over time (McCann & Pearlman, 1990) though the length of time varies from counsellor to counsellor. Other variables of vicarious trauma include age, sex, amount of interaction with exposed clients, length of time providing treatment and the clinician's own history, including his or her personal experiences of trauma (Cunningham, 2003, 2004; Dane, 2002; Way, Vandeusen, Martin, Applegate, & Jandle, 2004). There is also the comparatively new idea of compassion fatigue, a process that happens over time and is not the result of a one-time event as with secondary traumatic stress (Thompson, 2004). Compassion fatigue reflects a physical, emotional, and spiritual exhaustion that takes over all helpers, not only social work interns, and causes a decline in their ability to feel and care for others (Figley, 1995). It can occur to anyone as a result of serving in a helping capacity (Rothschild, 2006). These forms of trauma can bring about significant change in one's life. Fundamental assumptions regarding life that can be shattered by trauma include a belief in personal invulnerability, the perception of the world as meaningful and comprehensible, and the ability to view ourselves in a positive light (Janoff-Bulman & McPherson Frantz, 1996).

Along with the emotional effects of practice also come issues resulting from exposure to and experiences of physical trauma, encompassing both real and perceived harm, including threats of harm (Rey, 1996; Smith, McMahon, & Nursten, 2003). There are inherent physical risks associated with social work practice, such as visiting clients in the home, working with high-risk clients who have committed violent acts, and interaction with agitated clients who are in a crisis state. Newhill (1996) indicated that up to 20% of B.S.W. students had been verbally or physically assaulted during their practicum experience. Physical trauma is an ongoing concern, and social workers who have been threatened or abused by clients report higher levels of irritability, depression, anxiety, and burn-out compared to workers who have not experienced threats or abuse (Jayaratne, Vinokur-Kaplan, Nagda, & Chess, 1996).

Negative responses can also arise as a result of workplace harassment or bullying. Bullying is a global phenomenon that can take multiple forms: physical, relational, or verbal, and has long-lasting negative consequences (Berger, 2007; Esbensen & Carson, 2009; Smokowski & Kopasz, 2005). However, this phenomenon is less likely to happen to social work interns, since both bullying in an academic environment and workplace harassment arise as a result of an individual being repeatedly and systematically exposed over time to negative actions by one or more persons (Chapell et al., 2004; Parault, Davis, & Pellegrini, 2007; Zapf & Gross, 2001). The first requirement of bullying, a power differential, certainly exists between social work interns and both social work and non-social work employees. However, the shorter duration of most placements, typically less time in days than the probationary period of most employees, make the opportunity for a systematic pattern of negative behaviours against an intern less likely, though it is still possible, particularly in concurrent placements (Einarsen, Hoel, Zapf, & Cooper, 2011). Interns are more likely to have a negative response due to a specific incident rather than ongoing harassment over the course of placement.

Certain researchers have acknowledged that many social worker candidates enter schools of social work having already been exposed to substantial personal trauma (Furman et al., 2004; Russel, Gill, Coyne, & Woody, 1993). A study of the trauma experiences of a group of undergraduate and graduate students at King's University College found that prior to beginning their studies, over 50% reported being verbally harassed, 40% had been verbally threatened, 25% had been sexually harassed, and over 10% having been previously stalked (Table 13.1). However, only 25% of respondents had themselves sought out counselling for these issues and other related traumatic events that had occurred prior to them being accepted into the school of social work (Didham, Dromgole, Csiernik, Karley, & Hurley, 2011).

The same study found that virtually every respondent had experienced a personally upsetting or disturbing incident during their practicum. While researchers deemed the majority had minimal negative impact, these events still had the potential to become the foundation for the development of secondary and/or vicarious trauma, if not compassion fatigue, especially for the students who did not have the opportunity to deal with the issues in a timely manner (Table 13.2). In reviewing the written comments made by students regarding the impact of their practicum upon them, researchers saw little difference between

Table 13.1 Critical Incidents Experienced by Students (%)

	Within the last two years				Two or more years ago			
	3rd	4th	MSW	Total	3rd	4th	MSW	Total
	n=17	n=30	n=8	n=55	n=17	n=33	n=8	n=58
Verbally harassed	64.7	53.3	50.0	56.4	35.3	39.4	37.5	37.9
Verbally threatened	52.9	33.3	37.5	40.0	35.3	36.4	50.0	37.9
Sexually harassed	23.5	33.3		25.5	11.8	27.3	25.0	22.4
Threatened with physical harm	11.8	13.3		10.9	17.6	21.2	25.0	20.7
Threats to personal property	11.8	13.3		10.9	5.9	18.2		12.1
Racial/ethnic harassment	5.9	10.0		7.3	11.8	6.1		6.9
Physically assaulted–no injury	17.6	3.3		7.3	29.4	12.1		15.5
Physically assaulted –injured	11.8	0.0		3.6	17.6	6.1	12.5	10.3
Death of a parent	5.9	3.3		3.6	17.6	21.2	25.0	20.7
Sexually assaulted	5.9	0.0		1.8	29.4	12.1	12.5	17.2
Death of a child	5.9	0.0		1.8	0.0	6.1		3.4
Threatened with harm to family member or colleague	5.9	0.0		0.0	5.9	6.1		5.2
Stalked	0.0	0.0		0.0	17.6	15.2		13.8
Death of a partner	0.0	0.0		0.0	5.9	0.0		1.7
Death of other family member	0.0	0.0		0.0	5.9	0.0		1.7

these and the journals of other trauma survivors. There were significant changes in sleeping, eating, concentration, psychoactive substance use, confidence, and academic performance.

The most unexpected outcome, however, was that the significant critical events were not the result of worker–client interactions. Rather, the greatest negative impacts came from the few incidents involving field instructors and faculty consultants. Being yelled at or disciplined in front of others, or feeling verbally intimidated by a supervisor or co-worker either in private or in a group setting, and feeling threatened or harassed in the practicum setting by a colleague or field instructor produced the most negative impacts. Likewise, in the instances where faculty consultants were perceived to be unsupportive or

Table 13.2 Nature, Frequency, and Intensity of Traumatic Incidents (n=58)

	Experienced (%)	Frequency (0–4)	Severity (0–4)
Emotionally upset after meeting with a client	84.5	1.6	1.8
Emotionally upset after reading case files	69.0	1.7	1.3
Physically upset after meeting with a client	56.9	1.3	1.4
Emotionally upset as a result of seminar	53.4	1.8	1.6
Emotionally upset after meeting with another professional	50.0	1.6	1.7
Yelled at by a client	44.8	1.6	1.4
Emotionally upset after a home visit	34.5	1.7	1.1
Physically upset after reading case files	34.5	1.4	1.0
Verbally disciplined by field instructor	32.8	1.7	1.7
Verbally intimidated/threatened by a client	29.3	1.6	1.6
Physically upset after meeting with another professional	25.9	1.3	1.7
Physically upset as a result of a seminar	24.1	1.7	1.7
Physically upset after a home visit	15.5	1.4	1.4
Verbally Intimidated or threatened by a colleague/supervisor	13.8	1.8	2.3
Yelled at by a colleague/supervisor	12.1	1.9	2.4
Sexually harassed by a client	12.1	1.6	1.0
Physically intimidated/threatened by a client	12.1	1.4	1.6
Sexually harassed by a colleague/supervisor	8.6	1.6	3.0
Racially harassed/discriminated by a client	6.9	1.5	1.3
Racially harassed or discriminated against by a colleague/ supervisor	3.4	2.5	1.3
Physically intimidated or threatened by a colleague/ supervisor	1.7	2.0	3.0

unresponsive regarding the internship, some students said they felt oppressed and helpless. Due to the lack of power students have in the academic and field environments, they may purposefully choose the path of least resistance to avoid conflict with those who hold their future in their hands (Didham et al., 2011).

Case Studies

Mary Lou

Mary Lou, age 43, is a child and youth care worker with fifteen years' experience in a rural board of education. In her professional career, she typically worked with students with special needs and had been at the same high school for five years before returning to university to obtain her M.S.W. Her placement was in a large urban child welfare setting, and everyone in the placement process thought she would thrive because of her extensive experience in the social services field. However, she struggled academically with her first few assignments and had likewise encountered a range of frustrations in her internship. One seemingly small issue pertained to the team member who was assigned to orientate her in the community. This colleague kept being called out on emergency calls exactly when they had scheduled time together, and four weeks into the placement Mary Lou still had not gotten a feel for the city. After six weeks had passed, it seemed too late to go out together to do this, as Mary Lou had already begun to make independent home visits. Being only a student, Mary Lou did not want to complain or appear unable to accomplish a simple task, so she never discussed the lack of orientation with either her field supervisor or faculty liaison.

Two months into her practicum and just as she was starting to develop a routine, Mary Lou caught the flu and missed four days of her placement. She returned with trepidation, not knowing what had happened with her new case files and the families with whom she was just beginning to develop rapport. She was also concerned about making up the necessary time before the end of term given her heavy academic workload, which included two night classes. Her anxiety was not without cause, as one family file, the one she has been working on the longest, had been transferred to another worker in her absence, and a second family moved out of town, leaving her with only two active files. Despite this, she somehow fell behind in her recordings and was told simply to stay longer, as the only way she would become faster was to work on this part of her practice. However, because of her night classes, the only evening she could stay late was Friday, and after 5:00 p.m. there was typically no one in her unit available to ask about protocols and proper recording format. At the end of the third month of practicum, Mary Lou was still trying to catch up while other students were leaving on time and appeared confident. This was something she had had when she started her internship, but it was quickly giving way to feelings of panic and imposter syndrome. Prior to her midterm review with her faculty liaison, Mary Lou's field supervisor indicated that she could not use the extra time she was working on recordings to make up for the sick time she had taken earlier in the term, as she still needed to do the "real" work. Mary Lou was upset. In her previous professional position, she had always felt part of the team, and now, halfway through her practicum, she still felt unsure and "green" even though she was older and had more direct practice experience than the majority of the team. It made her wonder, was she too old to be back at school? When she had been the youth care team leader, she felt close to everyone in her workplace, but now she had no social contacts with anyone from her practicum.

Mary Lou made up her lost time over the Christmas/New Year's break in between writing her four take-home exams, but by early January she was very fatigued. She developed a severe migraine headache and lost another week of placement time. Upon returning, Mary Lou felt very self-conscious and was certain two senior team members resented her absence as they had had to cover her family crisis calls on top of their own workload while she was gone. In their view, the student was there to help with the team's workload, not add to it.

On a Friday afternoon at the conclusion of reading week, Mary Lou's mother, who lived several hours north, died suddenly. Mary Lou had to make travel arrangements and dip into her quickly diminishing savings. Even worse, during the funeral planning and visitation, she was worried about how this would impact her final evaluation which was only six weeks away, as she was missing yet another week of placement. Because she was a student, no condolences were sent from the placement agency, while those she had worked with before returning to school were unaware of her mother's sudden passing, and thus she received no social support from either group. When Mary Lou returned to placement, only one team member and her supervisor acknowledged her loss. In the middle of her first day back, after missing two weeks, Mary Lou started to cry in her cubicle, and could be overheard by a large segment of the staff. In turn, she thought she overheard one social worker from another unit say, "What's the matter with her? How is she going to make it as a social worker if she can't even manage her own emotions when she's only carrying a student caseload?"

Steve

Steve was a bright but very young social work intern who, despite his youth and lack of experience, was given the opportunity to be placed at an agency that worked with families in crisis because there were no other men currently employed there. Steve still lived at home, and had to commute nearly an hour by bus to get to the practicum. The trip home took even longer after 8:00 p.m., when bus service was reduced. However, he was always on time, stayed late as clients needed, and soon developed a reputation as someone who would take on any task offered.

One of the reasons Steve had chosen social work was because he had received a great deal of support early in life from a hospital social worker. Steve was born with a heart defect, and by the time he was 12 had undergone three open-heart surgeries. Thus, despite his age and healthy appearance, he suffered from extreme fatigue if he was physically overtaxed or sleep-deprived. Steve had hidden this health issue from most of his peers, not wanting to receive any unnecessary sympathy as he began his professional career. His field supervisor ensured that she offered Steve one to one and one-half hours of supervision weekly; however, she worked in a different office and on different evenings than Steve due to agency and client demands, and thus was not regularly available to him for informal consultation, or to allow Steve to drop in and check about routine matters.

Even so, the independence offered Steve led him to take on more tasks, more files and more complex cases than any of the other student interns. His supervisor was not disappointed in what she had been told about his intelligence, and by second term he had more responsibility than several of the M.S.W. and master's students from other disciplines, which resulted in Steve becoming a popular topic for gossip, particularly after the summer job openings were posted. How could someone that young be given so much responsibility so soon, especially when he took a nap during lunch every day instead of socializing with the other students on placement? Despite thriving in the environment and developing good relationships with clients, Steve wondered if it was worthwhile to continue on in this setting, where his earnest efforts to work with clients and assist them was met with jealousy and pettiness from his older and more experienced co-workers.

Laura

Laura, age 28, married and had a child immediately upon completion of her B.S.W. Her marriage lasted three years and she now had a beautiful daughter, but little support from her former partner. She decided that she wanted to obtain her M.S.W. before her daughter grew too much older, so she was working full-time and going to school part-time as well as being the primary caregiver for her child. Her M.S.W. studies invigorated her and gave her a new appreciation for social work that she did not have as an undergraduate student. While Laura had been committed to the profession upon being accepted into the B.S.W. program, she had not spent as much time studying as an undergraduate as she had going out with her future husband to clubs, bars, and other university events.

Upon beginning the part-time M.S.W. program, her new professors actively encouraged her to use her workplace to test out the theory, practice, and research ideas that she was learning in class. From the beginning, her clinical supervisor at work was equally ecstatic with Laura's new ideas and enthusiasm. However, upon beginning her placement, Laura moved from full-time to part-time employment, which put additional financial pressure upon her. As well, the agency did not have the budget to replace her, so for four months her peers and supervisor had to cover part of her caseload, and while everyone was supportive, she still felt obligated to do as much as possible with her regular clients when she was not in class or in placement.

However, when Laura began her M.S.W. placement, the skills and knowledge she brought as an experienced registered social worker and M.S.W. candidate were devalued, particularly by those from other health care disciplines. While the referrals and recommendations she made in her work setting were acted upon without hesitation, in her practicum they underwent extensive scrutiny, with every decision requiring written explanation along with a note from her supervisor indicating it was acceptable before any other member of the team would take action. Likewise, members of the interdisciplinary team were hesitant to refer new clients to her without first meeting separately with her field instructor, and it appeared that the skills and new ideas she had been developing in school that were welcome in her workplace were dismissed in her practicum environment.

Laura found herself becoming increasingly irritable and less interested in her placement, and in turn looked for reasons not to attend class or speak to anyone in the School of Social Work that had recommended and placed her in this environment to enhance her practice skills. Halfway through the practicum and three months away from graduation, Laura is actively considering dropping out, returning to her job, and spending more time with her child.

The Challenges of Social Work Internships

Adams and Csiernik (2002) discussed seven distinct challenges of work that can be readily applied to social work internships and the duality of being both a student and a beginning social work practitioner. After contemplating the difficulties faced in these three cases, we can increase our understanding of the stressors faced by social work interns by delineating seven specific challenges that Mary Lou, Steve, and Laura, and their peers across university settings, share.

The first is the practical aspects of being a new social work practitioner, be it as a brand new member of the profession, transferring skills from another helping discipline to social work, or enhancing existing knowledge and skills by returning to obtain a master's degree. This can include dealing with one's first caseload and the multiple tasks that require distinct skills and knowledge, some taught while interns are completing their initial practicum, and some not taught until near the end of the second practicum. It can also entail learning to work with a new population in a new setting after having already established one's abilities in a different setting.

Second is the physical aspect of practicum. This includes coping with the fatigue of a full-time course load and the equivalent of a new part-time job for which one is not yet fully prepared or trained, or trying to combine a full-time job with part-time school and a practicum. As well, since the practicum typically occurs through the day, most social work students must attend at least one evening class, often after spending an entire day in their practicum. Then they end up going home and are forced to decide what they have time to complete, their homework or their case recording.

Third, the behavioural challenge of the internship entails learning to develop a sense of professional practice and decorum while continually returning to the student role within the university setting with its unique power relationships. What can be a further challenge for those returning to school after several years of employment is the lack of acknowledgement for the skills and abilities they had developed even if it was not in social work or at a master's level.

Fourth, the emotional challenges of internships can be overwhelming at times for even the most mature of social work students. Still in a learning position, students must regularly respond to client issues while managing their own anxieties regarding competency and ability, constantly battling the imposter syndrome that is common among interns. Further, when the losses that enter all of our lives (typically at the least opportune times), occur during a time-limited placement, there may not be time provided to grieve or respond in the same manner as if the student were in a more permanent setting. As well, students who have not fully resolved their own traumas may be required to work with clients who have similar issues, leading to both countertransference and ethical dilemmas.

The fifth challenge of the social work internship is a cognitive one. This entails balancing the demands of the academic institution and the social work practicum, the need to learn textbook material and respond to lectures while simultaneously learning about agency policy, practice, and new community resources and programs. Some workers and even some supervisors may be threatened by the new knowledge, different ideas, youth, and exuberance of social work interns, and thus they may not be open to the new ideas interns express. They can be discouraging to rather than supporting of the intern.

The sixth challenge, the social, requires the development of a sense of professional self and fitting into a new social work team or agency while still maintaining ties to academic roommates, school friends, past colleagues, professors, and related academic service commitments such as student council or social justice committees.

The final and typically most neglected challenge is the spiritual one. Along with all the other challenges social work interns face during the course of their practicum, they must somehow also try to find a balance between all that is applied and their spiritual selves. Their spiritual wellness can be and often is overtly and covertly challenged when they face the duality of developing a professional identity as a new social work practitioner while still meeting the high academic standards to obtain a professional degree (Adams & Csiernik, 2002; Csiernik & Adams, 2002). In Mary Lou, Steve, and Laura's cases, was there any time and space offered them in consideration of their spirituality and the need to develop the whole person in their respective learning environments?

These seven areas are challenges faced by all social work interns, as they live in two worlds. However, they are not only the source of stress and frustration but also forces that can involve and motivate. These challenges are simultaneously obstacles that prevent students from acquiring and maintaining a level of wellness and the foundation of wellness that provides them with a sense of achievement and feelings of success, wholeness, and empowerment (Csiernik, 2005). However, one dynamic that can complicate the transition from learner to professional that has been insufficiently examined is the unresolved trauma issues many social work interns carry. The effects of these incidents have the potential to be further intensified by the trauma created during the completion of multiple internships over the course of attaining a social work degree.

Mediating Trauma: Wellness, Spirituality, and Social Work

Despite having a foundation based upon Judeo-Christian principles, social work education has historically not incorporated spirituality as a major theme. The relative minimization of education about spirituality and social work in Canadian schools of social work negates the importance of spirituality as one of the foundations of both client and student wellness. The origins for the contemporary definition of wellness are credited to Halbert Dunn, whose book, *High-Level Wellness* (1961) was initially premised upon the World Health Organization's (1946) definition of health: "Health is a state of complete physical, mental and social well-being, and not merely the absence of disease and infirmity" (p. 1). For Dunn, a complete state of well-being involved wellness of the mind, the body, the environment, family, community life, and a compatible work interest. Wellness also included a way of living that maximized one's potential, adaptation to the challenges of a changing environment, and a sense of social responsibility. Dunn postulated that being well does not merely constitute a state where one is not ill, or "unsick," a position that was echoed later by Ardell (1977).

Wellness consists of five core components: physical, psychological, intellectual, social, and spiritual health. Physical health includes physical fitness, nutrition, control of substance abuse, adequate rest and sleep, and medical self-care including the absence of disease. Emotional or psychological health involves one's subjective sense of well-being and the capacity to cope and maintain relative control over emotional states in response to life events. This includes the effective management of stress and emotional crises. Intellectual health encompasses the realms of education, achievement, role fulfillment, and career development. It also includes proficiency in thinking clearly, independently, and critically. Social health entails the ability to interact effectively with others, including the development of appropriate relationships among friends, families, co-workers, and the general community. It also entails the ideas of role fulfillment, caring for others, and being open to the caring actions of others. These three components have also been associated with spiritual health and well-being in addition to other factors such as love, charity, purpose, a positive sense of self, motivation, a longing for transcendence, and meditation (Drouin, 2002; Perry & Jessor, 1985; Schafer, 1992; Sefton, Wankel, Quinney, Webber, Marshall, & Horne, 1992). Morgan (1993) suggested that spirituality includes a person's ability to transcend the physical limits of time and space, the ability to reason, to will, to be creative, and to seek meaning. For him, spirituality also entailed self-awareness, adherence to values, being ethical, being connected with others, and maintaining a belief system that includes a religious dimension. Anderson and Worthen (1997) further suggested that our spirituality hinges on three critical assumptions. The first is an awareness of the existence of a supreme power or force. The second is the innate yearning people have for connection with this supreme entity, while the third is the belief that this power is interested in humans and acts upon this relationship in order to promote changes that benefit humans.

As components of wellness, physical, psychological, intellectual, and social health tend to have more empirical credibility than the idea of spirituality. Spirituality has been viewed by some professional practitioners as too ethereal, esoteric, and removed from practical concerns to merit systematic study or inclusion in clinical practice, and the idea itself remains somewhat ambiguous (Adams & Csiernik, 2002). However, in current social work practice, we are aware that when conducting a comprehensive psychosocial assessment that incorporates recognition of the importance of client diversity and strength, spirituality must be considered. Neglecting the spiritual dimension is contrary to our commitment to holistic practice. Positively or negatively, spirituality can be a fundamental contributor to personality formulation and cognition, the development of personal meaning and purpose, the creation and maintenance of interpersonal relationships within the family and community, and the acceptance of or the will to change a wide range of life, death, and bereavement-related concerns.

Within social work practice, spirituality can be an energizing and empowering principle in problem-solving with both individuals and groups, as well as a major factor in the formulation of health and social policies. In recent years, spirituality has gained increasing importance in medical social work, addiction, mental health, geriatrics, and palliative care, and has always been an integral component of First Nations social work practice (Boucher & Timpson, 1999; Brownbill, 2005; Brownbill & Etienne, 2010; Lederman, 1998; Stevenson, 1998). Some researchers also argue that an awareness and application of spirituality is essential for conducting culturally competent practice (Bell, Busch, & Fowler, 2005).

Historically, a key function of a strong spiritual self has been to enable us to effectively face, cope with, and overcome our personal and collective suffering (Maes, 1990). Spirituality is essential to our belief that our suffering will be removed or that we will be rewarded or compensated in some tangible manner for the suffering we have endured (Epstein, 1994; Frankl, 1984; Maes, 1990). Our spirituality provides us with hope, connects us with forces beyond the present, gives us inner strength to cope, encourages us to look for meaning in our tribulations, and aids us in managing our lives and transcending our suffering (Eaton, 1988; Highfield, 1992). Percy's (1997) concept of "shuddering," the process of living through the pain and experience of our suffering during past and current trauma, is a critical concept to consider when examining spirituality in the social work internship environment. Shuddering occurs when we succumb temporarily to our suffering. Caught up in the rapids of change in our daily and working lives, we react to the cumulative stress, overload, and trauma. While the process of shuddering draws upon and may deplete our spiritual strength, it may alternatively enhance our spiritual energy and motivate us to regain control, find new hope and new purpose in our lives. By shuddering, we learn that we can and will use our renewed energy to move forward and overcome the trauma that has enveloped our lives.

Spirituality is essential for enabling us to find faith in ourselves, in our beliefs, and in our connections to others. It is also vital in aiding us to find faith in an uncertain future. Within this context, shudderings can be viewed as transitional points. They provide us with unique insights and even enlightenment concerning our states of being. In a trauma-related or induced shuddering, interns can find the motivation, strength, and courage to face past traumas that may hinder their future practice, particularly if a supervisor or professor is attuned to the spiritual needs of people who are transitioning from being students to professionals. Shuddering enables us to take risks that demonstrate initiative, creativity, and innovation when we challenge stagnation or unhealthy or unreasonable changes. At the same time, shuddering may provide us with the impetus to re-order our academic, work, and family priorities, deal with personal life cycle crises, or take action against unresponsive systems with, or on behalf of, clients and for ourselves.

The literature discusses how one major impact of vicarious traumatization is the damage done to the counsellor's sense of spirituality (Trippany, Kress, & Wilcoxon, 2004; Way et al., 2004). However, just as readily one's spirituality can aid in minimizing or mitigating the effects of vicarious trauma and compassion fatigue (Palm, Polusny, & Follette, 2004). Spirituality does this simply by offering a belief system that counters what is witnessed in practice, offering hopefulness in light of the sadness and despair that social work interns may experience during their first field experiences. A strong sense of spirituality can provide a larger sense of meaning to one's life and one's beginning practice to counter the negative cognitive schemes that can emerge from one's initial practicum experiences. Spirituality is also reported to be a motivator for counsellors to counter the injustices they regularly see. It offers an alternative narrative to the trauma witnessed in the course of practice, either through practices within an organized faith, or by offering an organized system of social supports among those who hold a similar world view (Bell et al., 2005; Brady, Guy, Poelstra, & Brokow, 1999; Trippany et al., 2004).

Hesse (2002) discusses a range of practices associated with becoming more spiritually connected or maintaining one's connections, such as yoga, meditation, prayer, or participation in community or environmental activities. She also states that spending time with key crucial supports like family and friends is important to maintaining one's spiritual beliefs, thus further solidifying one's core identity in preparation for potential traumatic events. Spirituality entails experiencing basic joys while also allowing an individual the space to cry and grieve, for social work is a profession that deals fundamentally with loss and grief.

Spirituality is not merely one of the seven challenges of both academic and working life discussed earlier; rather, it can be viewed as the integral component that binds and helps to resolve all of the other challenges (Figure 13.1). Spirituality may provide the calm for a student, enabling her to find the tools to deal with the practical challenges of the internship successfully. It may assist her in coping with the physical challenges through encouraging self-care and the ability to balance the demands placed upon her physically. Spirituality may also contribute to meeting intellectual challenges by allowing room for humour and mutual support, particularly when she must manage demands from a multitude of academic and placement stressors. Behaviourally, spirituality may motivate her to care for and respect her peers, and perhaps move toward shared responsibility or ownership of the academic and applied environments as she learns to become a professional social worker. Respite, positive social interaction, and diversion may be further contributions spirituality provides to assist with the social challenges social work students must successfully manage in the dual environments. In summary, spirituality can bring serenity, energy, direction, creativity, connectedness, goal attainment, and perhaps most importantly, hope for the future (Adams & Csiernik, 2002). Spirituality has the power to assist students

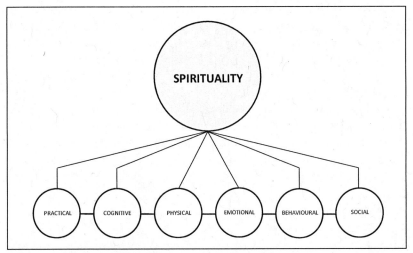

Figure 13.1   Spirituality as an Overriding Force in Meeting Social Work Intern Challenges

to move beyond past traumas, and through those that have occurred as part of their academic and applied education. Spirituality within a social work academic context can be an essential force, the overriding factor that allows students to successfully meet all the challenges they encounter.

However, the obstacles to applying spiritual principles to most academic environments and internship settings are many and formidable. Along with the discomfort many have when publicly discussing this topic comes a range of issues. These include fixed beliefs, chronic inaction, tolerance of employee abuse, neglect of clients and of one another, lack of status being a student on practicum, culture dicta, economic deficiencies, emotional overload, social isolation, third-party forces, the unrelenting flow of often trivial information, and demands created by the continually enhanced ability to transmit information that technology provides (Bell et al., 2005; Csiernik, 2005; Csiernik & Adams, 2002). Ironically, in the social work profession there is also often a lack of access to counsellors that can limit spiritual growth and development, and thus impede wellness. If a social worker does find her or his way to another social worker counsellor for assistance, there remains the concern about how comfortable the counsellor is discussing spirituality as part of the helping process.

Closing Reflection

Each school of social work faces its own unique challenges in educating, supporting, and developing a new group of hopeful social work candidates each year. Many of these candidates come to the profession because of issues they have overcome, though others enter with unresolved issues that the academic process, particularly the practicum, can exacerbate. Spirituality is a critical and readily accessible tool that is available to assist with resolving these issues, these sufferings, though one that has been historically underutilized. Thus it is critical to support interns during their time in university as they begin to develop their sense of professional selves, and to also establish both preventative and coping methods, spiritual and otherwise, to deal with the realities of our profession. It is crucial to normalize the emotional effects that social work has upon new practitioners; they need to be able to openly discuss the impact of their practice with field instructors, professors, and peers without fear of being viewed as unfit or not competent enough to graduate and thus to practice.

References

Adams, D. W. (1982). Terminally ill patients. In S. Yelaga (Ed.), *Values and ethics in social work.* Springfield, IL: C. C. Thomas.

Adams, D.W., & Csiernik, R. (2002). Seeking the lost spirit: Understanding spirituality and restoring it to the workplace. *Employee Assistance Quarterly, 17*(4), 31–44.

Anderson, D. A., & Wortham, D. (1997). Exploring a fourth dimension: Spirituality as a resource for the couple therapist. *Journal of Marital and Family Therapy, 23*(1), 2–12.

Ardell, D. (1977). *High level wellness.* Emmasus, PA: Rodale Press.

Bell, H., Busch, N., & Fowler, D. (2005). Spirituality and domestic violence work. *Critical Social Work, 6*(2). Retrieved from http://www.uwindsor.ca/criticalsocialwork/spirituality-and-domestic-violence-work

Berger, K. (2007). Update on bullying at school: Science forgotten? *Developmental Review, 27*(1), 90–126.

Boucher, R., & Timpson, J. (1999). Confronting HIV and AIDS: A personal account. *Native Social Work Journal, 3*(1), 39–53.

Brady, J., Guy, J., Poelstra, P., & Brokow, B. (1999). Vicarious traumatization, spirituality, and the treatment of sexual abuse survivors: A national survey of women psychotherapists. *Professional Psychology: Research and Practice, 30*(4), 386–393.

Brownbill, K. (2005). A First Nations' perspective on work, the workplace and wellness. In R. Csiernik (Ed.), *Wellness and work: Employee assistance programming in Canada.* Toronto, ON: Canadian Scholars' Press.

Brownbill, K., & Etienne, M. (2010). Understanding the ultimate oppression: Alcohol and drug addiction in Native Land. In R. Csiernik and W. S. Rowe (Eds.), *Responding to the oppression of addiction* (2nd ed., pp. 256–273). Toronto, ON: Canadian Scholars' Press.

Cadell, S. (2007). The sun always comes out after it rains: Understanding posttraumatic growth in HIV caregivers. *Health and Social Work, 32*(3), 169–176.

Canda, E. (1989). Religious content in social work education: A comparative approach. *Journal of Social Work Education, 25*(1), 36–45.

Canda, E. (Ed.) (1998). *Spirituality in social work, new directions.* New York, NY: Haworth Press.

Canda, E., & Furman, L. (1999). *Spiritual diversity in social work practice: The heart of helping.* New York, NY: Free Press.

Chapell , M., Casey, D., De la Cruz, C., Ferrell, F., Forman, J., Lipkin, R., Newsham, M., Sterling, M., & Whittaker, S. (2004). Bullying in college by students and teachers. *Adolescence, 39*(153), 53–64.

Coates, J., Graham, J., & Swartzentruber, B. (with Ouellete, B.) (2007). *Spirituality and social work: Selected Canadian readings.* Toronto, ON: Canadian Scholars' Press.

Coates, J., & Ouellette, B. (1997). *Spirituality and social work: Sponsoring responsible civil society, first annual report.* Fredericton, NB: St. Thomas University.

Coates, J., & Ouellette, B. (1998). *Spirituality and social work: Sponsoring responsible civil society, second annual report.* Fredericton, NB: St. Thomas University.

Coholic, D. (2006). Spirituality in social work pedagogy—A Canadian perspective. *Journal of Teaching in Social Work, 26*(3–4), 197–217.

Csiernik, R. (2005). Wellness and the workplace. In R. Csiernik (Ed.), *Wellness and work: Employee assistance programming in Canada.* Toronto, ON: Canadian Scholars' Press.

Csiernik, R., & Adams, D. (2002). The impact of social work education on students' spirituality. *Currents: New Scholarship in the Human Services, 1*(1). Retrieved from http://www.ucalgary.ca/currents/files/currents/v1n1_csiernik.pdf

Csiernik, R., & Adams, D. (2003). Social work students and spirituality: An initial exploration. *Canadian Social Work, 5*(1), 65–79.

Csikai, E. (2004). Social workers' participation in the resolution of ethical dilemmas in hospice care. *Health and Social Work, 29*(1), 67–76.

Cunningham, M. (2003). Impact of trauma work on social work clinicians: Empirical findings. *Social Work, 48*(4), 451–460.

Cunningham, M. (2004). Teaching social workers about trauma: Reducing the risks of vicarious traumatization in the classroom. *Journal of Social Work Education, 40*(2), 305–317.

Dane, B. (2002). Duty to inform: Preparing social work students to understand vicarious traumatization. *Journal of Teaching in Social Work, 22*(3/4), 3–20.

Derezotes, D. (1995). Spirituality and religiosity: Neglected factors in social work practice. *Arete, 20*(1), 1–15.

Didham, S., Dromgole, L., Csiernik, R., Karley, M. L., & Hurley, D. (2011). Trauma exposure and the social work practicum. *Journal of Teaching in Social Work, 31*(5), 523–537.

Drouin, H. (2002). Spirituality in social work practice. In F. Turner (ed.), *Social work practice: A Canadian perspective* (2nd ed., pp. 33–45). Toronto, ON: Prentice Hall.

Dudley, J., & Helfgott, C. (1990). Exploring a place for spirituality in the social work curriculum. *Journal of Social Work Education, 26*(3), 287–293.

Dunn, H. (1961). *High-level wellness.* Arlington, VA: R.W. Beatty.

Eaton, S. (1988). Spiritual care: The software of life. *Journal of Palliative Care, 4*(1/2), 94–97.

Ebears, J., Csiernik, R., & Bechard, M. (2006). Examining the role and practice of social work within the Catholic Church. *Critical Social Work, 7*(1). Retrieved from http://www.uwindsor.ca/criticalsocialwork/is-there-a-place-for-social-work-within-the-catholic-church

Ebears, J., Csiernik, R., & Bechard, M. (2008a). Applying the generalist model of social work practice for a Catholic Church parish team. *Journal of Religion, Spirituality and Social Work: Social Thought, 27*(1–2), 105–121.

Ebears, J., Csiernik, R., & Bechard, M. (2008b). Furthering parish wellness: Including social work as part of a Catholic pastoral team. *Social Work and Christianity, 35*(2), 179–196.

Einarsen, S., Hoel, H., Zapf, D., & Cooper, C. (2011). The concept of bullying and harassment at work: The European tradition. In S. Einarsen, H. Hoel, D. Zapf, & C. Cooper (Eds.), *Bullying and harassment in the workplace: Developments in theory, practice and research* (2nd ed., pp. 33–40). Boca Raton, FL: CRC Press.

Epstein, D. M. (1994). *The 12 stages of healing: A network approach to wholeness.* San Raphael, CA: Amber-Allen.

Esbensen, F., & Carson, D. (2009). Consequences of being bullied: Results from a longitudinal assessment of bullying victimization in a multisite sample of American students. *Youth and Society, 41*(2), 209–233.

Figley, C. R. (ed.) (1995). *Compassion fatigue—Coping with secondary traumatic stress disorder in those who treat the traumatized.* New York, NY: Brunner/ Mazel.

Figley, C. R., & Kleber, R. J. (1995). Beyond the "victim": Secondary traumatic stress. In R. J. Kleber, C. R. Figley, & B. P. R. Gersons (Eds.), *Beyond trauma: Cultural and societal dynamics* (pp. 75–98). New York, NY: Plenum.

Frankl, V. (1984). *Man's search for meaning.* Washington, DC: Square Press.

Furman, L. D., Benson, P. W., Grimwood, C., & Canda, E. (2004). Religion and spirituality in social work education and direct practice at the millennium: A survey of UK social workers. *British Journal of Social Work, 34,* 767–792.

Geller, J. A., Madson, L. H., & Ohrenstein, L. (2004). Secondary trauma: A team approach. *Clinical Social Work Journal, 32*(4), 415–431.

Gitterman, A., & Germain, C. (2008). *The life model of social work practice* (3rd ed.). New York, NY: Columbia University Press.

Graham, J. (2008). Who am I? An essay on inclusion and spiritual growth through community and mutual appreciation. *Journal of Religion and Spirituality in Social Work: Social Thought, 27*(1–2), 5–24.

Graham, J., & Al-Krenawi, A. (2000). Contested terrain: Two competing views of social work at the University of Toronto, 1914–1945. *Canadian Social Work Review, 17*(2), 245–276.

Graham, J., & Bradshaw, C. (2000). A forgiving state of heart: Narrative reflections on social work practice from a Christian perspective. *Social Work and Christianity, 27*(1), 40–48.

Graham, J., Coholic, D., & Coates, J. (2006). Spirituality as a guiding construct in the development of Canadian social work: Past and present considerations. *Critical Social Work, 7*(1). Retrieved from http://www.uwindsor.ca/criticalsocialwork/spirituality-as-a-guiding-construct-in-the-development-of-canadian-social-work-past-and-present-cons

Hesse, A. R. (2002). Secondary trauma: How working with trauma survivors affects therapists. *Clinical Social Work Journal, 30*(3), 293–309.

Highfield, M. F. (1992). The spiritual health of oncology patients—Nurses' and patients' perspectives. *Cancer Nursing, 15*(1), 1–8.

Hyman, O. (2004). Perceived social support and secondary traumatic stress symptoms in emergency responders. *Journal of Traumatic Stress, 17*(2), 149–156.

Janoff-Bulman, R., & McPherson Franz, C. (1996). The loss of illusions: The potent legacy of trauma. *Journal of Loss and Trauma, 1*(2), 133–150.

Jayaratne, S., Vinokur-Kaplan, D., Nagda, B. A., & Chess, W. A. (1996). A national study on violence and harassment of social workers in a rural state. *Child Welfare, 73*(2), 173–179.

Kamya, H. (2000). Hardiness and spiritual well-being among social work students: Implications for social work education. *Journal of Social Work Education, 36*(2), 231–240.

Kaplan, A., & Dziegielewski, S. (1999). Graduate social work students' attitudes and behaviours toward spirituality and religion: Issues for education and practice. *Social Work and Christianity, 26*(1), 25–39.

Kirst-Ashman, K., & Hull, G., Jr. (2008). *Understanding generalist practice* (5th ed.). Chicago, IL: Nelson-Hall.

Lederman, J. (1998). Trauma and healing in Aboriginal families and communities. *Native Social Work Journal, 2*(1), 59–90.

Maes, J. L. (1990). *Suffering: A caregivers' guide*. Nashville, TX: Abingdon Press.

McCann, L., & Pearlman, L. A. (1990). Vicarious traumatization: A framework for understanding the psychological effects of working with victims. *Journal of Traumatic Stress, 3*, 131–149.

Miller, M. (2001). Creating a safe frame for learning: Teaching about trauma and trauma treatment. *Journal of Teaching in Social Work, 21*(3/4), 169–187.

Moffat, K. (1994). Social work practice informed by philosophy: The social thought of Edward Johns Urwick. *Canadian Social Work Review, 11*(2), 133–149.

Morgan, J. D. (1993). The existential quest for meaning. In K. Doka & J. D. Morgan (Eds.), *Death and spirituality*. Amityville, NY: Baywood.

Newhill, C. E. (1996). Prevalence and risk factors for client violence toward social workers. *Families in Society, 77*(8), 488–496.

Palm, K., Polusny, M., & Follette, V. (2004). Vicarious traumatization: Potential hazards and interventions for disaster and trauma workers. *Prehospital and Disaster Medicine, 19*(1), 73–76.

Parault, S., Davis, H., & Pellegrini, A. (2007). The social contexts of bullying and victimization. *Journal of Early Adolescence, 27*(2), 145–174.

Pearlman, L. A., & Saakvitne, K. (1995). *Trauma and the therapist: Countertransference and vicarious traumatization in psychotherapy with incest survivors*. New York, NY: W. W. Norton.

Percy, I. (1997). *Going deep: Exploring Spirituality in life and leadership*. Toronto, ON: Macmillan Canada.

Perry, C. L., & Jessor, R. (1985). The concept of health promotion and the prevention of adolescent drug use. *Health Education Quarterly, 12*(2), 169–184.

Rey, L. D. (1996). What social workers need to know about client violence. *Families in Society, 77*(1), 33–39.

Rothschild, B. (2006). *Help for the helper.* New York, NY: W. W. Norton.

Russel, R., Gill, P., Coyne, A., & Woody, J. (1993). Dysfunction in the family of origin of MSW and other graduate students. *Journal of Social Work Education, 29*(1), 121–129.

Schafer, W. (1992). *Stress management and wellness.* Toronto, ON: Harcourt Brace/Jovanovich College.

Sefton, J., Wankel, L. Quinney, H., Webber, J., Marshall, J., & Horne, T. (1992, March). *Working toward well-being in Alberta.* Paper presented at the National Recreation and Wellness Conference, Coburg, Australia.

Sheridan, M., & Amato-von Hemert, K. (1999). The role of religion and spirituality in social work education and practice: A survey of student views and experiences. *Journal of Social Work Education, 35*(1), 125–141.

Sheridan, M., Wilmer, C., & Atcheson, L. (1994). Inclusion of content on religion and spirituality in the social work curriculum: A study of faculty views. *Journal of Social Work Education, 30*(3), 363–376.

Smith, M., McMahon, L., & Nursten, J. (2003). Social workers' experience of fear. *British Journal of Social Work, 33*, 659–671.

Smokowski, P., & Kopasz, K. (2005). Bullying in school: An overview of types, effects, family characteristics, and intervention strategies. *Children and Schools, 27*(2), 101–111.

Spencer, S. (1956). Religious and spiritual values in social casework practice. *Social Casework, 57*, 519–526.

Staral, J. (1999). Seeking religious and spiritual competence: The perceptions of BSW students at a private Catholic university. *Social Work and Christianity, 26*(2), 101–111.

Stevenson, J. (1998). The circle of healing. *Native Social Work Journal, 2*(1), 8–21.

Thompson, R. A. (2004). *Crisis intervention and crisis management: Strategies that work in schools and communities.* New York, NY: Brunner-Routledge.

Tower, K. (1994). Consumer-centered social work practice: Restoring client self-determination. *Social Work, 39*(2), 191–196.

Towle, C. (1957). *Common human needs.* New York, NY: National Association of Social Workers.

Trippany, R., Kress, V., & Wilcoxon, S. (2004). Preventing vicarious trauma: What counselors should know when working with trauma survivors. *Journal of Counseling and Development, 82*(1), 31–37.

Turner, F. (Ed.) (2002). *Social work practice: A Canadian perspective* (2nd ed.). Toronto, ON: Prentice Hall.

Way, I., Vandeusen, K. M., Martin, G., Applegate, B., & Jandle, D. (2004). Vicarious trauma: A comparison of clinicians who treat survivors of sexual abuse and sexual offenders. *Journal of Interpersonal Violence, 19*(1), 49–71.

World Health Organization. (1946). *Constitution.* New York, NY: Author.

Zapf, D., & Gross, C. (2001). Conflict escalation and coping with workplace bullying: A replication and extension. *European Journal of Work and Organizational Psychology, 10*(4), 497–522.

Chapter 14

Concluding Thoughts

Diana Coholic, Janet Groen, and John R. Graham

We have noted in this book how much growth has taken place over the past decade in the area of spirituality in social work and education, and that the time is ripe for considering how interdisciplinary collaboration can further advance our work in this broad field. We encourage emerging scholars, practitioners, and students to build on the solid foundation that has been created, to foster interdisciplinary dialogue, and to keep developing scholarship. There is much room for research and scholarship that considers holistic ways of practising, teaching, and critical thinking. In particular, we note that the broad area of social justice and change requires ongoing attention, as does the incorporation of Aboriginal perspectives.

"Spirituality" and how it is conceptualized in the Western world has long been criticized as being too individually focused on one's needs and desires. Often this latter conceptualization of spirituality is described as "New Age," and encapsulates the plethora of popular literature that encourages people to think good or positive thoughts to achieve the goals and attract the things they desire. This type of simplistic thinking about spirituality is potentially dangerous as, for just one example, people with illnesses such as cancer may blame themselves for not being able to eliminate their disease because they did not meditate or visualize effectively enough. While we support the connection between the mind, body, and spirit, a spirituality that is individually focused is highly problematic for many reasons, including the fact that it does not fit with social work's commitment to systemic anti-oppression, structural, critical, and feminist theories and practices, and the corresponding emphases in education (more specifically, in adult education) on challenging exclusionary societal discourses and practices to argue for research and practices that foster diversity and inclusion. Simply, within education and social work, we aim to interrogate and change societal structures that negatively impact people and the world, and we cannot achieve these aims by supporting a focus on personal desires.

Besides, for the most part, this is not how spirituality has been explored and conceptualized within Canadian education and social work. Indeed, spirituality and social justice movements have been strongly interconnected within the fields of social work and education, especially in adult education, as evidenced historically by the Antigonish Movement and more recently in adult literacy, adult environmental education, and the right to a sustainable livelihood. Certainly, the authors in this book have considered spirituality as something that could be an important part of developing people and communities, and changing broader ways of thinking and being in the world to provide more sustainable ways of living, better relationships, and improved ways of practising and teaching for the betterment of all concerned.

Along these lines, probably one of the most important areas in which the literature in spirituality and social work/education might grow is its analysis of social justice and social change. There has long been a relationship between religious formation and social justice: from liberation theology and the social gospel of the twentieth century, to the basic tenets of emancipation elaborated in religious texts and integrated in adherents' lives and social structures. However, much of the current literature on spirituality is anchored to small systems such as individual and family growth, rather than to the broader sociology of social change. Certainly, there are scholars such as Coates and McKay (1995) and Shahjahan (2009), who consider spirituality in our students and within our classrooms as a political act in itself, that its inclusion within our pedagogical approaches and content challenges the overriding higher educational epistemology of empirical rationality (Chickering, Dalton, & Stamm, 2006). As Shahjahan (2009) argued, "while spirituality is often discussed in the halls of higher education, the main challenge for spiritually-minded scholars has been to centre it in legitimate academic spaces, such as academic journals and classrooms" (p. 122).

But the whole area of social justice merits further consideration, especially given the current climate we live and work in, which includes the increasing corporatization of the university, the emphasis in helping/health professions on deliverables and "evidence," and the cutbacks in social services. While a number of complex matters have been considered by several authors in this book, these considerations are preliminary and suggestive. For example, Todd focuses on the challenges of incorporating spirituality within the secular classroom, particularly as one navigates the broad range of spiritual and religious experiences, both positive and negative, that students bring into the learning environment. And yet Vokey argues in his chapter that despite this range of associated memories and beliefs, we must promote spiritual maturity in our classroom in order to challenge the existing malaise that is responsible for much of our society's current breakdown. Spirituality as both a knowledge base and process of instruction within our social work and higher education classrooms serves as holistic preparation for a practice that challenges the status quo and seeks social justice and change.

We would also like to point out that we believe that Aboriginal scholars in Canada have something important to contribute to the ongoing discourse within social work/education and spirituality. It could be argued that not including a chapter written by an Aboriginal scholar is a serious omission in this book. At the same time, the resurgence in research and knowledge development in the area of spirituality in education and social work in Canada is just over ten years old, and to date, Aboriginal scholars have not been a significant voice within this literature. There is an important place for Aboriginal scholars within our growing community, and certainly, many indigenous world views are convergent with other spiritually sensitive viewpoints. Importantly, we could do much better to broaden social work and education knowledge/practice to focus on indigenous knowledge, particularly with regards to culture and spirituality. Gray, Coates, and Hetherington (2007) pointed out that social workers often do not take Aboriginal perspectives into account because they are more inclined to depend on cross-cultural or anti-oppressive practice literature (Recollet, Coholic, & Cote-Meek, 2009). We look forward to the important and significant contributions that Aboriginal scholars will make regarding indigenous spirituality within the fields of social work and education over the years to come.

Finally, there is no question that spirituality is a highly complex construct. It can also be a highly emotionally charged topic that challenges people's notions of what constitutes relevant research and knowledge development within the academe. We look forward to the day when "spirituality" is not dismissed by some as a legitimate focus of study and practice. As we look toward the future, it is our hope that with ongoing research and knowledge development in the area of spirituality in social work and education, spirituality will continue to move from the margins into the middle of our discourses. We have made considerable strides in the past decade in terms of conceptualizing and articulating what spirituality means for social workers and educators, how it may be incorporated into social work and education, and the rationales for doing so. But there is still so much more to explore, study, consider, develop, and debate. This book has been one step in bringing together a small group of scholars in social work and education to learn from one another, and to further advance our thinking in the area of spirituality and our respective professions. Hopefully, others will be encouraged by this process and will seek ways to deepen and extend the burgeoning knowledge in this area.

References

Chickering, D., Dalton, J., & Stamm, L. (2006). *Encouraging authenticity & spirituality in higher education.* San Francisco, CA: Jossey-Bass.

Coates, J., & McKay, S. (1995). Toward a new pedagogy for social transformation. *Journal of Progressive Human Services, 6*(1), 27–43.

Gray, M., Coates, J., & Hetherington, T. (2007). Hearing indigenous voices in mainstream social work. *Families in Society: The Journal of Contemporary Social Services, 88*(1), 55–66.

Recollet, D., Coholic, D., & Cote-Meek, S. (2009). Holistic arts-based group methods with Aboriginal women. *Critical Social Work, 10*(1). Retrieved from http://www.uwindsor.ca/criticalsocialwork/

Shahjahan, R. (2009). The role of spirituality in the anti-oppressive higher education classroom. *Teaching in Higher Education, 14*(2), 121–131.

Contributors

Veronika Bohac Clarke began her career as a secondary school science and math teacher, and later worked at the Alberta Ministry of Education in policy and finance. After completing her Ph.D., she joined the Faculty of Education at the University of Calgary. Her policy studies led to inquiries about values, and eventually to an examination of the role of spirituality in human development. To date, Veronika has supervised six successful doctoral dissertations based on the integral model.

Susan Cadell is a professor and Director of the School of School Work, Renison University College, affiliated with the University of Waterloo. Her research focuses on positive outcomes of trauma and grief, including caregiving, meaning-making, spirituality, and posttraumatic growth. She is involved in various multidisciplinary pediatric palliative-care research teams, and helped developed social work competencies in palliative care.

John Coates was professor and director at the School of Social Work in St. Thomas University, Fredericton, New Brunswick, upon his retirement in 2012. He is the current Chair and a founding member of the Canadian Society for Spirituality and Social Work (CSSSW). John is actively involved in advancing attention to ecology and spirituality within the professional and academic social work communities, and has chaired several conferences in these areas. His publications include *Ecology and Social Work* (2003), and *Indigenous Social Work Around the World* (2008, with M. Gray and M. Yellow Bird).

Diana Coholic is an associate professor at Laurentian University. Her current research program investigates the effectiveness of holistic arts-based group methods for the improvement of resilience. She is the author of *Arts Activities for Children and Young People in Need: Helping Children to Develop Mindfulness, Spiritual Awareness and Self-Esteem* (2010).

Rick Csiernik, professor of the School of Social Work, King's University College at Western University, has written and edited eight books, authored over 125 peer-reviewed articles and book chapters, and has been an invited presenter to 200 national and international conferences, workshops, and seminars. He has been on the King's University College Honour Roll of teaching 12 consecutive times, and is a past recipient of the McMaster University Instructor Appreciation Award.

Leona M. English is a professor of adult education at St. Francis Xavier University in Antigonish, Nova Scotia. She has an interest in the spirituality of adult education, especially as it affects community-based teaching and learning. She recently published *Learning with Adults: A Critical Pedagogical Introduction* (Sense Publishers) and *Adult Education and Health* (University of Toronto Press).

John R. Graham is Murray Fraser Professor of Community Economic Development, Faculty of Social Work, University of Calgary. He is the author, with A. Al-Krenawi, of *Helping Professional Practice with Indigenous Peoples: The Bedouin-Arab Case* (2009) and editor, with J. Coates and B. Schwartzentruber, of *Canadian Social Work and Spirituality: Current Readings and Approaches* (2007).

Janet Groen is an associate professor in adult learning in the Faculty of Education at the University of Calgary. Her research focus on spirituality began with her doctoral dissertation, *The Experiences and Practices of Adult Educators of Their Workplaces*. Recent publications can be found in the *Journal of Transformative Education, The Canadian Journal for the Study of Adult Education*, and *Teaching in Higher Education*.

John (Jack) P. Miller is the author/editor of 17 books on holistic learning and contemplative practices in education which include *Education and the Soul, The Holistic Curriculum, The Contemplative Practitioner*, and most recently, *Transcendental Learning*. The Holistic Curriculum has provided the framework for the curriculum of the Whole Child School (now named the Equinox School) in Toronto, where Jack has served on the Advisory Board. He teaches courses in holistic education at the Ontario Institute for Studies in Education at the University of Toronto, where he is professor.

Micheal L. Shier is a Ph.D. student, School of Social Policy and Practice, University of Pennsylvania, and Research Associate, Faculty of Social Work, University of Calgary. He has published articles and book chapters on spirituality and religion in social work practice and the role of spirituality and mindfulness practices on social worker perceived well-being.

Sarah Todd is an associate professor at the Carleton School of Social Work. Her main research interests are social work pedagogy, community practice, and sexuality. She is currently involved with a team of researchers exploring the impact of new managerialism on progressive social work education. In her most recent publications, Sarah explores the use of improvisational theatre in the classroom and issues of racism in community work.

Daniel Vokey is associate professor and Deputy Head in Educational Studies at the University of British Columbia. In his teaching and writing, he draws upon academic research in philosophy and religious studies, professional experience facilitating wilderness-based leadership programs, and years of Buddhist contemplative practice. Research areas include the role of intuition in ethics and potential contributions of contemplative pedagogy to transformative education. He is co-editor of *Paideusis: The Journal of the Canadian Philosophy of Education Society.*

Ian Winchester is presently a professor in the Faculty of Education at the University of Calgary, and a former Dean of Education in that institution. Prior to this, he spent 22 years at the University of Toronto in the Ontario Institute for Studies in Education, in both teaching and administrative roles. For the last decade and a half he has frequently offered a graduate course in Mind and Spirituality, and has worked with the research group mentioned in this paper over the last seven years looking at the claims of alternative healers.

Index

Aboriginal peoples: colonization/conversion of, 29, 126; lands of, 115; social justice work with, 125; social work practice with, 46

Aboriginal peoples, spirituality of, 42, 98; and adult education, 23, 26, 29; and approaches to social work, 87; in caregiving, 227; and environment, 44; and First Nations social work practice, 247; in healing, 207, 212, 213, 214; as included in curriculum, 108; in response to healing process/trauma, 170, 212, 214; and roots of social work, 38, 126; and shamanic practices, 151; and social justice, 127; and social work/ education practice/scholarship, 255, 257; and sweat lodge ceremony, 175, 227

Academy of Management, 25

Addams, Jane, 19

adult education, spirituality agenda in, 6, 15, 17–30; and Aboriginal peoples, 23, 26, 29; in community development, 24, 28–9; and culture/geography, 23; and gender, 23–4; in higher education, 27–8, 80; historical roots of, 17, 18–21; imagination and, 30; implications of, 29–30; and race/ethnicity, 20–1, 22–3; and religion, 17, 18–25, 26, 28–9; and shift from religion to spirituality, 21; and social class, 24; and social justice, 18–21, 22, 23–4, 29–30, 256; and spectrum of human emotion, 21–22, 29–30; in workplace education, 25–7

Advances in Developing Human Resources (journal), 25

African Americans: and spirituality as coping method, 174–5

African Canadians: as dealing with grief, 22–3; and significance of black churches, 44

Aga Khan Foundation, 125

Alberta Ministry of Education, 148–9

Alberta oil sands, 69

Alcoholics Anonymous, 178, 210

Aldridge, David, 205–6

Al-Krenawi, Alean, 35–6

Anthony, Susan B., 19

Antigonish Movement, 17, 18, 20, 22, 23, 24, 256

Arnold, Mary Ellicott, 17, 20

arts-based mindfulness programs, for children, 171–2

Bedouin/Arab communities: and traditional healing/spirituality, 3–4, 35–6, 205

Benedictine order, 23, 28

Berry, Thomas: *The Great Work*, 63, 69

Bohm, David, 146

BP explosion/oil spill (Gulf of Mexico), 69

Bruno, Giordano, 144

Buddhism, 42, 43, 111, 152; and holistic healing, 207, 210, 212, 213; meditation practices of, 27, 113, 147, 187, 195; on "non-dual" consciousness, 143; popular/accessible presentations of, 150–1; and self-examination, 83, 90;

160. *See also* environmentalism, spirituality and; social work and education faculties, teaching of spirituality in (curriculum)

Yeaxlee, Basil, 17, 20; *Spiritual Values in Adult Education*, 17

Yeshiva University, 46
YMCA, 17
yoga, 141, 147, 150, 248
Youmans, Letitia, 17

Zajonc, Arthur, 77, 78, 91, 130
Zoological Society of London, 58